Physical Golf

The Golfer's Guide to Peak Conditioning and Performance

Neil Wolkodoff

KickPoint Press

Denver, Colorado

Copyright ©1997 by Neil Wolkodoff

First Edition: November 1997
Published in the United States
KickPoint Press
8547 E. Arapahoe Road, Suite J-427
Greenwood Village, CO 80112
(303) 571-9335

Wolkodoff, Neil.
    Physical Golf
    ISBN 0-9657863-0-7

Library of Congress Card Catalog Number: 97-73250

The information in this book reflects the author's experience and current research, and is not intended to replace individual medical or professional advice. Before beginning this or any exercise or nutritional program, consult your physician or other appropriate health professionals.

Publisher's Cataloging-in-Publication Data

Wolkodoff, Neil.
        Physical golf : the golfer's guide to peak conditioning and
    performance / Neil Wolkodoff. — 1st ed.
        p. cm.
        Includes bibliographical references and index.
        Preassigned LCCN: 97-73250
        ISBN: 0-9657863-0-7

        1. Golf — Training. 2. Golf injuries — Prevention.   3. Physical
    fitness. I. Title

    GV979.T68W65 1997   796.352

Printed in the United States of America
10 9 8 7 6 5 4 3 2 1

Special thanks to the York Barbell Company for photographs of some of the early pioneers of strength training.

Those who think they have not time for bodily exercise will sooner or later have to find time for illness.
-Edward Stanley, Earl of Derby

Contents

About the Author

Neil Wolkodoff, Ph.D., sport scientist, trains both professional and amateur golfers in physical training and mental training for golf. He has trained a variety of athletes including NFL, NHL, MLB and Olympic athletes for over 15 years. A former strength and conditioning consultant for the Denver Broncos, the Colorado Rangers and the U.S. Freestyle Ski Team, Wolkodoff now devotes his efforts to helping golfers improve their performance. He holds certifications from the American Council on Exercise, the American College of Sports Medicine, the U.S. Weightlifting Federation and the National Strength and Conditioning Association.

He is a contributing editor for the American Council on Exercise, past editor for the American College of Sports Medicine, as well as contributor to various golf publications. Wolkodoff is a sport science consultant for Cherry Hills Country Club, Bear Creek Golf Club, Driving Obsession and The Ranch Country Club in Denver. His nationally recognized clinics on the physical and mental aspects of golf are sanctioned for continuing education credit by the PGA and LPGA.

His numerous awards and accolades include Best Personal Trainer in Colorado, 1997, by the *Denver Post;* State Director of the Year from the National Strength and Conditioning Association (twice); "80 People in Fitness to Watch in the '90s" by *Fitness Management Magazine;* and *Self Magazine* citing Wolkodoff as "one of the best exercise physiologists in the business."

Acknowledgments

Manuscript Reviewers

Carl Alexander, PGA Teaching and Touring Professional, Grand Cypress Academy of Golf, Orlando, Florida

Becky Armistead, Teaching Professional, Class A LPGA & PGA Apprentice, PROFORMANCE Research Organization, Phoenix, Arizona

Joe Assell, Director of Instruction, PGA member, Driving Obsession, Denver, Colorado

Julie Bartleson, Golf Professional, Class A PGA, Broadmoor Golf Club, Seattle, Washington

Bud Bellis, Teaching Professional and former Senior PGA Tour Player, Rancho Manana, Cavecreek, Arizona

Clayton Cole, Head Golf Professional, Cherry Hills Country Club, Englewood, Colorado

Richard Cotton, MA, Vice President, Certification and Public Information, American Council on Exercise, San Diego, California

Scott Hays, Author/Editor, Tustin, California

Carol Lingle, Assistant Golf Professional, PGA & LPGA Member, Rancho Bernardo Inn, San Diego, California

Dr. Rob Roy McGregor, DPM, Assistant Professor Orthopedics and Rehabilitation, University of Massachusetts Medical School

Dennis Murray, Head Golf Professional, PGA Member, Bear Creek Golf Club, Denver, Colorado

David Mutton, President and Founder, Driving Obsession, San Francisco, California

Harvey Newton, CSCS Executive Director, National Strength and Conditioning Association, Colorado Springs, Colorado

James F. O'Leary, PGA Member, Chelsea Piers Golf Club, New York, New York

Ed Oldham, Head Golf Professional, PGA Class 1, The Ranch Country Club, Westminster, Colorado

Dr. Sheldon Roger, Orthopedic Surgeon, Denver, Colorado

Susan Roll, LPGA & PGA Golf Professional, Cobra Golf, Carlsbad, California

Kerri Smith, *The Denver Post,* Denver, Colorado

Allison St. Claire, Clear Mountain Communications, Denver, Colorado

Jerry Telle, MS, Research/Exercise Scientist, Lakewood, Colorado

Scott Welsh, PGA Golf Professional, San Diego, California

John Wheatley, Ashdown Teaching Center, Newington, Connecticut

Dr. David Wilder, Former Radiology Department Head, Rose Medical Center, Denver, Colorado

Carey Zwahr, Director of Golf, Ft. Morgan Golf Club, Ft. Morgan, Colorado

Better Golf Is Physical Golf

Golf is a sport and, from the physical perspective, a very complex and demanding sport. As a golfer you are an athlete and should approach golf as you would any other sport, using physical conditioning to improve your game.

Golf is a good deal more physical than most people imagine. It requires the use of more muscle groups, strength, flexibility and endurance than most golfers would dream possible. However, with the exception of an enlightened few, the so-called fitness boom hasn't made a dent in the ranks of the nation's golfers.

As a society, Americans are getting older, and the notion that one can continually improve performance in any sport for an indefinite period of time is quickly diminishing. It's harder to teach an old dog new tricks, especially when the new trick is a complicated sport like golf, which involves precise repeatable movements as well as a specific set of psychological and tactical skills. The aging process brings losses in flexibility, strength, power and cardiovascular fitness — key components for any sport and especially for golf. Thus, it's necessary to train for golf to maintain levels of strength and flexibility as well as to offset the effects of the aging process.

> As a golfer you are an athlete and should approach golf as you would any other sport, using physical conditioning to improve your game.

1

One premise of this book is that physical conditioning programs retard the aging process and in some cases can return the body to physical performance levels reached 20 to 30 years earlier. The adage, "If you don't use it, you'll lose it" definitely applies to fitness and golf, though in a way one might not expect, for although golf requires physical skills, it doesn't build real fitness. In fact, it doesn't even stress the physical system to a level where fitness can be maintained.

Golf is a physical sport for reasons that are obvious and not so obvious. Physically, a golfer loads or compresses — storing power during the backswing — and uncoils or uncompresses, utilizing that power during the swing forward. This requires tremendous muscular control, coordination and endurance for up to 5 hours per round. Golf is mentally stressful in terms of the concentration required; how well this is managed depends upon physical energy levels. Physical energy levels are influenced by aerobic fitness levels, so regular aerobic training is a must for successful golf performance.

Changes in equipment, although making the game easier for many, have resulted in increased physical demands upon golfers. Longer clubs and perimeter-weighted irons, many of which are heavier than their counterparts of former years, can add significant force and control requirements during the swing. As little as 1/4 ounce added to a club head moving at 90-plus miles per hour can place significant demands on your body to both control and accelerate the club head. The ability to swing more mass in the club head faster can lead to more injury potential for an unconditioned golfer.

The growing experience of tour players, as well as the body of scientific research on the subject, points to some interesting conclusions about physical conditioning and golf:

Physical training enables the golf athlete to maintain golf-related physical abilities despite aging.

Resistance training improves the power and endurance to use modern golf equipment effectively.

- 50% of golf injuries could have been prevented by proper conditioning programs.
- Of those golfers who suffered a golf injury, healing time was reduced by 40 to 70% if the golfer had been in a conditioning program before the injury.
- After the age of 30, a golfer is likely to get a nagging golf injury every 3 years, and after the age of 50 that likelihood increases to almost every year.
- Physiological effects of aging, such as decreased strength, flexibility, endurance and coordination, negatively affect the golf swing and can be countered with a scientific conditioning program.
- Golfers who exercise regularly significantly lower their handicaps compared to golfers at similar skill levels who don't exercise.

Golfers who exercise regularly significantly lower their handicaps compared to golfers at similar skill levels who don't exercise.

What does this mean if you're already a better than average golfer, or even a scratch golfer? Can physical training do anything for you? Would it be better to spend the time you would devote to physical training to practice instead? Won't new clubs improve your game to the same level that physical training would?

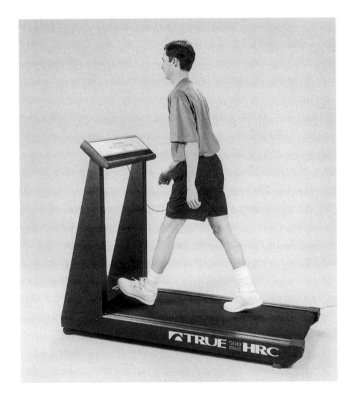

Aerobic conditioning will improve golf abilities by reducing overall fatigue and increasing the ability to mentally focus for 18 holes.

An important premise of this book is that a good physical training program, one geared to your skill level and the requirements of golf itself, will increase performance for a golfer at any level of mastery. Because of the specific physical requirements of golf, your physical training program has to target both those requirements and your own specific needs. Nonspecific and nonscientific conditioning will result in minimal improvement at best.

No two golf swings should be the same, and no two conditioning programs for golf should be the same! Golf isn't basketball or football, and

Remember, golf is a sport. As a golfer you are an athlete. This book will help you train effectively and safely for the sport of golf.

conditioning for golf, to be effective, needs to match what golf requires. No two golfers are equal in strength, flexibility, or cardiovascular (aerobic) endurance abilities, and each golfer responds somewhat differently to any training stimulus. If your conditioning program is specific, your performance and consistency will improve whether you are a tour player or a beginner.

The keys to training for golf are applicability, specificity and consistency. For example, one of the most common training mistakes is to add too much muscular bulk without additional flexibility training. The result will be a golfer who may have gained strength yet lost flexibility. Just as in other sports, the tool and the application of the tool are equally important. Whether strength training, aerobic or cardiovascular conditioning, or flexibility training, the application to golf has to be specific and tailored to your individual needs.

So what can the conditioning program outlined in this book do for your golf game? Why should you start or enhance a golf fitness program? Here is a summary of the ways the principles in this book will improve your golf performance and quality of life.

Power off the tee: The name of the distance game in golf is club-head speed, and resistance training improves your ability to generate club-head speed.

Decreased injuries: When you exercise regularly, you strengthen not only muscles but also the tendons and ligaments that support your muscles. The result is that you have resistance to overuse injuries from repeated motions like the swing, and when you hit a "fat shot," you are less likely to tear or strain a muscle, tendon or ligament.

Strength and muscular endurance for consistency: Consistency in golf is made in part by swing consistency. Resistance training improves your ability to repeatedly make a more consistent swing through improving strength in the necessary muscle groups.

Energy for mental focus: No matter whether you walk or ride, golf usually takes over 4 hours per round. Your aerobic or cardiovascular endurance is important in maintaining your energy and focus for this duration.

Finding your best swing: As you improve yourself physically, you will be able to explore new techniques in your golf swing and even in making specialty shots through increased muscular strength, flexibility and control.

Effortless swings: With increased physical strength and power, you will be able to make more "smooth" swings with greater distance and control with less effort. Increased confidence from physical training will let you swing easier with better results.

Back goes the clock: Exercise and proper nutrition can help slow the aging process. By increasing your conditioning, you can function physically at a level up to 30 years younger than your chronological age.

Apply the principles in this book, and your golf game will become correspondingly more consistent, and you'll lower your average score. Exercise for golf doesn't have to take 4 hours a day to be effective; rather, it must be applied consistently.

Remember, golf is a sport. *As a golfer you are an athlete.* This book will help you train effectively and safely for the sport of golf.

References

Baltes, P.B., and M.M. Baltes. 1980. *Plasticity and Variability in Psychological Aging: Methodological and Theoretical Issues in Determining the Effects of Aging on the Central Nervous System.* Berlin: Shering.

Benson, G. 1989. Research underscores potential pitfalls in golf's future. *Golf Market Today* 29:12-16.

Blair, S.N. et al. 1989. Physical fitness and all-cause mortality: A prospective study of healthy men and women. *Journal of the American Medical Association* 262:2395-401.

Bortz, W.M. 1996. *Dare to be 100.* New York: Fireside.

Buchan, J.F. 1990. Golf injuries: treatment and prevention. In S.D.W. Payne, ed., *Medicine, Sport and the Law.* Oxford: Blackwell Scientific Publications.

Carter, D. 1990. Pumping (a seven) iron. *American Fitness* (March-April):30.

Casperson, C.J. et al. 1996. Status of the 1990 physical fitness and exercise objectives — evidence from NHIS 1985. *Public Health Reports* 101:587.

Chopra, D. 1991. *Perfect Health.* New York: Harmony Books.

Delmonteque, B., and S. Hays. 1993. *Lifelong Fitness.* New York: Warner Books.

Duda, M. 1987. Golf injuries: They really do happen. *Physician and Sportsmedicine* 15(7):190-192, 194-196.

Evans, W., I.H. Rosenberg, and J. Thompson. 1992. *Biomarkers: The 10 Keys to Prolonging Vitality.* New York: Fireside.

Pernaut, J.F. 1988. Golf, sport de loisir ou sport de competition? (Golf, Leisure or Competitive Sport?) *Cinesiologie* 117:21-25.

Pratt, W.A., and K. Jennison. 1979. *Year-Round Conditioning for Part-Time Golfers.* New York: Atheneum/SMI.

Sharkey, B.J. 1997. *Fitness and Health.* Champaign, IL: Human Kinetics.

Wilmore, J.H. 1986. *Sensible Fitness.* Champaign, IL: Human Kinetics.

Wolkodoff, N.E. 1989. Building strength. *IDEA Today* 7:46, 49-55.

Understanding the Golf Swing

The Perfect Swing?

Golfers love to hit the ball. And not just hit it, but hit it squarely on the "sweet spot" — what's known as "catching it on the screws." All a golfer has to do is catch it "pure" one time, and they are hooked on golf. The Zen of the shot becomes a life-long pursuit.

However, the "perfect" golf swing does not exist — only the perfect shot for a particular situation. There are more swing techniques, variations, swing training devices and paths to get there being advocated today than ever before. There is only the perfect swing for you, and sometimes that is elusive!

Physical Dimensions of Golf

To improve your performance on the links, you need to understand the fundamentals of the golf swing, as well as how your body works during the swing. The golf swing is a highly complicated activity that takes coordination from both sides of your body for both movement and maintaining body position. You need balance, flexibility, specific psychological skills, power, coordination endurance and strength. These are needed in the right quantities in the proper muscle groups for the optimum golf swing.

The average PGA touring pro has a swing time ranging from approximately .95 to 1.25 seconds (which includes the start of backswing to impact). This data comes from Driving Obsession Learning Centers, which feature three-dimensional computer measurements and analysis. The speed of the swing means that so much occurs in about a second, it's difficult to feel which muscles are activating or firing. The time of the swing is so short that it is almost impossible to increase muscular efficiency or activation from just the golf swing itself.

This is also the reason that golf isn't enough to build or maintain fitness. There simply is not enough physical training stimulus in any one area to result in a fitness training effect. Improved golf performance relies on these abilities, yet these abilities are not built from golf itself.

> The golf swing is a highly complicated activity that takes coordination from both sides of your body for both movement and maintaining body position.

Computer measurements
and learning systems
enable the golf athlete
to improve technique
and gain an understand-
ing of which physical
components need
improvement.

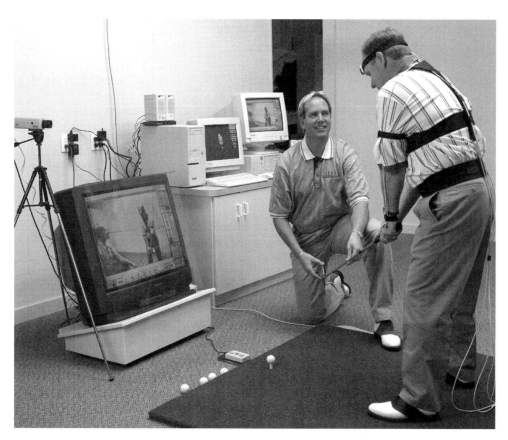

Golf instruction, until recently, focused on the mechanics of the swing. For example, should your arms initiate the downswing in some shots? Should the hips lead the motion in the swing for the greatest club-head speed? This focus on mechanics is definitely changing as proper conditioning is viewed as more essential to golf performance and consistency at any level of golf. Enhanced levels of physical conditioning lead to the ability to perform optimal mechanics repeatedly.

It is obvious that flexibility and strength are important for the golf swing. Knowing what to do with a body part or muscle group during the golf swing does not mean you have the physical ability to do it. In other words, trying to be more powerful in the golf swing does not mean the muscles necessarily have the ability to function more powerfully. To act in a coordinated, consistent and powerful motion in golf, the muscles must have the right blend of power, strength, endurance and flexibility. The physical capabilities of the muscular system will in large part determine your golf swing. Unless you are genetically gifted, physical training — rather than trying harder or with more concentration — determines these physiological abilities.

This chapter will help you understand the basic physical demands of the golf swing and which muscles are most important. Do the hands initiate the movement to the ball? How much does the body act like a whip? No matter how you swing, one thing is certain: the golf swing uses a good many more muscle groups than you ever would have thought, and those muscle groups and their capabilities can be improved through physical training.

Power: The Source

Like a chain, the golf swing is dependent on all the needed muscle groups making a contribution. The golf swing is a function of your physical ability to have all the mechanical elements contribute in the right timing and repeatable execution of the swing. Optimal conditioning allows the muscle groups used in golf to work in harmony to produce a powerful and consistent swing. The result is simply better, more consistent golf.

Many golfers think that the power in the swing comes only from the hips. Other muscle groups contribute to the coil/uncoil movement in golf. If other muscle groups such as the shoulders, trunk, forearms or back don't possess the right physical qualities, the hips can't contribute optimally to the golf swing. An effective golf swing is one in which the arms, legs, trunk and shoulders coil or store energy, and then that energy is released and directed so that maximum consistent impact occurs with the golf ball. Any weak link in the chain, and force is lost somewhere in the golf swing.

From this perspective, golf is a total-body athletic event; almost every major muscle in the body contributes to the golf swing and could be enhanced by physical training.

Optimal conditioning allows the muscle groups used in golf to work in harmony to produce a powerful and consistent swing.

As a whole-body activity, golf uses almost every muscle in the body and both sides of the body.

The path to a better golf swing is really quite simple — your physical abilities will directly affect your respective swing characteristics. And we're not talking about your physical size and appearance (tall, short, fat, thin), but rather about a more personal understanding and application of how the human body works, specifically, which major muscle groups contribute to the golf swing so you can increase their capabilities. Increase their abilities, and you have the physical foundation to improve the golf swing whether your goal is distance, consistency or accuracy.

Personal Swing Power

Discovering and understanding your own physical limitations and strengths is of paramount importance when attempting to find a swing that's right for you. Unlike other athletes, golfers have been somewhat slow to accept the role of physical conditioning in performance improvement. For example, you can improve your basketball skills and conditioning by simply playing on weekends. You can improve your racquetball skills and conditioning whacking a ball 3 times a week. But these are physically demanding sports. It's physiologically reasonable to expect the human body to improve itself from mere participation. In golf, the connection between physical capabilities, conditioning and mechanical improvement is not always obvious. Lessons and computer measurements, in conjunction with a professional instructor, can help point to weak areas in physical conditioning. In many cases, the inability to consistently perform a specific movement in golf is caused by the inability of the muscular system to perform that maneuver or movement.

The fitness conditioning effect from just playing golf is minimal at best. Merely playing a round of golf on weekends won't improve your golf-specific fitness. Strong back, abdominal and hip muscles are important to golf yet aren't developed effectively from playing golf. In an average round, where the golfer shoots 100, only 2 minutes of total time is spent swinging the club, including practice time.

Golfers haven't taken golf conditioning seriously because golf fitness is extremely complex. It is difficult to develop a plan of improvement for what you can't quantify or understand clearly. Too often, you can simply blame your poor performance on something else. You can blame it on stress, lack of practice, even your clubs. Even athletes on the PGA and LPGA tours have found that maintaining a fitness program, even if minimal, will result in better performance under more demanding conditions. *Improving fitness improves golf performance.*

The Physical Nature of Golf

To understand how to train your body for a better swing, you first have to understand what the sport of golf requires physically, both during performance and practice and during the swing. Like other sports, what you do during practice is different from what you do during performance. Your golf training should reflect what you need in a match as well as what you need to practice effectively. While there is a definite mental side of golf, the focus here is on the physical characteristics and abilities, which allow that mental side to produce its best golf.

Merely playing a round of golf on weekends won't improve your golf-specific fitness.

Your golf training should reflect what you need in a match as well as what you need to practice effectively.

For example, the pace of your shots during practice is faster than normal. Also, if you're hitting a bucket of balls, you don't get the chance to rest between shots. This requires muscular endurance or the ability to repeat the same movement because of the high number of swings during a short period of time. During a round of golf your swing patterns are different. Your pace isn't fast, and you do get a chance to rest between shots.

Practice takes a higher level of muscular endurance than actual golf performance. Golf performance is power, strength and flexibility, while practice requires more muscular endurance. In addition, actual performance of a golf round, lasting over 4 hours, depends on aerobic or cardiovascular conditioning levels to maintain focus, fight fatigue and maintain a consistent swing. Golf is golf, not physical training.

In either case, golf is not enough training stimulus to build any fitness component on which the golf swing relies. In this sense, golf may be the most unique sport in the world in its use of muscular power, endurance, aerobic/cardiovascular capacity and golfer-specific flexibility. Because of the breadth and depth of these components, you simply can't expect golf to build any fitness quality. If golf did build fitness, golfers would have all the forearm strength they need just from hitting range balls.

Therefore, to understand the golf swing, you need to understand the basic physiological components (power, strength, endurance, aerobic/cardiovascular capacity and flexibility) of golf and the major muscular movers of the swing phases. Each phase has a different blend of physical parameters, which, depending on the level of your game, require more or less attention. Understanding the muscle groups and physical requirements of the swing as well as the total game enables you to effectively adapt physical training to improve your golf game.

For example, if you're under a 7 handicap and play 4 or more times per week, your goal for conditioning may be to counterbalance the muscle groups that get overused and to correct postural imbalances. If you're a 23 handicap who only plays occasionally, then your goals and needs might be more in the areas of flexibility and general strength in order to maintain a more consistent swing pattern and prevent injury.

Golf Compared to Other Sports

Most sports require some degree of strength, power, endurance and flexibility. Golf is no different in that it requires specific physical abilities that include:

- Strength, which is defined as the maximal force you can exert regardless of duration.
- Power, or the ability to perform a movement as rapidly as possible.
- Muscular endurance, the ability to repeat a movement without fatigue.
- General endurance or aerobic capacity, which is the ability of the whole body to work steadily over an extended period of time.
- Flexibility, which is your range of motion around a joint or set of joints.

Golf is a sport that requires muscle endurance because the swing is repeated, especially on the practice range in short succession between shots. Power is necessary for each shot because in most cases, a golfer is best off generating as much controlled club-head speed as possible. Strength is important

Golf performance is power, strength and flexibility, while practice requires more muscular endurance.

If golf did build fitness, golfers would have all the forearm strength they need just from hitting range balls.

Power is necessary for each shot, because in most cases, a golfer is best off generating as much controlled club-head speed as possible.

What makes golf unique is that you use both sides of your body, and both sides are active during the swing.

to maintain body position and posture, such as the spine angle during the swing. Aerobic capacity or cardiovascular endurance is important because the average golf round is over 4 hours.

A major difference between the pro tour players and amateurs is golf-specific flexibility. The tour players get a greater degree of shoulder turn from trunk rotation than most amateur players, who gain this turn mostly from the shoulders. Without the spine and trunk twisting along its own axis and the back knee serving as an axis point, you're forced to use other muscles to generate both the swing and club head speed. The results are often a less than repeatable swing with high injury potential and fatigue. In this scenario, you have to use smaller muscles that fatigue faster given the power and control requirements of golf.

Swing Basics

During the golf swing, a number of complex movements occur that are interlinked in flexibility, muscular endurance, strength and power. During the basic stance, in a flexed position, you rely on support from your hamstrings, or the back of the upper leg. Without adequate strength or flexibility, the hamstrings will tighten, causing the right or non-target knee to straighten during the backswing. In addition, strong muscles in the back and abdominals are essential for support and maintaining support during the golf swing. Balance, posture and swing mechanics are, in this case, direct results of physical capabilities.

What makes golf unique is that you use both sides of your body, and both sides are active during the swing. During the take-away or backswing in a one-piece take-away, your shoulders turn away from the ball while your arms stay initially fully extended, with a relaxed grip on the club. In some players, there is an active hinging of the wrist and elbows, which requires more muscular activation of the arms, shoulders and forearms for control.

Your weight then shifts from being evenly distributed between the feet to the back foot, or non-target foot, while the hips turn away from the ball. The hips turn as a result of the shoulders turning, not as an independent movement. In this "coiled" position, you then uncoil the hips with a slight to moderate hip motion toward the target while coordinating with the arms and shoulders to meet the ball with as much speed and force during impact as possible. The swing continues with a weight shift to the target foot and a followthrough with the club, arms and shoulders.

Phases of the Modern Golf Swing

For the purpose of this book, five golf swing phases will be matched with the major muscle groups primarily responsible for movement and golf posture. Because the golf swing is a movement with individual variations, swings may look similar, yet they are not 100% identical. The human body is a lever system for golf, rotating around the shoulder closest to the target. The side closest to the target is referred to as the "target side," whereas the opposite side of the body, in the case of a right-handed golfer, the right side, will be referred to as the "non-target side."

Some research indicates that the muscle groups used are essentially the same for amateurs as professionals, just the efficiency and consistency varies based on proficiency. For example, tour pros fire the muscles in short bursts only when they are needed. High-handicap amateurs may fire or activate the muscle throughout the entire golf swing. It may be that, as an amateur, your need for conditioning from this perspective is substantially higher than tour players'. For example, the tibialis anterior, or front of the shin — a muscle used in balance — often is fired repeatedly by amateurs with high handicaps to maintain balance. On the other hand, the swing mechanics of the tour professionals are so consistent that they rarely get out of balance, so this muscle group is much less activated than with amateurs.

Address/Basic Stance

In this position, the golfer has weight equally distributed with approximately 60% on the non-target side and 40% on the target side. Most golfers can fit the hips in between the width of the ankles during address. The knees are slightly bent (10 to 20 degrees) with the back bent slightly forward, partially as a result of the hips tilting forward 5 to 15 degrees. The fingers and hands grip the club in this position with a straight or close to straight arm, with the back of the palm or the target hand facing the target. The target shoulder is slightly higher than the non-target shoulder. Some muscles of the upper body adjust and stabilize the distance from the golf ball.

Primary Muscles Used/Action

Upper Body
- Palmaris longus (forearms): isometric contraction to grip club.
- Triceps (upper arm/back): isometric contraction to hold target arm straight.

Trunk
- Erector spinae (back): posture/balance.
- Rectus abdominis (abdominals): posture/balance.

Lower Body/Legs
- Biceps femoris, semimembranosus, semitendinosus (hamstring group): posture/balance.
- Gluteus maximus (hips): posture/balance.

Training Implications

Golfers are rarely aware of the contribution of the hamstrings both to posture and hip rotation. Proper and consistent address posture is also aided by adequate strength and muscular endurance in the abdominal and back muscles. If you don't possess strength and muscular endurance in the golf stance and basic address, you won't maintain consistent posture through your round. As you change your golf posture over 18 holes, your mechanics have to change. Unfortunately, this usually means less than optimal results. Physical training will improve your ability to maintain golf-specific posture at address.

Some research indicates that the muscle groups used are essentially the same for amateurs as professionals, just the efficiency and consistency varies based on proficiency.

If you don't possess strength and muscular endurance in the golf stance and basic address, you won't maintain consistent posture through your round.

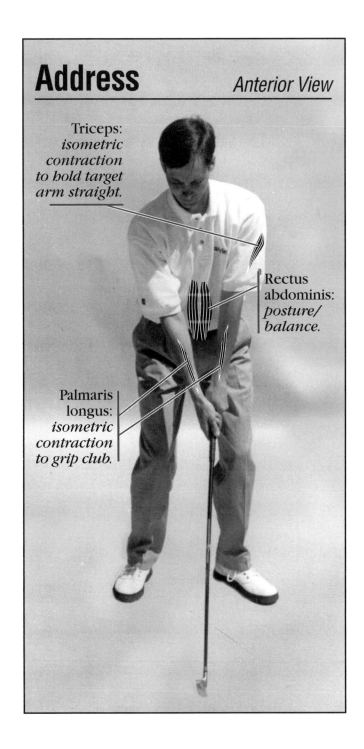

Address   *Anterior View*

Triceps: *isometric contraction to hold target arm straight.*

Rectus abdominis: *posture/ balance.*

Palmaris longus: *isometric contraction to grip club.*

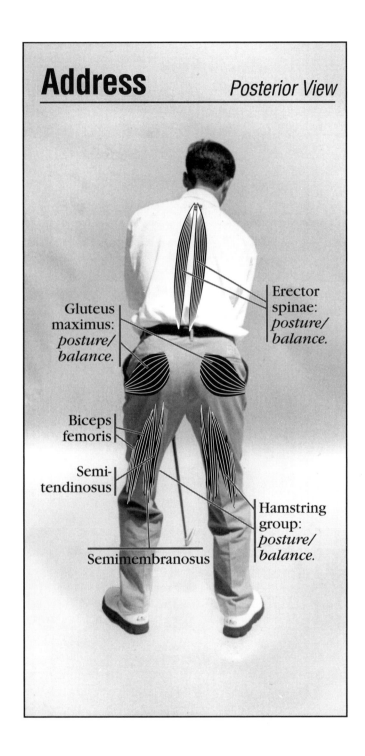

Address   *Posterior View*

Erector spinae: *posture/balance.*

Gluteus maximus: *posture/balance.*

Biceps femoris

Semi-tendinosus

Hamstring group: *posture/balance.*

Semimembranosus

Backswing

During the backswing, a number of muscle groups become active that were not active in the stance. In the backswing, most golfers will start to take the club and arms back as a unit, with the club being perpendicular to the plane of the shoulder.

Your hips and shoulders begin to rotate (with motion started by the shoulders) away from the target, with the shoulders ultimately 35 or more degrees of rotation away from the target than the hips. This difference between the shoulder and hip turn is referred to as the "X factor." During the backswing, the weight shifts from a fairly equal distribution to weight approximately 85% on the rear or non-target foot because of the redistribution of upper body mass.

As the arms and shoulder try to move backward as a unit, more muscle groups are called into play, and those that were active have become more active. For example, the triceps must stay active to keep the target arm straight, while the forearm muscles are used to keep the club "cocked" as long as possible. The hands move over the non-target shoulder. The rotator cuff muscles are used both in stabilizing the shoulder girdle and well as turning with the shoulders and arms. This is why these small muscles are key to the golf swing: their stabilization and action leads to power and control.

The external obliques (side abdominals) on the target side, as well as the hamstrings, contribute to hip rotation and controlling hip rotation during the backswing. The entire upper body moves slightly away from the target toward the non-target foot. Both the target arm/side and followthrough side/arm contribute to the take-away.

Primary Muscles Used/Action

Upper Body

- Biceps, non-target side: raising the club/support during last phase of backswing.
- Pectoralis major, target side: aids in moving target arm away from target.
- Flexor carpi ulnaris (forearm): stabilizes/cocks the wrist.
- Extensor carpi ulnaris (forearm): stabilizes/cocks the wrist.
- Teres minor, non-target side (rotator cuff): pulls the club back, stabilizes the shoulder girdle.
- Supraspinatus, non-target side (rotator cuff): assists in club take-away, shoulder stabilization from abduction of arm.
- Infraspinatus, non-target side (rotator cuff): pulls the club back, stabilizes the shoulder girdle, external arm rotation.
- Deltoids (shoulders), both sides: pulls the club back, aids in swing initiation forward.

Trunk

- External oblique (side abdominal), target side: rotation along spinal axis.
- Internal oblique (side abdominal), non-target side: rotation along spinal axis.
- Rectus abdominis, non-target side: rotation/stabilization.
- Erector spinae, non-target side: back stabilization, rotation along spinal axis.

Lower Body/Legs

- Biceps femoris, semimembranosus, semitendinosus (hamstrings): hip rotation, stance and posture.
- Adductor brevis, longus, magnus (adductors), target side: inward/lateral movement of thigh.
- Gluteus minimus, target side: inward/lateral hip movement.

Golf Training Implications

The shoulder girdle, or scapula area, can elevate, descend and even move forward and backward in sport movements. In golf, the corresponding muscle groups that keep this area stable form the physical basis for optimum mechanics. Golf athletes are dependent on a large number of muscle groups, including the trapezius, latissimus dorsi, deltoids and rotator cuff group, to keep the shoulder girdle stable and move when appropriate. This is part of the reason that sport simulators that try to build strength for the swing don't work effectively. They can't simulate the exact forces, movement requirements and acceleration patterns of the shoulder or other muscle groups during the golf swing.

One muscle group or side will pull up the club, while the other side of the body — sometimes the exact muscle group on the other side of the body — will be responsible for portions of the downswing and followthrough. Remember, golf uses both sides of the body almost equally and almost all muscle groups. You can't just train the target side. Some muscles are responsible for the control in the backswing, while some create the power in the downswing.

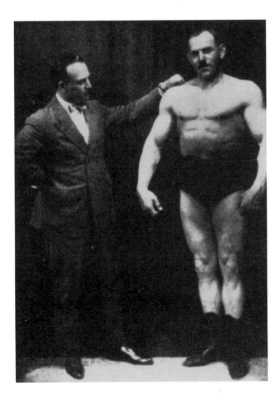

By increasing your physical abilities for golf, you will amaze your friends, decrease your handicap and intimidate your opponents. Such was the case with old-time weightlifter Herman Gorner, who reportedly was barred from Scotland because of his tremendous distance off the tee combined with finesse around the pin, which led to his being declared to have an insurmountable advantage over his opponents.

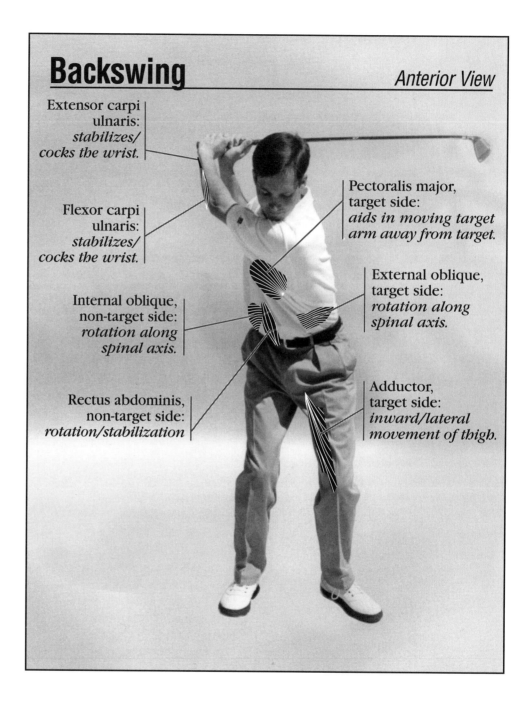

Backswing

Anterior View

Extensor carpi ulnaris: *stabilizes/ cocks the wrist.*

Flexor carpi ulnaris: *stabilizes/ cocks the wrist.*

Internal oblique, non-target side: *rotation along spinal axis.*

Rectus abdominis, non-target side: *rotation/stabilization*

Pectoralis major, target side: *aids in moving target arm away from target.*

External oblique, target side: *rotation along spinal axis.*

Adductor, target side: *inward/lateral movement of thigh.*

Backswing

Posterior View

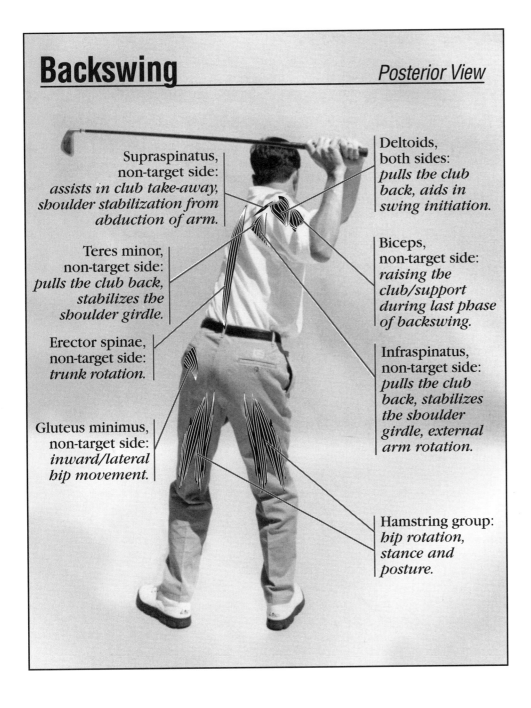

Supraspinatus, non-target side: *assists in club take-away, shoulder stabilization from abduction of arm.*

Teres minor, non-target side: *pulls the club back, stabilizes the shoulder girdle.*

Erector spinae, non-target side: *trunk rotation.*

Gluteus minimus, non-target side: *inward/lateral hip movement.*

Deltoids, both sides: *pulls the club back, aids in swing initiation.*

Biceps, non-target side: *raising the club/support during last phase of backswing.*

Infraspinatus, non-target side: *pulls the club back, stabilizes the shoulder girdle, external arm rotation.*

Hamstring group: *hip rotation, stance and posture.*

The Downswing/Initiation Forward

During the downswing, the weight distribution moves to the target side both from the uncoiling/turning of the hips into the target as well as the shift of the entire body toward the target as a rotating, lateral and pivoting movement. Before the downswing, the shoulders are turned approximately 35 degrees more than the hips. The stored energy in the muscles, ligaments and tendons, plus the stretch reflex (see chapters on strength and flexibility physiology) as well as your brain saying "now swing" all contribute to the movement.

Better golfers move their hips as the initial movement of the downswing, while others move the hips/shoulders simultaneously. Like throwing sports, the movement of the hips in golf initiates the motion. The non-target arm and elbow angle should be less than 90 degrees, which facilitates the generation of angular velocity. Keeping the club/arm system shorter means you can generate more club head speed at this point. For example, modern tennis players have gained greater velocity from keeping the racket arm in tighter to the body, generating more racket speed before full extension into the ball.

Primary Muscles Used/Action

Upper Body
- Pectoralis major, non-target side: arm swing to ball especially during acceleration just before impact.
- Posterior deltoid, non-target side: activation as stabilizer.
- Triceps: extension and isometric, or holding contraction.
- Teres minor, infraspinatus (rotator cuff): shoulder stabilization and movement of target arm.
- Trapezius: shoulder stabilization.
- Subscapularis (rotator cuff): internal rotation of non-target arm toward target.
- Extensor carpi radialis longus (forearms): return from wrist cock.
- Latissimus dorsi (lower back): shoulder girdle stabilization, adduction/stabilization of non-target arm, pull downward.
- Extensor carpi radialis brevis (forearms): return from wrist cock.

Trunk
- External oblique, non-target side: stabilizer, pulling of shoulders toward hips and rotation toward target.
- Internal oblique, target side: trunk rotation.
- Erector spinae, target side: trunk rotation.

Lower Body/Legs
- Biceps femoris, semimembranosus, semitendinosus (hamstrings): hip rotation.
- Gluteus medius, gluteus minimus (hips): hip abduction with non-target leg.

Golf Training Implications

The downswing requires the rotator cuff muscles to remain active to stabilize the shoulder girdle while the non-target arm remains "tucked" to generate speed before full extension. This is why the rotator cuff muscles, especially the external rotators on both sides, should be trained regularly in your conditioning program. Resistance training not only increases their physiological capabilities, but also your awareness of these various muscle groups in sport movements.

Better golfers move their hips as the initial movement of the downswing, while others move the hips/shoulders simultaneously.

The external rotators on both sides should be trained regularly in your conditioning program.

Full extension of the hands/forearms at impact is required for maximum club head speed.

Downswing
Initiation forward

Anterior View

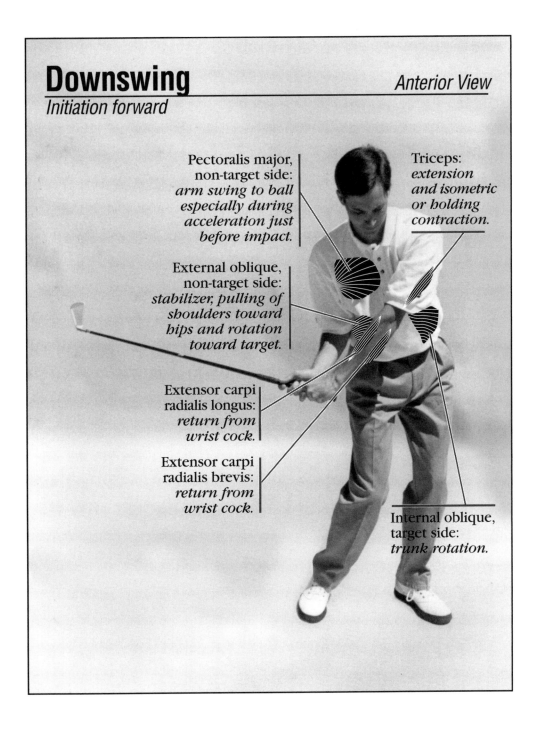

Pectoralis major, non-target side: *arm swing to ball especially during acceleration just before impact.*

External oblique, non-target side: *stabilizer, pulling of shoulders toward hips and rotation toward target.*

Extensor carpi radialis longus: *return from wrist cock.*

Extensor carpi radialis brevis: *return from wrist cock.*

Triceps: *extension and isometric or holding contraction.*

Internal oblique, target side: *trunk rotation.*

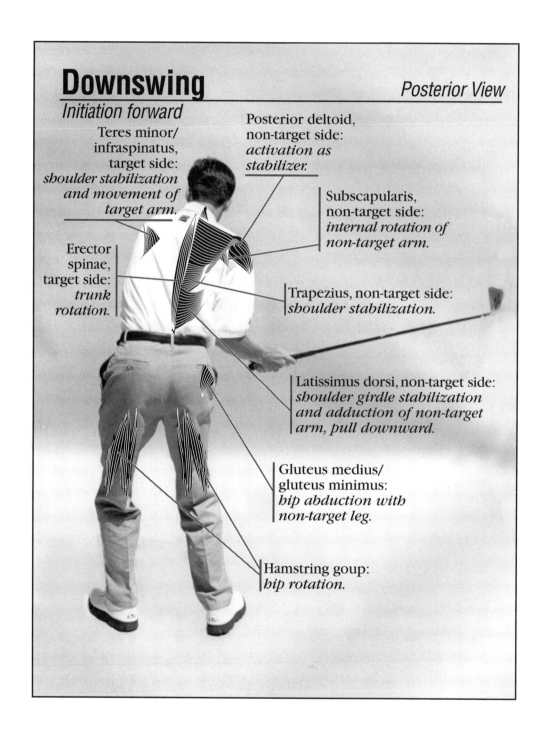

Downswing

Initiation forward

Posterior View

Teres minor/
infraspinatus,
target side:
*shoulder stabilization
and movement of
target arm.*

Posterior deltoid,
non-target side:
*activation as
stabilizer.*

Subscapularis,
non-target side:
*internal rotation of
non-target arm.*

Erector
spinae,
target side:
*trunk
rotation.*

Trapezius, non-target side:
shoulder stabilization.

Latissimus dorsi, non-target side:
*shoulder girdle stabilization
and adduction of non-target
arm, pull downward.*

Gluteus medius/
gluteus minimus:
*hip abduction with
non-target leg.*

Hamstring goup:
hip rotation.

Impact

During impact, the target arm and non-target arm and club should be extended as a singular unit with maximum length. The non-target side, especially in the trunk area, has activated the abdominal region to help launch the movement of the body, forward and laterally, to the target. At ball impact, certain muscle groups, such as the target side internal obliques as well as the pectoralis, are extremely active. At this point in the golf swing, the muscle groups activated in the initiation and acceleration of the downswing either remain active or decrease activity.

Timing of the various lever systems at impact is critical to club head speed and control. The hips and shoulders narrow the gap between them in terms of amount of turn, due in part to the rotational speed of the shoulders being faster than the hips. Full extension of the hands/forearms at impact is required for maximum club head speed. This lateral, then rotating, movement toward the target is another determinant of developing club head speed.

Primary Muscle Used/Actions

Upper Body
- Pectoralis major, non-target side: club swing, minor contribution.
- Latissimus dorsi, non-target side: internal rotation and movement of non-target arm.
- Triceps: extension and isometric or holding contraction during swing.
- Teres minor, infraspinatus (rotator cuff), target side: shoulder stabilization, external rotation of target arm.
- Subscapularis (rotator cuff), non-target side: internal rotation and movement of non-target arm.
- Extensor carpi radialis longus (forearms): return from wrist cock.
- Extensor carpi radialis brevis (forearms): return from wrist cock.
- Flexor carpi ulnaris (forearms): initiation of wrist snap/roll.

Trunk
- External oblique, non-target side: pulling of shoulders to hips and rotation toward target.
- Internal oblique, target side: trunk rotation.
- Rectus abdominis: stabilization.
- Erector spinae, target side: trunk rotation.
- Quadratus lumborum: side bend of trunk on non-target side.

Lower Body/Legs
- Gluteus medius (hips): rotation to target with non-target leg.
- Gluteus minimus (hips): hip abduction/lateral weight shift to target.
- Biceps femoris, semimembranosus, semitendinosus (hamstrings): hip rotation, hip extension.
- Adductor brevis, longus, magnus (adductors), non-target side: lateral weight shift/hip movement toward target.
- Gastrocnemius/soleus (calf group): push off/stabilization during weight change.

Golf Training Implications

The combination rotation/lateral movement toward the target of the entire body is based on hip and leg rotation. Exercises for the adductors, abductors and other hip muscles are essential to adding hip power. The hamstrings aid in maintaining posture and help rotate the femur and hips toward the target.

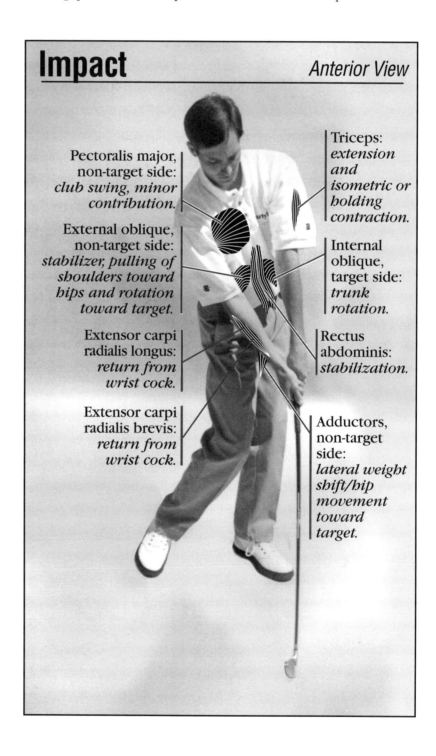

Impact
Anterior View

Pectoralis major, non-target side: *club swing, minor contribution.*

External oblique, non-target side: *stabilizer, pulling of shoulders toward hips and rotation toward target.*

Extensor carpi radialis longus: *return from wrist cock.*

Extensor carpi radialis brevis: *return from wrist cock.*

Triceps: *extension and isometric or holding contraction.*

Internal oblique, target side: *trunk rotation.*

Rectus abdominis: *stabilization.*

Adductors, non-target side: *lateral weight shift/hip movement toward target.*

Better golf depends on training the hamstrings. The rotator cuff group and abdominals are very active during this phase of the swing. Forearm strength and power is a determinant of not only club head speed but control and accuracy at impact.

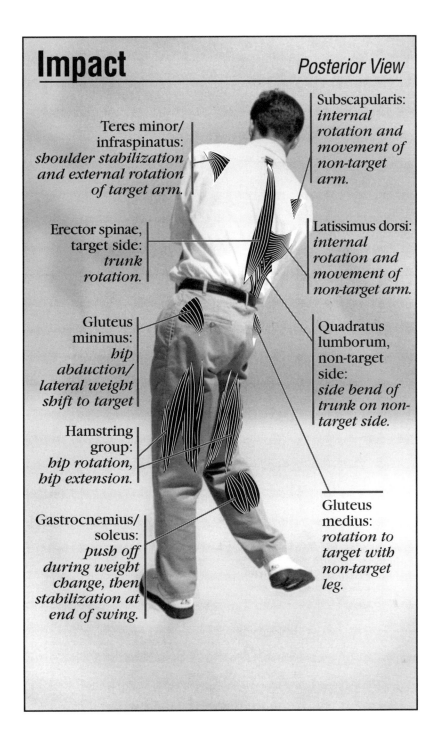

Impact   *Posterior View*

Teres minor/infraspinatus: *shoulder stabilization and external rotation of target arm.*

Subscapularis: *internal rotation and movement of non-target arm.*

Erector spinae, target side: *trunk rotation.*

Latissimus dorsi: *internal rotation and movement of non-target arm.*

Gluteus minimus: *hip abduction/lateral weight shift to target*

Quadratus lumborum, non-target side: *side bend of trunk on non-target side.*

Hamstring group: *hip rotation, hip extension.*

Gastrocnemius/soleus: *push off during weight change, then stabilization at end of swing.*

Gluteus medius: *rotation to target with non-target leg.*

The combination rotation/lateral movement of the entire body toward the target is based on hip and leg rotation.

Followthrough

During this phase of the golf swing, most muscle groups don't have as much activity; the swing, with a few exceptions, is a continuation of momentum and weight change. Even though momentum carries a large part of the follow-through, it is aided by certain muscle groups that continue the movement toward the target while maintaining balance. In addition, some muscle groups, such as the rectus abdominis, contract or perform a "braking" function to keep the golfer from hyper-extending the back.

In this phase of the golf swing, the golfer's center of gravity has shifted totally to the target leg. In addition, the shoulders and hips have rotated toward the target so they are facing the target, with the non-target side shoulder slightly closer to the target.

Primary Muscles Used/Action

Upper Body

- Teres minor, target side: shoulder stabilization and external rotation of arm.
- Subscapularis, non-target side: internal rotation and movement of non-target arm.
- Infraspinatus, target side: external rotation of target arm.
- Extensor carpi radialis longus (forearms): maintaining club grip.
- Flexor carpi ulnaris (forearms): maintaining club grip.
- Extensor carpi ulnaris (forearms): maintaining club grip.
- Extensor carpi radialis brevis (forearms): maintaining club grip.

Trunk

- External oblique, non-target side: stabilizer, pulling of shoulders toward hips and rotation toward target.
- Internal oblique, target side: trunk rotation.
- Rectus abdominis: stabilization and isometric contraction at end of swing to prevent excessive hyper-extension of the back.
- Erector spinae, both sides: brings upper body/trunk upright at end of swing.

Lower Body/Legs

- Biceps femoris, semimembranosus, semitendinosus (hamstrings): hip rotation, hip extension.
- Gluteus minimus, non-target side (hips): hip abduction with non-target leg, hip rotation.
- Gastrocnemius/soleus (calf group), non-target side: push off during weight change, then stabilization at end of swing.
- Tibialis anterior (front of shin), target side: stabilization of lower target leg.

Training Implications

The rotator cuff muscles are still very active during this swing phase. They both provide movement from the target side and stabilization from the non-target side. The abdominals are still active, both in the end of rotation and in stabilization. Strong trunk muscles, not just the abdominals, are important for golf, since they are active in every phase of the golf swing.

Followthrough   *Anterior View*

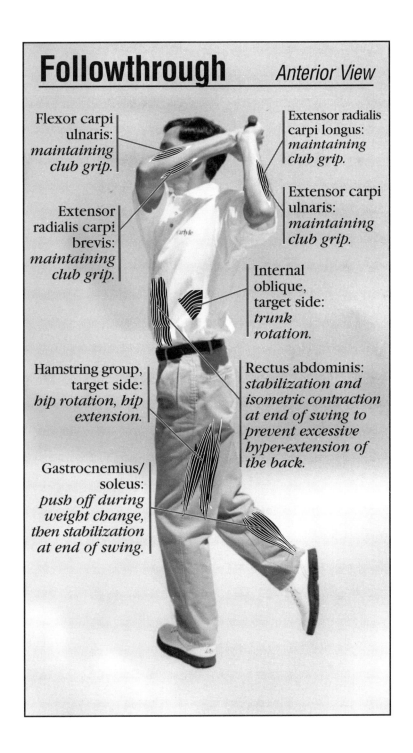

Flexor carpi ulnaris: *maintaining club grip.*

Extensor radialis carpi brevis: *maintaining club grip.*

Hamstring group, target side: *hip rotation, hip extension.*

Gastrocnemius/soleus: *push off during weight change, then stabilization at end of swing.*

Extensor radialis carpi longus: *maintaining club grip.*

Extensor carpi ulnaris: *maintaining club grip.*

Internal oblique, target side: *trunk rotation.*

Rectus abdominis: *stabilization and isometric contraction at end of swing to prevent excessive hyper-extension of the back.*

Golf is a unique sport in that, in one athletic movement, your muscles are required to perform with abilities ranging from muscular endurance to power.

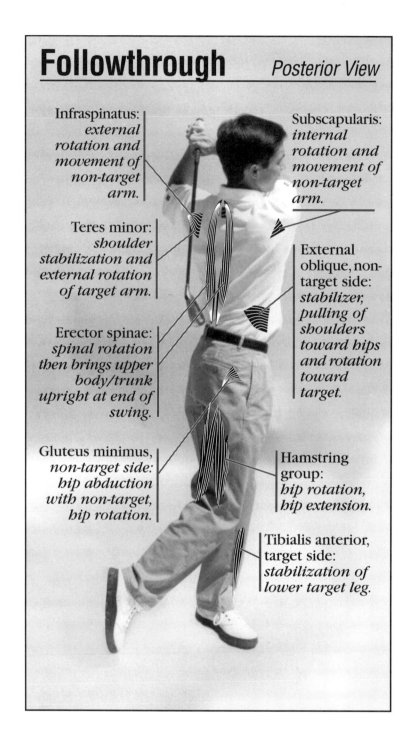

Followthrough   *Posterior View*

Infraspinatus: *external rotation and movement of non-target arm.*

Teres minor: *shoulder stabilization and external rotation of target arm.*

Erector spinae: *spinal rotation then brings upper body/trunk upright at end of swing.*

Gluteus minimus, *non-target side: hip abduction with non-target, hip rotation.*

Subscapularis: *internal rotation and movement of non-target arm.*

External oblique, non-target side: *stabilizer, pulling of shoulders toward hips and rotation toward target.*

Hamstring group: *hip rotation, hip extension.*

Tibialis anterior, target side: *stabilization of lower target leg.*

Observations that Dictate Physical Training

The Golf Swing as Whole-Body Movement

The golf swing uses upper, trunk and lower body muscles. Muscle groups that might not contribute to the active swing play just as important a role in posture or maintaining consistent swing planes. To a large degree, the right and left sides of the body function as mirror images of each other, even though your force and movement is directed toward the target. The target side, the left side if you are a right-handed golfer, is not necessarily more important than the other side of the body.

One of the training principles that can be derived from this analysis is that golf training should encompass the whole body. Neglect any part in training, and the linkage of the entire system will be impaired. For example, when performing resistance training, you should have some exercise for every major muscle group used in the golf swing. If you neglect hip strength or flexibility, you don't have much chance of making up for it with arm strength. This is also part of the reason why a nonspecific resistance training routine will somewhat improve golf performance — you use most muscles of the body in the golf swing.

> If you neglect hip strength or flexibility, you don't have much chance of making up for it with arm strength.

Spanning the Globe of Strength

Golf is a unique sport in that, in one athletic movement, your muscles have to perform with abilities ranging from muscular endurance to power. Your physical training should reflect the specific abilities these muscle groups need. For example, the rotator cuff group needs more emphasis on strength and muscular endurance because of the effect of these muscles on the stability of the shoulder girdle. They are active during almost the entire swing. For maximum effectiveness and applicability for golf, resistance training should address muscular endurance, strength and power.

Injury Potential

Golf results in many injuries that just shouldn't occur when considering the nature of the sport — a highly coordinated, whole-body movement. In other words, since the golf swing relies on so many muscle groups, there shouldn't be enough distress on any muscle group during the swing to cause injury. In actuality, the golf swing is dynamic, powerful and somewhat unnatural.

Old-time weightlifters like Anton Matysek probably would have made great golfers because of their blend of power and flexibility.

The sheer magnitude of the force that you generate dictates that the weak links will be more susceptible to injury. The average golf ball weighs 45+ grams, yet it is stationary at impact while your body is accelerating as fast as possible. The back, elbows, wrists, shoulders and knees are susceptible to injury if they are the weak links in this powerful and dynamic motion.

And that is the point: golf is powerful yet unnatural at the same time. Without specific conditioning for all the muscle groups required, there is a significant chance that one of those muscle groups will not possess the characteristics necessary for the singular, explosive performance of a swing. Even if the proper swing can be made, without golf-specific conditioning, the swing will not be repeated with regularity. These necessary physical characteristics include all the different qualities of strength from muscular endurance to muscular power and flexibility. If you lack in an area, another muscle group in the chain will have to compensate for that lack of ability. Unfortunately, compensation rarely works well in golf because the resulting mechanics have a high injury potential.

The answer to physical training for better golf is to better understand what golf requires. Treat golf as a sport, and train physically to improve your swing, lower your score and reduce your risk of injury.

Understanding the Golf Swing KEY POINTS

• Golf uses almost all the muscles in the body for an effective golf swing.

• The golf swing is not a natural motion, therefore physical training will enhance the abilities to make the swing effective and repeatable.

• The golf swing simultaneously uses strength, power, muscular endurance and flexibility.

• Almost every major muscle in the body is used in the golf swing.

• The target side and non-target side are both essential to a sound and repeatable golf swing.

• Practice on the range depends on muscular endurance, while actual golf performance requirements rely more on muscular power.

• These unique requirements of golf mean that a scientific conditioning program will improve performance and reduce injury potential.

References

Bechler, J.R., F.W. Jobe, M. Pink, J. Perry, and P.A. Ruwe. 1995. Electromyographic analysis of the hip and knee during the golf swing. *Clinical Journal of Sport Medicine* 5(3):162-166.

Cochran, A., and J. Stobbs. 1966. *The Search for the Perfect Golf Swing.* New York: J.B. Lippincott Co.

Hogan, G., and H. Spencer. 1994. *The Challenge: Fact Versus Theory in the Golf Swing.* Sydney: H.E.S. Video Productions.

Kao, J.T., M. Pink, F.W. Jobe, and J. Perry. 1995. Electromyographic analysis of the scapular muscles during a golf swing. *American Journal of Sports Medicine* 23(1):19-23.

Kawashima, K. 1993. Comparative analysis of the body motion in golf swing. International Society of Biomechanics. Congress (14th: 1993: Paris, France); Societe internationale de biomecanique. Congres. (14e: 1993: Paris, France). In, *Abstracts of the International Society of Biomechanics, XIVth Congress, Paris, 4-8 July, 1993,* vol. I, Paris, s.n., 1993, 670-671.

Kirby, R., and J.A. Roberts. 1985. *Introductory Biomechanics.* Ithaca, NY: Movement Publications Inc.

Knudson, G., L. Rubenstein, and N. Harris. 1989. *The Natural Golf Swing.* Bellevue, WA: Kirsh & Baum Publishers.

Lowe, B., and I.H. Fairweather. 1994. Centrifugal force and the planar golf swing. World Scientific Congress of Golf (2nd: 1994: St. Andrews, Scotland). In, Cochran, A.J. and Farrally, F.R. (eds.), *Science and Golf II: Proceedings of the 1994 World Scientific Congress of Golf,* London, E & FN Spon, 59-64.

McLaughlin, P.A., and R.J. Best. 1994. Three-dimensional kinematic analysis of the golf swing. World Scientific Congress of Golf (2nd: 1994: St. Andrews, Scotland). In, Cochran, A.J. and Farrally, F.R. (eds.), *Science and Golf II: Proceedings of the 1994 World Scientific Congress of Golf,* London: E & FN Spon, 91-96.

McTeigue, M., S.R. Lamb, R. Mottram, and F. Pirozzolo. 1994. Spine and hip motion analysis during the golf swing. World Scientific Congress of Golf (2nd: 1994: St. Andrews, Scotland). In, Cochran, A.J. and Farrally, F.R. (eds.), *Science and Golf II: Proceedings of the 1994 World Scientific Congress of Golf,* London: E & FN Spon, 50-58.

Montague, L. 1993. The ABC of a perfect golf swing. *Golf News,* 4-7.

Nesbit, S.M., J.S. Cole, T.A. Hartzell, K.A. Oglesby, and A.F. Radich. 1994. Dynamic model and computer simulation of a golf swing. World Scientific Congress of Golf (2nd: 1994: St. Andrews, Scotland). In, Cochran, A.J. and Farrally, F.R. (eds.), *Science and Golf II: Proceedings of the 1994 World Scientific Congress of Golf,* London: E & FN Spon, 71-76.

Sanders, R.H., and P.C. Owens. 1992. Hub movement during the swing of elite and novice golfers. *International Journal of Sport Biomechanics* 8(4):320-330.

Wallace, E.S., P.N. Grimshaw, and R.L. Ashford. 1994. Discrete pressure profiles of the feet and weight transfer patterns during the golf swing. World Scientific Congress of Golf (2nd: 1994: St. Andrews, Scotland). In, Cochran, A.J. and Farrally, F.R. (eds.), *Science and Golf II: Proceedings of the 1994 World Scientific Congress of Golf,* London: E & FN Spon, 26-32.

Weir, B. The Attacking Golf Swing. 1992. *Golf Australia* 31-35.

White, A.L. 1991. *Validation and Comparison of a Model Golf Swing with the Mechanical Profiles of Beginning Golfers.* Thesis (Ph.D.) Ann Arbor, Michigan: University Microfilms International.

Energy for the Long Haul

How important is endurance in golf? Imagine walking 18 holes, anywhere from 4 to 5 miles on average, and being winded before and after every shot. Obviously, without general endurance you won't play optimal golf. In addition, if you walk the course carrying a heavy bag over hills, the physical effort you expend, unless you're in good shape aerobically, will draw physical and mental energy away from your game. This is one of those situations where you don't realize how important something is until it's missing.

Does this mean golf is a sport of endurance? Not exactly. Golf is a sport of timing, tempo, power and mechanics. By strict definition, it's not the same as running a marathon or cycling. However, general endurance or energy system fitness is important in golf. It may not improve your swing, but it will reduce overall fatigue and improve your mental game.

General endurance will reduce overall fatigue and improve your mental game.

Does Golf Build Energy Fitness?

Golf is usually thought of as a leisure-time activity. Walking 18 holes at the normal pace is not enough to significantly increase your aerobic capacity or general endurance. Why? Because you are walking, stopping and hitting the ball, then waiting, then walking again. You aren't exercising hard enough or long enough to improve aerobic or endurance capacity beyond a minor level. Even walking up a hill is an intermittent effort and too short in duration to produce a training effect.

Some studies have shown that walking a golf course has minor health benefits. If you want moderate or higher health benefits or fitness levels, then golf is not an optimal exercise. The actual physiological effects of walking a course depend on how fit you are, the weight of your bag, the topography of the course — including the number of hills — and the temperature and humidity at the time you're walking. For example, being less fit, carrying a heavier bag and walking over a hilly course on a hot day will increase the level of aerobic effort it takes to walk the course. Obviously, you need endurance for golf, yet golf won't build significant endurance. Unless you play regularly in Tibet.

You need endurance for golf, yet golf won't build significant endurance.

33

What Is Aerobic Capacity?

To play optimal golf, you have to improve your aerobic capacity. This term, aerobic capacity — also called cardiovascular capacity — is the ability to use oxygen and fuel efficiently during extended exercise. Aerobic capacity is developed through sustained, less than maximum capacity, whole-body exercise. Whole-body exercise that is rhythmical, such as cross-country skiing or bicycling, satisfies the physiological requirements. These types of exercises can be sustained at varying levels for significant amounts of time — they're not all-out sprints.

Aerobic activity occurs when any group of large muscles moves rhythmically for at least five minutes at a sufficient intensity or work level.

As an example, imagine your car on cruise control set for 55 miles per hour. The gas in your tank and the air running through your fuel injectors combine in the proper amounts to match the engine speed. You are not going as fast as the car will go, yet you aren't at a dead stop either. To keep running, the engine needs the proper combination of oxygen and fuel on a continuing basis. The car runs because it has enough fuel to keep going. At the same time, the fuel and air mixture is flowing through the car's cylinders constantly and evenly to maintain a steady speed.

Aerobic-fitness exercise is similar to this process. The fuel in your tank (fats and carbohydrates) combines with the oxygen you're breathing into your system to keep your muscular engine running at its most efficient middle speed. As you gain aerobic fitness, you're simply increasing the cruise-control-speed capacity of your body.

What Is Anaerobic Capacity?

Unlike a car, however, the human body takes time to adjust to the "cruise control" settings. If you work too hard, your body switches to anaerobic, or sprint, metabolism. In this process, the body uses only carbohydrates as fuel for this high-intensity exercise, without any oxygen. An example would be in a game of football where players are constantly sprinting for 30 to 100 yards at a time. The same thing occurs in basketball and racquetball, where players regularly expend short bursts of high-intensity energy.

Unfortunately, even though it burns lots of calories, this type of all-out sprint activity can only be maintained for 1 or 2 minutes, so it isn't practical or even very applicable as a regular training method for golf. A drag racer can only maintain all-out speed for less than 5 seconds and does not get 30 miles to the gallon. However, levels of anaerobic activity, those that are higher than the normal aerobic levels prescribed later in this chapter, can be excellent training methods when time is short or you desire very quick fitness gains. This type of activity would include running sprints, cycling or a stair-climbing program, which alternate periods of high intensity with periods of recovery.

Energy system training refers to training that covers the spectrum from the low end of aerobic levels of training to the high end of anaerobic, or sprint, training. Golf is a sport that relies primarily on fitness at aerobic and not anaerobic levels. The majority of your energy system training for golf should occur in the aerobic zone.

Aerobic Training and Physiological Changes

Aerobic activity occurs when any group of large muscles moves rhythmically for at least 5 minutes at a sufficient intensity, or work level. Keep in mind, though, that if you're training, 20 minutes of sustained activity is the minimum standard. During this time the body shifts to a "steady-state" metabolism. Physiologists have noted that, during this state, changes occur that positively influence the body's ability to function aerobically. These physiological changes include:

The Benefits of Aerobic Conditioning for Golfers

- Burns calories.
- Helps maintain optimum weight.
- Improves hand-eye coordination through decreased fatigue.
- Enhances mental concentration resulting in lower scores.

Golf is a sport that relies primarily on fitness at aerobic and not anaerobic levels.

- More capillaries, or small blood vessels, deliver fuel and oxygen to the working muscles.
- More mitochondria (the "power plants" in the muscle).
- Total blood cholesterol drops, and HDL (the so-called "good" cholesterol that helps prevent heart disease) levels increase.
- Resistance to stress increases.
- Weight loss occurs through direct burning of calories during exercise in addition to increased overall metabolism immediately after exercise.
- General fitness improves, making it easier to perform advanced exercises effectively.
- Ability to perform higher levels of aerobic exercise is enhanced.

Energy Fitness and Golf Performance

You should always train at an aerobic level that is 5 to 10% higher than that required to play a round of golf.

Your golf performance will improve if you've got a finely tuned, fuel-efficient engine. A higher than average aerobic fitness program increases your overall energy level. Better conditioning will allow you to focus on the mental aspects of your game because you won't be taxed physically; you will have more energy to put into course and shot management.

You should always train at an aerobic level that is 5 to 10% higher than that required to play a round of golf. That extra energy can be applied to other aspects of your game — you'll feel stronger, swing better and be a more confident player. Once you add an aerobic component to your golf fitness program, you'll never have to worry about a round of golf taxing your system to the point where it interferes with your game. And because your swing relies on muscular endurance, which is enhanced by aerobic activity, you'll also improve the consistency of your golf swing.

Regular aerobic training away from the golf course is the best means to build general endurance for improved golf performance.

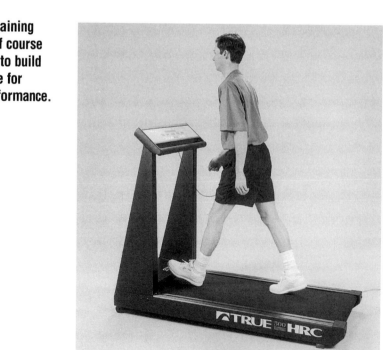

Psychologically, higher aerobic fitness levels translate into a higher confidence level. Golf is a sport that is kinder to the confident player; in fact, confidence can make or break a golfer. Setting goals and reaching them has a direct and positive effect on your self-confidence. Simply put, doing something like exercising regularly teaches you that you can achieve your goals in other areas.

Golf is just as tough mentally as it is physically. Each shot takes a specific set of thinking skills that must be repeated over the course of four or more hours. The mental energy of concentration takes real physical fuel. Better physical energy capabilities mean the effects of mental stress are diminished. The aerobically fit golfer can maintain energy levels and focus so that the putt on the 18th hole at noon is as balanced and controlled as the one that was made on the practice green at eight.

> **Psychologically, higher aerobic fitness levels translate into a higher confidence level.**

Exercise Variables: Keys to Effectiveness

How do you adjust your exercise program to gain aerobic fitness for golf? You need to form your golf conditioning program with four variables in mind: intensity, duration, frequency and mode.

Intensity is the physical difficulty of, or effort used during, the exercise. It can also be measured in the amount of calories used per hour or per minute. Some experts note that intensity is the single most important factor in developing aerobic fitness. Intensity can be measured by heart rate during exercise, the exerciser's perceived exertion and calories used per hour.

Duration is the number of minutes spent per training session. In general, 20 minutes at the appropriate training intensity is recommended to increase aerobic fitness levels. There is also a relationship between intensity and duration: As you increase intensity you must decrease duration. If you decrease the intensity, you can increase the duration.

Frequency, or the number of individual workout sessions per week, depends on individual goals. Building aerobic fitness takes a minimum of 3 sessions per week when someone first begins an aerobic exercise program. To significantly improve aerobic fitness, 4 or more sessions per week are required. Maintaining conditioning once a certain level of aerobic fitness has been achieved generally requires a frequency of 3 sessions per week. However, if you are a golfer walking the course more than 3 times per week, you could probably cut back to 2 weekly aerobic sessions once you've achieved your target conditioning goal.

Mode, or modality, is the type of exercise engaged in. Aerobic modes normally include brisk walking, running/jogging, cycling, stair climbing, slideboard training and swimming. If your goal is to compete as a runner, then running should be the means you use to train so your body gets more efficient. If your goal is to improve your golf performance, then a mix of activities (which wouldn't allow your body to become as energy-efficient as a marathon runner) will produce the best fitness gains in the shortest amount of time.

Adjusting the Variables

How you adjust these variables depends on your fitness level. If you are exercising for the first time or after an exercise hiatus of some duration, start with a lower intensity and a duration of less than 20 minutes. Even though most experts agree that the most important variable in developing aerobic capacity is intensity, novice golf exercisers should progress to higher intensities, not start there. Before you get fit, higher intensity is uncomfortable physically and mentally.

In order to get the quickest fitness benefit, you've got to exercise hard enough to get your heart rate and rate of energy expenditure up to a level where positive changes occur. Scientifically, there are a number of ways to set this level. Each method has a correlation to your maximum oxygen uptake (VO_2 max), which is the highest level of aerobic performance you can reach at the time you're measuring it. The normal training-effect zone is defined as 60% to 80% of your VO_2 max, or 60% to 85% of your maximal heart rate (MHR). No matter what exercise is engaged in, to get an aerobic training effect, the intensity must be at this level. This training zone is most easily calculated by using an age-predicted MHR.

Your MHR in the age-predicted method is roughly 220 minus your age. A 40-year-old man, for example, would have an MHR of 180 beats per minute (bpm). If he were interested in staying within 60% of that target range (a lower training level), he would multiply 180 by 60% to get 108 bpm. A disadvantage with this method is that it is an estimate based on averages, and your actual maximum heart rate can actually vary by as much as 12 bpm up or down from the number you get with this calculation.

What should your training heart rate be? It depends on your current fitness level and age. New exercisers work at the lower end of the training zone,

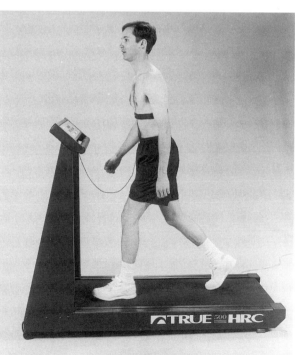

Heart-rate monitoring and control, integrated into equipment such as treadmills, gives the golf athlete a significant training edge in designing golf-specific programs.

55% to 70% of their MHR; golfers with average fitness levels and some exercise experience work at 70% to 85%; and trained athletes can go as high as 90% of MHR. As long as you can elevate your heart rate to the proper level, you can give your system a meaningful aerobic workout.

Always check with your physician or other health professional before starting any exercise program, especially if you are over 40, have significant risk factors for heart disease, or have symptoms of heart disease.

Measuring Your Desired Intensity

One of the easiest ways to monitor your heart rate is to use a heart-rate monitor during both aerobic and anaerobic exercise. Although a marathon runner will have a good idea of relative effort and intensity because of extensive experience, most recreational exercisers don't have this kind of mental data bank to draw from. And since most golf athletes haven't had enough experience with training intensity, they may overshoot or undershoot the desired training zone if they try to rely on perceived effort alone.

Heart-rate monitors consist of a transmitter and receiver unit. A chest strap is the most common transmitter and when placed around an exerciser's chest will transmit to a special heart-rate watch. Some energy system machines, such as treadmills and stair machines, have receivers built into a control panel that will receive the signals from a chest strap.

There are other ways to measure aerobic intensity, should you want to use other methods besides target heart rate. For instance, you can take a treadmill or bicycle test. This test measures the volume of oxygen (VO_2) you use during the test exercise. This information can be used to help you adjust your training levels. These tests are administered by trained physiologists and physicians and usually cost at least $200 per test.

Another method of measuring exercise effort or intensity, the Borg Scale of Perceived Exertion, compares actual energy used in exercise to how the exerciser perceives exertion. This scale uses a number system whereby a number is assigned to various levels of physical effort. In exercise science studies, there has been a strong relationship between the scale numbers and effort levels. Once a person can link his or her experience of exertion to the specific numbered exercise intensity, this method becomes another valid means to measure aerobic intensity. The scale uses the following number system:

6	No exertion at all
7	Extremely light
9	Very light
11	Light
13	Somewhat hard
15	Hard or heavy
17	Very hard
19	Extremely hard
20	Maximal exertion

> One of the easiest ways to monitor your heart rate is to use a heart-rate monitor during both aerobic and anaerobic exercise.

In using this scale, aerobic exercise should fall between 12 and 16. In other words, the exercise should feel somewhat hard to very hard to be effective in building aerobic fitness for golf. However, this scale is not valid for those people who have little exercise experience. They simply have no established reference points from which to judge exertion.

When time is an issue or you want to lose weight, train harder! If you have medical clearance and average or above average fitness, working at 80% to 90% of MHR can have significant benefits. It raises your resting metabolism when compared to moderate-intensity aerobic training, and this burns more calories even after the exercise is over. Remember, this is for golf athletes with medical clearance, at least average fitness and no orthopedic problems.

Most aerobic activities are effective if performed according to these physiological variables. Of course, not all exercises pay off equally in fitness results or sport-performance improvement. In most cases, treadmill walking or running makes the most sense for golfers, because the exercise simulates the demands of the golf course.

Getting Started

If you are a beginning exerciser or haven't exercised for 30 days, then lower the intensity (to less than 70% of MHR) and decrease the duration (to less than 20 minutes) of your workout. A good starting point is to engage in easy aerobic exercise for 15 to 20 minutes 3 times per week. After the first week, add slightly more intensity or duration so your weekly total is slightly longer or more difficult. Physiologically, it takes about 3 weeks before you will see noticeable changes in your aerobic fitness. However, you will get a psychological boost after the first week because you will have set and met a tangible goal.

> **Physiologically, it takes about 3 weeks before you will see noticeable changes in your aerobic fitness.**

The higher the impact or intensity of your choice of exercise, the higher your risk of injury. It's harder to run 5 times a week, because of the pounding the knees take, than it is to cycle 5 times a week. Mixing different types of exercise, such as alternating jogging with cycling on a day-by-day basis, will help most exercisers ameliorate the negative effects of high-impact exercise.

Choosing the Right Piece of Aerobic Equipment

The type of exercise you choose can affect your mental state as well as your physical conditioning. Pick one that you enjoy and that suits your personality, budget, available space and physical characteristics. If you enjoy it and it feels right for you, you'll be more apt to keep doing it. At home, try placing your equipment in front of the TV set or near your CD player. This can increase your enjoyment and help you realize long-term benefits in your golf game and your health, especially if you watch golf tapes.

Choosing the right piece of equipment is about as difficult and as personal as choosing a putter. Any machine you choose should be able to accommodate a range of intensities, because on some days you'll work harder than you will on others. Aerobic equipment can also be used for your days of long, slow distance training, where light endurance activity fits your needs.

Training Variables and Their Fitness Effects

Intensity

50% to 60% MHR: Burns some fat, results in very low fitness gains, minor impact on health by raising HDL cholesterol (the "good" cholesterol) a minimal amount. Minor improvement in golf performance (this is the aerobic level that is reached by many golfers as they walk the course), yet a starting point for golfers formerly inactive.

60% to 70% MHR: Results in minor fitness gains, moderate impact on health by raising HDL cholesterol and moderate improvement in golf performance.

70% to 85% MHR: Moderate to high fitness gains, positive relationship to health and major impact on golf-related aerobic fitness.

85%+ MHR: High fitness gains, high caloric burn results in rise in resting metabolism, efficient use of time, higher injury potential from high intensity and impact activity.

Duration

20 minutes: Produces minor gains in aerobic fitness unless intensity is raised to 80% or more of maximum heart rate in most cases or sessions occur more than three times per week.

20 to 40 minutes: Produces moderate to high gains in aerobic fitness, health and endurance-related sports performance.

40+ minutes: Produces high gains in aerobic fitness; may detract at this level from strength and power gains by recruiting different muscle fibers, and subtracts from time for resistance and flexibility training.

Frequency

2 sessions per week: Will not normally produce aerobic gains or even maintenance unless other activity is added.

3 sessions per week: Minimum necessary for both building and maintaining aerobic fitness if intensity and duration criteria are met.

4 to 5 sessions per week: Develops moderate to high aerobic fitness.

5+ sessions per week: Will build aerobic fitness at the high levels needed for aerobically based sports such as running, cycling, or swimming.

Mode

1 aerobic activity: Promotes caloric and mechanical efficiency (ability to perform more efficiently with the same amount of energy, such as running faster) to improve performance in the specific activity, such as running, cycling, or swimming.

2 aerobic activities: Develops caloric and mechanical inefficiency to burn more calories per exercise session due to the body's use of additional muscle groups.

3 or more aerobic activities: Fosters the highest level of inefficiency to burn more calories and is the ideal approach in using aerobic exercise for weight loss.

Energy Training Systems

Athletes use a number of energy training systems in conjunction with strength and flexibility programs to achieve optimal sports fitness. Golfers should use a mix of these techniques and systems. Each method of training can be used to make a training phase more effective for golf performance.

Long, slow distance (LSD) training is performed at 50% to 70% MHR for 40 minutes or more. Golf uses: Recovery from strength workouts, stress reduction, development of aerobic fitness for novice exercisers.

Normal aerobic (NA) training is performed at 70% to 85% MHR for 20 minutes or more. Golf uses: Development and maintenance of aerobic fitness for golf, weight loss.

Interval high-intensity (HI) training is performed at 85%+ MHR. It may be composed of a single interval of high-intensity exercise followed by a period of low-intensity exercise for recovery; or shorter intervals of high-intensity exercise may be alternated with periods of low-intensity exercise for recovery. Golf uses: Maintenance and development of aerobic fitness when time is a problem; excellent system to use concurrently with strength training because it makes strength training more effective by providing the ability to work harder during resistance training; significant boost in self-confidence.

Treadmills

Treadmills have become popular because an exerciser can walk or run on them. They are especially good for golfers, who can choose different speeds and gradients in order to design their own programs. The amount of perceived exertion, or how hard you think your body is working, will be lower on a treadmill because you're using a natural, whole-body motion. In other words, you can exercise harder and it won't feel more difficult.

In order to simulate the demands of walking hills on the golf course, your treadmill's gradient adjustment should reach a minimum of 10%. Expect to pay at least $1,500 for a motorized treadmill with electronic speed and grade controls that will last more than 5 years with regular use.

Golf grade:

A+: Motorized versions with speed and grade control, programming, heart-rate monitoring and heart-rate control features

A: Motorized versions with speed and grade control and programming features

C: Nonmotorized treadmills

> The amount of perceived exertion, or how hard you think your body is working, will be lower on a treadmill because you're using a natural, whole-body motion.

Stair Climbers

Stair climbers first became common in health clubs and have now become popular for home exercise centers. Like treadmills, the motorized versions offer electronic resistance changes and variable programs that are conducive to golf training.

There are two major types of stair climbers: independent climbers, where one step will move down independent of the other step; and dependent climbers, where, as one step moves down, the other moves up. Many fitness experts believe the independent step climbers offer a better workout because they allow each leg to set its own range of motion or depth of step. With electronic controls and programming, you can devise your own golf-specific workout to simulate the demands of the course. However, depending on an exerciser's body position and any orthopedic problems, these machines have been found by some to aggravate back pain and some degenerative knee conditions. Newer designs with vertical arms significantly decrease stress to the back.

Golf grade:

    B+: Electronic climbers with programming features
    C: Nonelectronic resistance climbers

Stationary Bicycles

Stationary bicycles are a mainstay both in athletic clubs and homes. The reasons are simple: you can control the workload, and everyone can ride a bike. It's also possible to read while riding a stationary bicycle.

There are two basic types of stationary bicycles: upright and recumbent. The upright bikes are traditional exercise bikes; recumbent bikes are more like chairs with a large wheel attached to the front. Recumbent bikes allow you to sit down, with your back supported, while you pedal.

Newer models of both kinds of stationary bicycles include electronic and air-resistance cycles, which can exercise arms as well as legs. The benefits depend on a number of factors, including resistance settings. However, using your arms in addition to the pedaling motion can significantly raise the amount of calories you burn — a plus when time is tight.

If you have back problems that are aggravated by golf, or if you play golf more than 5 days a week, you should consider a recumbent model. It will help alleviate back stress by placing you in a supported position. Air-resistance models with arm and leg options offer the best opportunity for overall aerobic fitness gains because they require the use of more muscle groups and therefore will burn more calories.

Golf grade:

B+: Recumbent models
B+: Dual-action and air-resistance models
B-: Upright stationary bikes

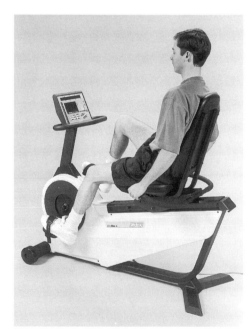

Total-Body Exercise Machines

One of the most recent developments in exercise equipment is the total-body exercise machine. These machines work a very large number of muscles per session and are rapidly becoming popular in athletic clubs. The rationale for their development is simple: Find a motion different than running or walking that burns a substantial number of calories by using major muscle groups. These machines facilitate an elliptical motion, which simply means the lever arms or foot pedals move one direction, later changing direction with a slight circular motion. These machines provide a novel motion that burns a substantial number of calories in a low-impact manner. There are three types of these machines: Cross-country ski simulators, leg-only elliptical machines and combination elliptical machines, which combine arm and leg motions.

There's no doubt that a ski machine can provide a good aerobic workout that involves both the upper and lower body. However, some fitness enthusiasts have found that balancing on the machine requires the legs to push into the support pad to maintain balance. This requires the user to work at least at a moderate pace just to maintain balance. Leg-only elliptical machines, which facilitate a movement akin to running or hiking, provide an excellent low-impact aerobic workout. The combination elliptical machines, which combine both arm and leg motion, have the most applicability to golf because they build aerobic capacity in the arms *and* the legs.

The combination elliptical machines have the most applicability to golf because they build aerobic capacity in the arms *and* the legs.

Golf grade:

A: Elliptical machines that involve arms and legs and have an electronic control

B: Elliptical machines with leg-only motion and an electronic control

C-: Cross-country ski machines

Aerobic Riders

One of the newest pieces of aerobic equipment is the "rider." With handles and pedals, this bicycle-like device forces you to pull/push with the upper body, mainly the shoulders/arms while pushing with the legs. The appeal of riders is the promise of a whole-body workout without impact.

In reality, the mechanics of the machine and positioning may mean your forearms and back may fatigue before you reach your training zone. In addition, body-weight resistance models may only provide enough fitness challenge when you are relatively unfit. Not all models fit everyone equally, therefore not all people get the same physiological effect from just one size of machine. Some of the newer, club-like electronic models have improved mechanics and electronic resistance and, therefore, will provide a superior workout for golf fitness compared to body-weight riders.

Golf grade:
B: Electronic models
D: Body-weight/pneumatic models

Slide Boards

Slide boards started out as a rehabilitation tool for people with injuries, particularly injured knees. These people began using them to get fit once they noticed slide training builds energy system fitness. Using a slide board also builds strength and trunk stability.

You can get a significant workout on a slide board. If you're not already in moderately good shape, you'll probably have trouble lasting more than 10 minutes at first, though. Once you master the movements, you can build an effective golf workout that uses the lateral hip muscles. These muscles help drive the golf swing and add power to it. Slide boards also develop muscular endurance in the legs and hips in a low-impact manner.

Golf grade:
B+

Heart-Rate Monitors

No matter what piece of aerobic exercise equipment you choose, heart-rate monitoring will provide a significant advantage. On any given day, your stress level, sleep requirements and other factors influence how you feel about exercise. Monitoring your exercise intensity through heart rate ensures that you can work at the best level that day for your golf performance and your health. In addition, if you have an aerobic machine that will not control intensity through heart rate, or won't even read heart rate, a monitor is a sound investment.

Monitors generally include a chest strap, monitor unit and heart-rate watch. In addition to their use in exercise, they can be useful tools in monitoring your reaction to physical stress and psychological variables during a round of golf. Models cover the range from basic monitoring and setting specific target zones all the way to versions with computer download capabilities.

Golf grade:
A

Monitoring your exercise intensity through heart rate ensures that you can work at the best level that day for your golf performance.

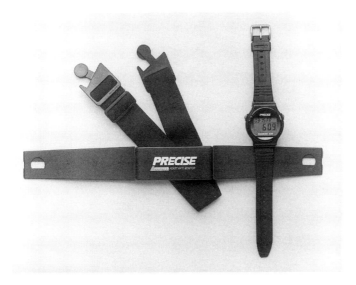

Energy for the Long Haul KEY POINTS

- Energy system fitness is necessary for golf because rounds last more than 4 hours.

- Aerobic exercise is any exercise that involves large muscle groups, is rhythmical and lasts for more than 20 minutes per session (i.e., jogging, cycling and stair climbing) at a sufficient intensity (at least 60% of your maximum capacity).

- Improving aerobic fitness reduces the effects of the mental stress of golf and improves overall health, reducing the risk of heart disease. Aerobic fitness is related to how much oxygen your body can use in combination with fats and carbohydrates to sustain aerobic exercise. Higher fitness levels allow you to combine more oxygen and fuel at any given time. You can simply work at a higher sustained level.

- Aerobic exercise improves the quality of life; you will be able to play golf longer as well as better.

- Walking the golf course does not contribute significantly to building aerobic fitness.

- Golfers have to complete at least 2 aerobic sessions per week in addition to regularly walking the course to maintain a reasonable level of aerobic fitness.

- Your golf game will improve based on how you adjust intensity (difficulty or level of energy use or rate), duration (minutes per exercise session) and frequency (number of sessions per week), as well as what exercise mode you choose.

- Certain types of exercise equipment will give better results for golf training. These include motorized treadmills, recumbent and dual-action bicycles, total-body exercise machines, stair machines and slide boards.

References

American College of Sports Medicine. 1990. Position statement on the recommended quantity and quality of exercise for developing and maintaining cardiorespiratory and muscular fitness in healthy adults. *Medicine and Science in Sports and Exercise* 22:256-274.

Astrand, P.O., and K. Rodahl. 1986. *Textbook of Work Physiology.* 3rd ed. New York: McGraw-Hill.

Ballor, D.L., J.P. McCarthy, E.J. Wilterdink, and S.J. Hanson. 1989. Exercise intensity does not affect the composition of diet and exercise-induced body mass loss. *Medicine and Science in Sports and Exercise* 21(2).

Borg, G. 1973. Perceived exertion: A note on history and methods. *Medicine and Science in Sport* 5:90-93.

Coyle, E.F. et al. 1985. Effects of detraining on responses to submaximal exercise. *Journal of Applied Physiology* 59:853-859.

de Vries, H.A. 1986. *Physiology of Exercise.* Dubuque, IA: William C. Brown.

Drinkwater, B.L, and S.M. Horvath. 1972. Detraining effects on young women. *Medicine and Science in Sports and Exercise* 4:91-95.

Gaesser, G., and G. Brooks. 1984. Metabolic bases of excess post-exercise oxygen consumption: A review. *Medicine and Science in Sports and Exercise* 16:29.

Gordon, E. 1967. Anatomical and biochemical adaptations of muscle to different exercises. *Journal of The American Medical Association* 201:755.

Orlander, J., K.H. Kiessling, and J. Karlsson. 1977. Low intensity training, inactivity and resumed training in sedentary men. *Acta Physiologica Scandinavia* 101:351.

Palank, E.A., and E.H. Hargreaves. 1990. The benefits of walking the golf course. *The Physician and Sportsmedicine* 18(10):77.

Pollock, M.L., J. Dimmick, H. Miller, Z. Kendrick, and A. Linnerud. 1975. Effects of mode of training on cardiovascular function and body composition of middle-aged men. *Medicine and Science in Sports and Exercise* 7:139-145.

Wolkodoff, N. 1995. *Consumer Treadmill Study.* Denver, CO: ExerTrends.

Zeni, A.I., M.D. Hoffman, and P.S. Clifford. 1996. Energy expenditure with indoor exercise machines. *Journal of the American Medical Association* 275(18):1424-1428.

Strong for Golf

Golf Power, Golf Consistency

Most golfers will work on their flexibility and may consider engaging in some aerobic training in order to improve their health. But they'll ignore weight training (also called strength or resistance training) because of past misconceptions. Resistance training has been rumored to result in golfers becoming "bulky," ruining their golf swing. Yet of all the fitness components of golf, resistance training holds the most promise for golf performance improvement.

Most golfers don't use resistance training simply because they don't know the best way to apply it. They don't understand what constitutes "golf strength." Traditionally, golf athletes have not differentiated between types of strength in their training programs. Like other fitness factors, if strength is applied to golf without specificity, your golf game won't improve. "Strength" really covers a wide range of abilities, from muscular endurance to power. Depending on the sport's requirements and on how one trains, sport-specific strength is a unique blend of physical abilities and sport performance needs. Obviously, golf is very different from football or bodybuilding in terms of strength. As a golfer, you aren't trying to build muscle for the sake of appearance, and golf is not a game of brute strength, such as football, especially on the green. Optimal golf requires repeatable power combined with finesse.

Because there are many forms of resistance that can be used to increase strength, the term "resistance training" is preferred to "weight training." For golf, you can use weights (machines or free weights), bands, cords, medicine balls, and even your own body weight. They all constitute resistance, with some more preferable for producing maximum golf improvement.

Over the last ten years, training for just about every sport from swimming to mountain climbing has used resistance training. Why? Resistance training improves your muscular ability to exert more force, power, and endurance. It even helps improve your coordination and self-confidence. Especially important for golf, resistance training improves the strength of the support tissues, ligaments, and tendons, thus lowering the risk of injury. Traditionally used

> **Optimal golf requires repeatable power combined with finesse.**

51

only in power sports such as football, resistance training has recently been applied successfully to training for endurance sports such as running, and now is being applied to golf.

Golf is a demanding sport from a strength and power perspective. Every time you coil and uncoil as you swing, you're storing a tremendous amount of energy. To release that energy you need to count on your ligaments, tendons, and muscles to store and direct it. Club-head speed dictates the length of your shots, and resistance training helps you generate more club-head speed. Resistance training is also crucial in giving you the muscular endurance to keep your swing repeatable as well as powerful.

Resistance training, used for years by other sports, can significantly improve power and muscular endurance for golf.

The mental benefits of resistance training are just as important for golf as are the physical and performance improvements, in generating club-head speed and in consistency, for example. And as you increase the capabilities of your muscles in power and muscular endurance, your self-confidence gets a boost. The reason for this is simple: The tangible progress you make as you lift weights or use other forms of resistance training, and the stronger you get, the more confident you become. But before you begin, you must first rethink much of what you already believe you know about resistance training and golf.

Five Myths About Resistance Training and Golf

Myth #1: Golf is a Game of Coordination, and Resistance Training Doesn't Improve Coordination

Both scientific research and the experience of a broad base of athletes over the last 30 years demonstrates that resistance training actually improves coordination. If you strengthen your system, you're more able to maintain balance and posture during performance, especially in off-balance shots. Golf in particular requires balance and coordination. Resistance training gives a golfer the ability to more precisely fire the appropriate muscle groups for finesse shots. In general, the strongest golfers have the best short games for this reason.

Myth #2: Resistance Training Ruins Flexibility

In fact, resistance training can improve flexibility. Olympic weightlifters, for example, consistently come up with better-than-average flexibility scores. Why? Because if you train or exercise through full range of motion (ROM), you enhance rather than detract from flexibility. The application to golf is that the right training methods that include full range of motion will enhance flexibility. In addition, certain muscle groups, such as the hamstrings, which are used extensively in golf to maintain posture, require a certain amount of strength in order to stay flexible because of repeated demands from the golf stance and swing.

Myth #3: Hitting Balls on the Driving Range Will Build all the Strength I Need for Golf

Golf requires strength, muscular endurance, flexibility and coordination, but no single one of these fitness components can be developed when all are being used simultaneously. These separate qualities must be built in isolation. Think of it this way: Running a marathon won't build big biceps even though you use your biceps during running. Remember, on the PGA tour, the average time from start of swing to impact with a driver is .95 to 1.25 seconds. That's not enough time for a singular muscle group to adapt, let alone a complex system of muscles that must fire at precise times. Just hitting golf balls, even if it built strength, would not give you a reserve when you hit a fat shot or get out of your swing plane. And just hitting on the range won't develop that extra strength or ligament support that will keep you from getting injured.

Myth #4: I'll Get Hurt Lifting Weights

You're more likely to become injured from playing a round of golf or driving to the course than from resistance training. Proper form, proper equipment and the right training methods will significantly decrease your injury potential from resistance training. You might get an occasional strain from pushing too hard, but that's no different than in any other sport or activity. Statistically, you are 10 times more likely to get a back injury from golf itself than from resistance training.

Resistance training gives a golfer the ability to more precisely fire the appropriate muscle groups for finesse shots.

Myth# 5: If I Lift Weights, I'll Lose My Touch Around the Green

Actually, resistance training increases your ability to regulate force. When you lift weights, you're conscious of balance and posture. That helps you focus on posture during tricky and delicate shots with less than optimal footing. With regular resistance training, you boost your ability to use small muscles to regulate force, especially in the arms and hands. This is critical to golf performance, from putting to sand play.

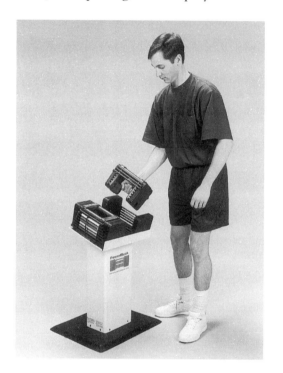

Resistance training will significantly boost golf performance if applied specifically and scientifically.

The Big Picture

Your muscles will respond differently to various types of resistance training. Not only must you perform the right exercises for golf, but at the optimal level and with the best method for both your golf game and level of training. There is no one "strength" but a whole continuum of qualities ranging from muscular endurance to strength to power. Understanding these qualities and how they affect golf performance will help you select the right methods to maximize your golf potential.

With regular resistance training, you boost your ability to use small muscles to regulate force...from putting to sand play.

You have to pick the right exercise at the right intensity and resistance and in the right progression to improve your golf game. Resistance training for golf should address the muscle groups most responsible for movement and posture. The most obvious groups are the rotator cuff muscles, lower pectorals, hips, forearms, hamstrings and the trunk/back region. But just because the golf swing uses these muscle groups doesn't mean other groups would not benefit from some form of resistance training. In fact, the muscle groups that help put your body back into balance and proper alignment also should be trained. These include the hip flexors, upper pectorals, trapezius and lower latissimus dorsi. For example, your golf posture and the effectiveness of your latissimus dorsi, which helps pull and stabilize during the swing, is enhanced by a moderate amount of incline presses, which strengthen the opposite muscle groups.

So, which "strength" qualities are needed for golf?

Muscular Endurance

On one end of the strength spectrum is muscular endurance. This is the ability to perform submaximal, or less than all-out, effort for an extended period of time. In competitive cycling, for example, muscular endurance is important because of the large number of leg revolutions needed at 80+ rpm to complete a 25-mile race. In golf, muscular endurance is key because a golfer swings repeatedly during a round. Even though the golfer has adequate time for the muscles to recover between strokes and the workload is relatively short, muscular endurance is needed because he or she may hit more than 200 shots in practice and the actual round.

But golfers really need muscular endurance on the driving range, where the pace of the shots is much higher than on the course. A significant number of the strains and sprains seen on the driving range don't result from lack of strength but from lack of the muscular endurance needed to keep up a quick pace of shots.

> **Muscular endurance is key because a golfer swings repeatedly during a round.**

Muscular Strength

Strength is defined scientifically as the ability to produce maximal force regardless of the duration involved in doing so. A good example is a wrestler trying to maneuver his opponent while also maintaining his position.

Certain muscle groups in golf use significant strength levels. The hamstrings, back, shoulders and forearms (including the hands and fingers) maintain certain positions during a swing. Strength is needed in order for these muscle groups to maintain golf-specific posture, balance and control.

Even though strength is only one factor in golf performance and applies to certain muscle groups more than to others, it should be included in general training for other reasons. Certain areas, such as the shoulders, knees, elbows and back, can benefit from training for strength to develop ligament and tendon density. Consequently, it's important for golfers to include some training in these areas for injury prevention. The entire body needs attention if a sound resistance program for golf is to be developed. This is especially important in the off-season and the early part of the golf season.

> **Golfers really need muscular endurance on the driving range, where the pace of the shots is much higher than on the course.**

Power

Power is an area golfers are starting to recognize as crucial for generating club-head speed and control. Power is defined as the ability to move as rapidly as possible or to overcome a resistance in the shortest possible time. Golf is definitely becoming a game of power. In fact, a number of golf experts recognize that the best way to swing a golf club is to swing it consistently as fast as possible. However, the source of power in golf is not as simple as an upward movement of the major leg muscles and the trunk, like in basketball. In golf, power is created by a rotation of the shoulders, trunk, hips and legs combined with activation of the arms and other small-muscle groups in a counter-rotating movement.

> **Power is defined as the ability to move as rapidly as possible or to overcome a resistance in the shortest possible time.**

Why Haven't More Golfers Used Resistance Training?

One of the reasons golfers have had negative experiences with resistance training is a lack of education: They haven't known how to correctly apply the principles of resistance training to golf. This has been especially true with regard to traditional "bodybuilding" resistance training methods, which most golfers find builds limited strength and power at the expense of flexibility. These golfers get larger muscles that aren't necessarily more powerful and actually retard flexibility, especially in the shoulders and trunk region. In response to this, some golfers have moved in the opposite direction, using light weights and tubing to build muscular endurance. Even though muscular endurance will improve somewhat from this type of program, it won't build strength or power for golf. It's not that resistance training is bad for golf. It just needs to be well thought out and applied specifically to the sport. The key to your workouts is to build the right proportions of muscular endurance, strength and power specifically for golf.

The key to your workouts is to build the right proportions of muscular endurance, strength and power specifically for golf.

Think Specificity

How you train determines the results you achieve. Very specific modalities, or types of resistance training, produce very specific effects in and around muscle. These changes can be one of two types: physiological, or those changes that involve the muscle-fiber structure, size and use of fuels; and neurological, or how the muscle fiber is activated and used. Most resistance training programs result in changes to both areas. However, muscular endurance is

John Davis, Olympic weightlifter from the 1940s, demonstrated that power can be developed with flexibility.

primarily a physiological set of changes because the muscle is learning how to generate fuels and recover between work sessions. Strength changes are a combination of physiological changes that revolve around fuel, changes in muscular size, increase in the strength of the support structures (ligaments and tendons) and, depending on training method, changes in the way the muscle is used or activated.

Power training doesn't produce many changes in physical structure; rather, changes are due to the increased efficiency and activation of the wiring or neural system. This is part of the reason why Olympic weightlifters can rapidly and explosively lift more than 300 pounds over their heads without the huge muscles normally found on bodybuilders. They improved the efficiency of the wiring, not the size of the muscle.

One of the tenets of resistance training for golf is that it shouldn't hinder golf-related flexibility. It would be desirable for resistance training to actually increase flexibility as well as strength. There are some methods and applications of resistance training that actually build flexibility rather than retard it.

How Muscle Works

Muscles are composed of different types of fibers, the structural units that cause movement. Each fiber is composed of protein filaments, which are the smallest unit of contraction or movement. The filaments are composed of two proteins, actin and myosin, which pull against each other during movement somewhat the way a caterpillar inches up a vine.

There are two basic kinds of muscle fiber: fast and slow. Slow-twitch (ST) fibers are the muscle fibers first used in movement. These fibers are very good at producing aerobic energy over the long term, yet they have poor power capabilities. Fast-twitch (FT) fibers are at the other end of the spectrum and are very explosive. They can work anaerobically, or without oxygen, for short periods of time, as in a 200-yard sprint. However, they aren't particularly useful for endurance.

There is a third kind of fiber that has characteristics of both the ST and FT fibers. Depending on how you exercise, this kind of fiber can be trained to act either as an endurance or a power fiber. This type is called fast oxidative/ glycolytic (FOG) because it shares characteristics of the ST and FT fibers. If

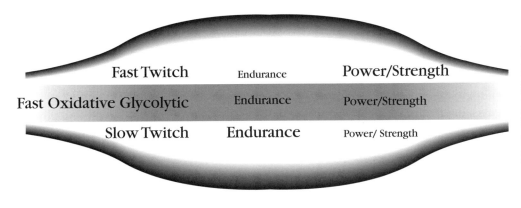

Fast Twitch	Endurance	Power/Strength
Fast Oxidative Glycolytic	Endurance	Power/Strength
Slow Twitch	Endurance	Power/ Strength

Each muscle fiber type has specific properties that improve golf performance, with golf requiring activation of the FOG and FT fibers for power development.

Specific training loads and methods produce specific adaptations.

you train FOG muscle for cycling, it becomes endurance-oriented, and power training makes it more powerful. Because each individual's muscles are a unique blend of these three dominant fiber types, different golfers will not realize the same results from identical training regimens.

These fibers have specific ways of adapting based on their capabilities and the training stimulus or on the level of resistance used in training. Fibers are very specific in their adaptations because there is only so much crossover potential that any type of fiber can have. Specific training loads and methods produce specific adaptations. For instance, you can try to make a slow-twitch fiber more explosive, and it will get more powerful to a small degree. This is why specificity of training is so important. You have to know how to target the particular fibers in your training to get them to do what you want regarding golf performance. As an example, to increase club-head speed, your training methods need to make changes in the fast-twitch fibers, making them more explosive, as well as to enhance the slow-twitch units.

Basic Muscular Fiber Activation Progression

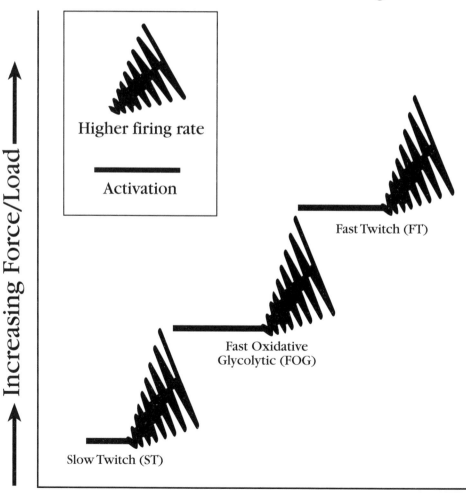

Muscle is activated based on force and workload requirements, with higher force requirements recruiting the power fibers.

Muscles are organized in groups of fibers called "motor units," groupings of ST, FOG and FT fibers. Unlike a car, where all engine cylinders are firing all the time, the human muscular system is organized by an energy-efficiency system that is based on how muscle is activated neurologically. In other words, the body will choose the most energy-efficient fibers first then add additional fibers as the workload or metabolic demands increase. It will first try to meet the requirements of the exercise with ST fibers, which fire very slowly and have the smallest motor neurons, or activation cells. If full activation of those fibers is not sufficient for the workload imposed on the muscle, the body will begin to add more ST motor units. As the workload requirements increase, the body will continue this recruitment pattern first with the FOG and then the FT fibers. This process has a number of interesting implications for golfers.

Lots of Little Weights Don't Equal One Mega Weight

The first implication is that you can lift a light weight a great number of times in an attempt to activate the FT and FOG fibers and still not access these fibers with optimal power-enhancing conditions. Muscular endurance is not the same thing as power, and you can't get muscular power from repeated bouts of muscular endurance. The body will either activate a rotation among the ST fibers or activate the FT fibers at low power levels. Thus, you can lift a light weight 25 to 30 times and gain very little power or strength, merely muscular endurance. This is the forte of the ST fibers. As weight or resistance increases, however, you probably will begin to add some FOG fibers later in training.

All muscle fibers can grow in size given the right kind of training stimulus or load. For example, some research and practical experience has shown that lifting weights in the 8- to 12- repetition range will build muscular size, especially in the ST and FOG fibers. However, even though some of the strength gained in this repetition range is useful for golf, it does little to engage the FT fibers. If the resistance is great enough that only 6 or fewer repetitions can be performed, there is a greater chance that the FT fibers will be recruited, thus undergoing a change in both activation pattern and size.

Heavy weights or resistance have been rumored to result in large muscles. The opposite is really the case. Training loads of less than 6 repetitions are so brief that there is little chance the muscle can gain significant size when compared to traditional bodybuilding methods. Consider the amount of time spent in a 1- repetition effort in Olympic-style weightlifting, where there is a relatively minor gain in muscular size. In fact, this is one of the training premises of successful golf conditioning: To build strength and power without building size, you have to work at a load of 6 or less repetitions at some point.

Muscle Fiber Types and How They Change with Training

Based on how muscle adapts to resistance training, sport scientists have identified resistance training loads with their effects on muscular components. This is based on a principle of training called Repetition Maximum, or RM. A 12 RM weight is a weight with which a particular person could only perform 12 movements. Neurological and physiological changes in muscle correlate with

Lifting weights in the 8- to 12- repetition range will build muscular size, especially in the ST and FOG fibers.

To build strength and power without building size, you have to work at a load of 6 or less repetitions at some point.

Neurological and physiological changes in muscle correlate with these specific repetition ranges.

these specific repetition ranges. For golf, this means that for each type of muscle fiber, training level and muscle group, there are repetition ranges that will produce the best golf-specific results. Knowing these ranges and their effects will help you apply resistance training for golf more effectively.

The following chart shows data about neurological and physiological adaptations and experiences of athletes using resistance training.

15+ Repetitions

Minor changes in fiber size (ST), very minor strength or neurological activation (ST). Most changes are physiological, affecting enzymes and fuels that are related to muscular endurance.

Golf Implication: This is a good starting point for most training and a good range for building muscular endurance in such groups as the rotator cuff muscles.

12-15 Repetitions

Minor changes in fiber size (ST, FOG), minor strength gains, and some neurological activation and synchronization, especially for those individuals who have never participated in a formalized resistance training program.

Golf Implication: This repetition range is useful to build high-intensity muscular endurance, which is needed as a base for strength or power.

8-12 Repetitions

Changes in muscle size, especially ST and FOG muscle fiber. Some additional neurological activation when compared to more than 12 repetitions. This is the range where bodybuilders usually train and where the most gains in muscle size are realized.

Golf Implication: Although the range of 8 to 12 repetitions will build some strength, too much emphasis here will develop "bulk" that might interfere with flexibility for golf.

6-8 Repetitions

Medium to large changes in muscle size (FT and FOG), but less than in the 8 to 12 range. Very small changes in fuel enzymes, some in the anaerobic or "sprint" enzymes, significant changes in synchronization and neurological access to more powerful fibers.

Golf Implication: Golfers who are beginning a resistance program should aim for this range to develop power in selected exercises.

Less than 6 Repetitions

Minor changes, if any, in muscle size and FT fibers. Very little change in the enzymes and catalysts used in fuel. Very significant changes in synchronization and neurological access, or how the FT fiber is accessed.

Golf Implication: Once a golfer has developed resistance training experience, progressing to this range will develop true power without bulk.

Rest Periods Between Sets

The amount of rest taken between sets of repetitions will partially determine whether the desired results are realized. Muscle is dependent on a chemical fuel, Adenosine Triphosphate/Phosphocreatine (ATP-PC), which is used during resistance training and lasts less than 20 seconds. In the same way a rocket needs fuel for high-power bursts of speed, your muscles need adequate ATP-PC, and how you rest and recover between sets determines whether there is enough of this fuel to meet your strength goals.

ATP-PC has a half-life of 30 seconds in recovery, which means that 30 seconds after exercise stops, about half of the ATP-PC you started with will be replenished. For muscular endurance activities you don't need much replenishment of this compound, so short rest periods of 30 seconds are adequate. But if you want to develop strength, then 45 to 60 seconds of rest are required between sets in order for enough of this fuel to be replenished to make strength gains. High-level strength and power training requires at least 120 seconds rest between sets to replenish this fuel, which is needed for this highly intense muscular work.

Whatever your level of strength or training, you need the right recovery period coupled with the right number of repetitions for optimum golf results.

> **You need the right recovery period coupled with the right number of repetitions for optimum golf results.**

Types of Muscular Contractions or Movements Used in Golf Training

To improve golf performance, you need the right combination of strength factors. In addition, you have to train or exercise your muscles so as to derive the full benefit of their capabilities. In resistance training, these basic movements are called muscular contractions. There are four basic types of contractions you can use in resistance training for golf. Not all provide the same benefit for golf performance, so you need to be aware of which types will give you the greatest benefit.

Concentric contractions occur when the muscle shortens, as when you pull a weight toward your shoulders in a bicep curl. Lowering the weight back down as the muscle lengthens is an example of an eccentric, or lowering, contraction. Normally, you can lower 50% more weight or resistance than you can raise because of the physiological nature of muscle contractions. Some bodybuilders have used very heavy eccentric contractions (from which comes the term "forced negatives"). When their programs reach a plateau, they add more weight in the lowering phase to actually "rip" the muscle fiber and stimulate new muscle growth.

Too much eccentric or lowering movement, and muscles become sore. Some electronic weight machines have programs that actually increase the weight load by 30 to 50% during the lowering phase of exercise. Eccentric exercise, especially at these heavy levels, does cause a significant physiological tearing of the muscle. For most people on a golf training program this is neither needed nor useful. However, do not forsake the normal eccentric exercise of most resistance training modes in favor of special equipment, whose manufacturers (especially makers of isokinetic or speed-controlled

Types of Muscular Contractions

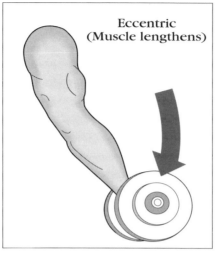

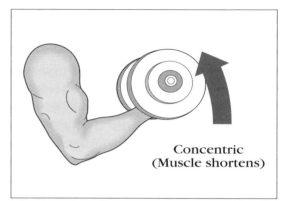

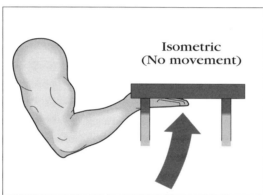

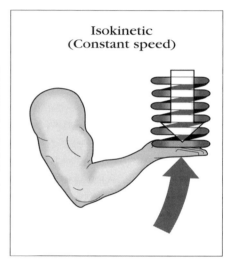

Resistance training for golf should focus primarily on concentric and eccentric movements.

equipment) claim their products will produce the same results without the discomfort of eccentric exercise. Walking downhill in golf requires eccentric muscle activity to control your speed and keep you from falling, which is an example of why normal eccentric exercise should be included in golf training.

Isokinetic contractions take their name from a concept popular in sport science and sports medicine, that of controlling speed. In this type of movement, muscles move at a more or less constant speed. Generally, most isokinetic resistance machines require a push-pull motion. An example would be a shoulder press followed by an alternate lat pull-down. Isokinetic exercise is more useful in testing and rehabilitation than in sport training. Except for swimming, most sports do not use movements that occur at a constant speed. In addition, most isokinetic machines are not set for eccentric contractions, a key component in sport and fitness training.

The fourth type of contraction important to golf performance is the isometric contraction, where muscle is used to push against resistance that is sufficient to prevent much, if any, movement. An example of this type of contraction is a wall-sit, in which a person sits with his back to a wall and with his legs stretched straight out and his feet pressing against the wall. No matter how hard he pushes in this position, he can't possibly move. In the golf swing, the forearms, fingers and wrists are locked in an isometric contraction during parts of the swing.

Isometric exercise, which gained popularity in the 1920s and again in the 1960s and 1970s, builds strength only in the joint angles used in the contractions. Although it is helpful to remedy "sticking points," or areas of weakness present in such exercises as the bench press, isometric training is not widely prescribed for a number of reasons: Other exercises are generally much more effective at building dynamic or movement strength, and the rises in blood pressure caused by isometric activity can be a health concern if you have high blood pressure.

> **Isometric exercise builds strength only in the joint angles used in the contractions.**

How Golf Strength Improves During Resistance Training

Weeks 1 Through 3

Early in your resistance training program you learn how to more effectively fire your muscles. You develop more force because the muscle fibers learn to fire as a unit and also fire more rapidly. These changes occur progressively during training as you gradually add more weight. When you first start lifting and haven't seen any increase in muscle size yet find that you can lift more weight than when you started, the improvement in muscle-fiber firing speed and efficiency is responsible.

Weeks 3 Through 7

After 3 or more weeks of resistance training, your ability to lift more weight and to add sets of repetitions is due partly to your muscles' increased ability to fight localized fatigue. For many beginners, working the bench press or lat pulldown is the first time they have stressed their muscles repeatedly in a high-intensity endurance workout. In this case, the body responds to the work demands by increasing production of the enzymes that help with fuel production. It is not uncommon for new exercisers to see a 20% increase in the weight they can lift from this factor alone.

Week 8 and Beyond

If you train long enough in the 8- to 12- repetition zone, you will increase the size of your muscles. This enlargement is known as hypertrophy. As the protein filaments are stressed in muscle, they respond by gaining size and therefore more specific protein filaments. This aids in coping with the higher workloads that are being forced on the muscle. Some parts of a muscle may actually "split," or form new fibers, yet this process is not responsible for much strength gain compared to hypertrophy.

For any athlete, let alone a golfer, too much work in the 8- to 12- repetition zone will cause muscular enlargement. However, if you mix your training principles and methods and combine muscular power and endurance training, this shouldn't happen to you. Remember, most competitive bodybuilders train 6 days a week, resistance-training 2 hours or more a day primarily in the 8- to 12- repetition range. Unless you are going to approach resistance training this way, you shouldn't worry about developing excessive bulk.

Resistance Training Benefits for Golfers

- Increased muscular endurance to improve swing consistency.

- Increased strength to reduce injuries.

- Enhanced power for greater club-head speed.

- Development of targeted muscle mass, which raises metabolism and aids in weight loss.

- Increased flexibility.

- Correction of muscular imbalances.

- Higher self-confidence.

- Enhanced kinesthetic sense, or body awareness, during golf.

It is in this phase of your training program that you'll see even greater gains in power development. During the first 3 weeks of training you gain some "neurological" power from activating more muscle. If you train at a high enough intensity (high weight with low repetitions), after 8 weeks you'll develop more power from your FT muscles. You simply will have recruited or activated more FT muscle through resistance training than was previously available. Generally, the most significant gains in neural activation occur in this training phase because your gains are dependent on proper form and localized muscular endurance, which takes up to 8 weeks to develop.

Resistance Training Systems and Golf

Resistance training for golf works best when it is based on a combination of different training systems. This approach allows golfers to use the best methods for a particular muscle group to satisfy varying golf needs. If you understand the basic systems and how they work, you can refine and tailor your golf resistance training program for greater results.

Bodybuilding

This set of training methods focuses on developing muscular mass in specific muscle groups. Most bodybuilding exercises stress one muscle group only, such as the triceps. Strict bodybuilding methods reduce overall body fat because of the intensity of the training and the high volume or the total amount of weight that is lifted.

Bodybuilding is a discipline of physique development, not of athletic performance based on movement. In most cases, bodybuilders use high volumes of 8 to 12 repetitions in conjunction with short rest periods of 45 to 60 seconds. This promotes muscular mass, largely in the ST and FOG fibers. In addition, bodybuilding methods use isolation exercises (exercises that work a single muscle group in isolation from other muscles) with structured variations, such as bicep curls. Bodybuilding can develop joint integrity and strength, but it shouldn't be the cornerstone of a golf training program.

Power Lifting

This sport became popular as a method of training for football. Power lifting includes competitive bench-press, squat and dead-lift maneuvers, in which maximum effort is exerted in one attempt. Most power lifters train with less than 8 repetitions to build size in the fast-twitch or explosive fibers, and to maximize neurological activation in the target lift.

The power lifts themselves are excellent multi-joint exercise strength developers. Most of the benefit comes from the repetition range of less than 8 repetitions and from the multi-joint muscle group lifts that mobilize the large muscles of the body. This is essential to overcoming inertia in sports such as basketball and football. For golfers, power-lifting methods and loads applied at the right training phases can increase muscular strength and power.

Olympic Weightlifting

Popularized in professional and collegiate football, these training methods revolve around the "snatch" and "clean and jerk" exercises. These two exercises involve rapidly "cleaning" the bar off the floor and then, depending on the lift, moving it overhead in 1 or 2 additional movements. These lifts — and others that are variations of them, such as the "power clean" — are tremendous developers of power. They activate the fast-twitch muscle fibers with sets of 1 to 4 repetitions. As in power lifting, the benefit is partly derived from the lifts' mobilization of the major muscles of the body. The major muscles are used to overcome inertia and the specific weight that is lifted. This activates the FT muscle fibers in the large muscles of the body.

You can successfully borrow Olympic weightlifting principles to increase golf power (1976 Olympic silver medalist Lee James).

Though you may never perform an Olympic exercise, you can successfully borrow Olympic weightlifting principles to increase golf power. For example, after sufficient base training, you could improve your power for golf by working with very heavy sets/low repetitions of dumbbell bench presses or seated rows.

Circuit Training

While not a formal weightlifting sport, circuit training, where the exerciser moves rapidly from exercise to exercise has been popular over the last 30 years. The benefit for golf athletes is limited because of the physiological focus of circuit training.

Circuit training was originally conceived to attempt to increase both aerobic and strength fitness in a short time period of training, generally 30 to 45 minutes. In most circuits, there is a quick progression from machine to machine, with repetition ranges of over 15 repetitions or 30 seconds of total resistance work per machine or exercise. Each resistance exercise is followed by a short recovery of 30 seconds, or aerobic activity such as cycling or aerobic dance before moving to the next exercise.

The very nature of circuit training means it may be useful for basic fitness needs, yet not optimum for specialized golf fitness. The short rest periods, long work intervals and the use of machines means you will at best build some non-specific muscular endurance and lower levels of strength when compared with focused resistance training. Circuit training will not build maximal strength or muscular power when compared to pure resistance training where the loads/repetitions and rest periods can be carefully controlled. The same limited result is also true for energy system fitness. Circuit training definitely will improve general endurance yet not with the results that focused energy system training, such as using as a treadmill, will produce.

If you are going to use circuit training, use it in a limited fashion at the beginning of the off-season when you are trying to build basic fitness. However, circuit training will not allow you to focus on the specific muscular balance that the off-season should develop, which is better addressed by tailoring your resistance training program. In addition, circuit training is a poor substitute for focused training during the in-season as it does not allow emphasis on specific muscle groups, such as the external rotators of the shoulder, and does not build or maintain muscular power.

Other Forms of Training

Other systems traditionally used in sports training should be factored into a golf program. Body-weight resistance exercises — push-ups, pull-ups, sit-ups and others — are successfully used by experts in sports training. Such exercises develop muscular endurance, but compared to resistance training they are less adequate at building strength or power. However, in the early phases of golf training such exercises can help establish a base of muscular endurance.

A new method of training is plyometric training, or the use of explosive exercises. Originally used in track and field, these exercises build power in such sports as running, where muscle goes through rapid stretching then a contraction in the opposite direction. In plyometric exercises, a lengthening, or eccentric (lowering against the force), movement is followed by a rapid movement in the other direction, which attempts to combine as many forces as possible to move the other direction. For example, by stepping off a bleacher step, compressing your body, then jumping upward, you would be performing a plyometric exercise.

Although plyometric leg exercises are not especially useful for golf, plyometric training using medicine balls for the trunk and abdomen can benefit your golf game. That's because their use mimics the twisting, "load then explode" movement of the trunk during golf.

Each system has something to offer the golfer looking to improve his or her performance through resistance training. For the golf athlete, the scientific combination of all systems produces superior results to reliance on just one system.

For the golf athlete, the scientific combination of all systems produces superior results to reliance on just one system.

Factors Involved in Strength Development

In addition to the way muscle reacts to resistance training, there are other factors that help determine your training program's effectiveness in improving your golf game.

Age, Fitness Level and Training Experience

The older you get, the tougher it seems to be to maintain and build strength — especially if you've never formally exercised with weights. As one ages, there is a lessened tendency to build muscle mass and an increased tendency to gain strength and power from the activation of neurological factors. Regardless of your age, though, you can drastically improve your golf game with resistance training. If you're a resistance-training beginner, your body will make great strides because of the novelty of the exercise and training experience. On the other hand, if you're an old pro at resistance training, your gains from training for golf won't be as great — though they'll still be significant, especially in neural activation.

Choice and Order of Exercise

For most golf athletes, it's best to start a resistance-training workout with larger muscle group exercises such as the dumbbell bench press, bent row and leg press or squat. "Multi-joint" exercises stress more than one muscle group and joint. They are best placed at the beginning of the training session, when the large muscles are rested and capable of their best effort. Even if you are training smaller muscle groups, such as the arms or shoulders, a few sets of multi-joint exercises are still a recommended warm-up. Single joint and muscle group exercises, such as the triceps pressdown, are generally best done at the end of your training session. Once you have developed sufficient strength, you can place smaller muscle group exercises at the beginning of your workout for variety.

> "Multi-joint" exercises are best placed at the beginning of the training session, when the large muscles are rested and capable of their best effort.

Progressive Overload

Without consistently increasing the intensity or volume of your training, you won't progress. Whether it is muscular endurance, strength or power you want, it is necessary to make your training workouts progressively more difficult. At each training session you should strive to do 1 more set, 1 more repetition, add 1 more pound, or rest a little less between sets.

Training Variety

The more ways you can perform the same resistance training exercise, the better. For example, if you have free weights at home and your golf club has a variety of weight machines, you might be able to develop three or four different variations on a bench press. Having exercise choices for a specific muscle group is important in keeping the muscle stimulated into making continual gains. Training variety also maintains strength during the golf season, when you may only pursue resistance training once per week. Variety can help you make the most of limited training time.

Rest: The Key to Training Gains

If you are going to stress a muscle, take time to let that muscle recover. The length of the rest break is crucial to improvement. Generally, you should not resistance train for two consecutive days with the same muscle group. For example, if you perform side-lying flyes for the rotator cuff on Monday and Tuesday, that muscle group won't have time to recover and adapt. You need at least 48 hours between sessions of resistance training of a specific muscle group.

> **If you are going to stress a muscle, take time to let that muscle recover.**

Adapt and Move On

The best training program remains the best training program only for a period of 2 to 3 weeks. Plan both your pre-season and in-season training to avoid overdoing any particular training phase. After a certain amount of time your muscles adapt to your program and you must move to the next training phase or your muscles get "stale." If you are a beginner, basic physical changes take up to 6 weeks, so staleness isn't a real issue for your first 2 training phases. However, if you have regularly been using resistance training for some time, staying in a training phase for over 3 weeks means you might not realize maximum fitness benefits.

> **After a certain amount of time your muscles adapt to your program and you must move to the next training phase or your muscles get "stale."**

Don't Forsake Practice and Play for Getting Physical

In golf, timing, "touch" and target orientation are the key features of successful performance. Time spent in the weight room should be just enough to maintain or build the necessary strength qualities. The majority of training time should go toward developing technique, tactics and strategy. You have to identify the key character-istics you need and efficiently develop those qualities, be-cause your time for in-season conditioning is limited. Even during off-season resistance training, you should work on your swing. As you gain strength, you will constantly adapt your swing to increases in your strength, power and endurance.

Get Back to the Basics

The golf season can last all year long in some parts of the world. Unfortunately, if you attempt perpetual maintenance of your physical abilities, you will actually lose fitness. In sports like golf, where the sea-son is so long, it's necessary to periodically rebuild key areas of fitness. For example, when

In sports like golf, where the season is so long, it's necessary to periodically rebuild key areas of fitness.

you have a 3-week lull between tournaments, take 1 week to reestablish mus-cular endurance with sets of 15 to 20 repetitions. This adds training variety, but more important for golfers, it helps rebuild muscular endurance. Trying to maintain fitness by using the same routine will cease to be maintenance after 3 to 4 weeks of the same routines.

Work Intelligently Around Injuries

If you've had injuries or have areas where you tend to experience problems (such as recurring tendinitis), additional strength training is advisable because it will strengthen the problem joint's integrity. Most golfers, based on individual body mechanics, have one or more injury-prone areas. After you have suffi-ciently recovered from tendinitis, for example, you should strengthen all the muscle groups related to the affected joint, which in turn will strengthen the integrity of the joint. Plan on 3 sets of additional exercise (at slightly different joint angles) a week to strengthen the affected area after recovery. For exam-ple, for prevention of further elbow tendinitis, use different versions of triceps exercises, such as presses and push-downs, for each set.

Focus, Focus, Focus

Although exercise variety boosts golf conditioning, too much variety in the performance of actual sets and repetitions can be detrimental. Rather than per-forming varied sets of, say, 15, 12, 10, 8 and 4 repetitions in one workout ses-sion, stick with narrow bands of the same number of repetitions. Vary the number of your set-by-set repetitions only by 2 or 3, and you'll obtain better results because of specific muscular adaptations.

Resistance Training Model for Golf

For golf, the following model is useful in determining resistance training priorities during various training phases. For golf purposes, muscular endurance is built in 15 or more repetitions per exercise; strength-endurance is built in 12 to 15 repetitions per exercise, strength is built in 8 to 12 repetitions per exercise, maximum strength is built in 6 to 8 repetitions per exercise, and power is built in less than 6 repetitions per exercise.

Off-season

This is the period following the end of the golf season and lasting until 8 to 15 weeks before the next golf season starts.

Resistance Training Goals: Strengthen injury-prone areas; work the entire body without too much specificity; work to correct strength imbalances such as overly strong quadriceps as compared to the hamstring group.

The off-season is a good time to develop a feel for exercises that work best for each muscle group. Also, this is an excellent time to experiment with your equipment, either at home or the fitness club. This is especially important as advance planning for the in-season training phase. Accurately plan which exercises will result in the most benefit over the shortest period of time.

Training Emphasis: Muscular endurance, 45%; muscular strength, 45%; muscular power, 10%.

Methods: Mixture of resistance training, cross-training and body-weight resistance exercises, such as slide training, dips/pull-ups.

Pre-season

This is the period covering roughly the 8 to 15 weeks before your golf season starts.

Resistance Training Goals: Further refine the overall balance of strength and start to focus on the specific muscle groups needed in golf performance (such as the latissimus dorsi, rotator cuff and hamstrings) as well as on an extensive abdominal and back routine. Start with major-muscle-group multi-joint exercises and, after 2 to 3 weeks, add additional single-joint exercises, such as triceps extensions and rotator cuff exercises.

Specific time progression for the 8 weeks before the golf season:
1. Muscular endurance, 2 weeks
2. Muscular strength, 2 weeks
3. Muscular endurance, 1 week
4. Muscular strength, 1 week
5. Muscular power, 1 week
6. Training-method mix, 1 week

Training Emphasis: Muscular endurance, 35%; muscular strength, 30%; muscular power, 35%.

Methods: Structured resistance training, some trunk and upper-body plyometrics.

> The off-season is a good time to develop a feel for exercises that work best for each muscle group. This is an excellent time to experiment with your equipment, either at home or the fitness club.

In-season

This is the period of the golf season.

Resistance Training Goals: The goal of this training phase is to maintain maximal muscular endurance, strength and power with a minimal training-time allotment. For most golf athletes, this means adding 2 additional 30- to 45-minute sessions each week devoted to resistance training.

Training Emphasis: Muscular endurance, 30 to 45%; muscular strength, 30 to 35%; muscular power, 30 to 45%.

Methods: Structured resistance training, structured power training after a significant warm-up and selected trunk and upper-body plyometric exercises. One training session per week should be power-oriented, and another should emphasize strength and muscular endurance. During the in-season, muscular endurance should be emphasized for a single week period every 4 weeks with an additional training session focusing on this repetition range. Every other week, vary the total training balance slightly in favor of strength or power.

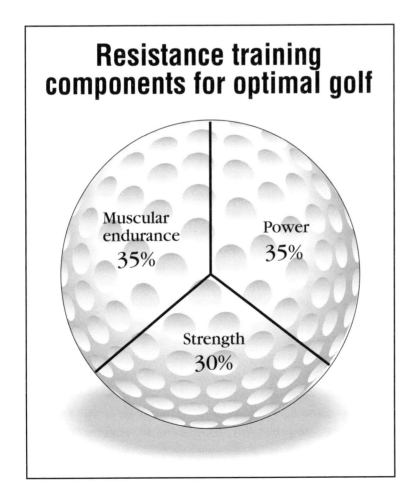

Resistance training components for optimal golf

Muscular endurance 35%

Power 35%

Strength 30%

Resistance training for golf should concentrate slightly in favor of muscular endurance and muscular power.

Training Equipment: Maximize Your Results

The resistance training industry has seen an explosion in recent years in different types of training equipment. This means that you now have more resistance training options. And the old standbys — free weights — are just as popular as ever.

Although it's not essential that you understand everything about how different training equipment systems work the muscles, you must know a certain amount in order to purchase or use appropriate training equipment for your home or office. If you exercise at a club, the following information will help you select the best method or piece of equipment from your available choices.

Manufacturers of resistance training equipment, especially home gyms, have improved over the last 15 years. Whereas some improvements in equipment help train muscle groups with greater effectiveness, other advances relate to improved equipment adjustment and fit. Both have profound effects on your progress. The better the fit, the more precise the adjustment, the better the likelihood that the apparatus will increase training effectiveness.

Elastic Tubing

Elastic tubing is popular in physical therapy programs, especially for home use. It's inexpensive, portable and can be used for a variety of exercises. However, its best use may be for support muscle groups, such as the rotator cuff, in cases where traditional resistance training may not be initially advised. Elastic tubing is also useful during periods of travel when no other form of resistance training is available.

Because tubing or elastic systems increase resistance as they stretch, they can't match the force capabilities of the muscles. Machines that use elastic resistance function in much the same way as using elastic tubing with handles. In essence, they only overload muscle at the end of the movement, at its weakest point, producing results that are least applicable to better golf performance. In some cases, such as the performance of arm curls with tubing, the angle of pull moves against joint stability when the tubing is held below the working arm. If you increase the tubing or elastic resistance and overload the muscle, this may place the joints in injury-prone positions. Although high-level athletes have used tubing and elastic resistance for purposes of rehabilitation, this method is not used extensively for serious strength or power development.

Free Weights

Free weights are the most variable and cost-effective training system available. Many athletes and industry experts consider free weights to be superior in most cases to machines.

There are, however, a couple of disadvantages to free weights. One is that most people require some initial spotting when using free weights. Another is that to use free weights properly, you must learn correct form. On the plus side, you'll activate more muscle groups with free weights than with the same exercise on a machine. That's because with free weights you must balance the weight in addition to guiding the motion. Free weights have the best cost-to-benefit ratio — they are amazingly inexpensive considering their variety and effectiveness.

Barbell exercises are good for multi-joint, multi-muscle group exercises like squats and lunges. Dumbbells provide added benefits, using additional muscle groups that not only move the weight but also balance and direct the weight through the exercise. Dumbbells, if used correctly, build flexibility as well as

Dumbbells, if used correctly, build flexibility as well as strength because they require increased range of motion for most exercises when compared to barbells.

Dumbbells, for maximum effectiveness and convenience, should be pop-pin or spin-lock in design.

strength because they require increased range of motion for most exercises when compared to barbells. Dumbbells do not allow the body's weak side to dominate or cheat in any exercise, as barbells can. For example, most right-handed golfers are far stronger in their right arms. By exercising with dumbbells, right-handed golfers can eventually build the strength in their left arms to almost the same level as in their right arms. For this reason, dumbbells should be the cornerstone of any resistance training program for golf.

Machines

Machine exercises can truly isolate muscle groups. However, not all machines are engineered the same in terms of fit and sizing. Some definitely have better fit adjustments than others. Weight machines have a fixed angle of movement, so the balance and stabilizer muscle groups are not developed in comparison to using free weights. Traditional exercise machines use a dynamic, constant resistance, which maintains force through the range of motion. Cam-based machines, on the other hand, attempt to match force with what a muscle can generate at any given point. In general, you can lift more in the middle of an exercise's range of motion and less at the beginning and end. Cam-based machines mechanically add resistance at the middle of the range of motion and subtract weight mechanically at the start and the end. Home gyms have progressed to the point that a multi-station home machine has almost the same quality of exercise offered on individual machines at an upscale athletic club.

Isokinetic machines limit the speed of movement either through electronic or mechanical means. This speed-controlled training does not provide for negative, or eccentric, resistance, but only for pushing or pulling motions. For this reason, strength results are not as complete on isokinetic machines as with free weights.

Home multi-station gyms now have a number of quality exercises in a space-efficient package.

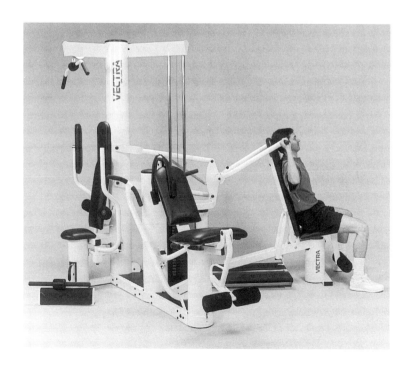

Another area in which machines may not be as effective is in abdominal and back training. Here, the variety and modifications you can make with body-weight resistance exercises generally outweigh the benefits of machines. And body-weight resistance exercises produce great results.

Although some abdominal/back machines can be useful in isolation resistance training, the best models are generally the fitness club versions, which, at over $2000 a machine, are impractical for home use. The space requirements are high considering the limited benefit. Some of the abdominal devices available for under $100 do work, however, especially the "roller" devices designed to assist you in learning the correct "crunch" motion for the abdominals. If such devices provide motivation, they are well worth an investment.

Medicine Balls

Plyometric exercises, where muscle is stretched and then forcefully contracted in the other direction, are easily accomplished with medicine balls. These balls, which can be as large as a basketball or as small as a softball, weigh from 3 to over 25 pounds. They're useful in trunk-rotation exercises and in shoulder and arm exercises such as side and overhead throws. However, medicine-ball training requires a knowledgeable partner and a sound training progression. Generally, this is best designed by a professional strength coach with experience in plyometric training. If you can meet these requirements, medicine-ball training can be a great asset to your resistance program.

Remember that the best resistance training system for golf is one that starts with a basic selection of important exercises and builds from that point. Free weights and especially dumbbells, selected machine exercises such as hamstring curls, and body-weight abdominal and trunk exercises should constitute the core routine for most individuals. If you can supplement the basic exercises with machine versions, so much the better.

Strong for Golf KEY POINTS

- Golf requires muscular endurance, strength and power for successful performance.

- Muscular endurance is the ability to repeat a movement without fatigue.

- Strength is the ability to exert maximal force regardless of the duration involved in doing so.

- Power is the ability to exert maximal force in the shortest possible time.

- Different muscles used in golf have varying requirements for the best combination of muscular endurance, strength and power.

- Hitting golf balls will not build the necessary strength, power or muscular endurance required for optimal golf performance.

- Resistance training is the most effective means to build the specific strength qualities for golf.

- Resistance training will enhance flexibility for golf if performed correctly.

- Overloading, or constantly presenting more challenge to the muscle, is the key to both building and maintaining strength gains.

- To build muscular endurance, perform 15+ repetitions maximum (RM).

- To build muscular strength, perform 6 to 12 RM.

- To build muscular power, perform less than 6 RM.

- The best resistance training model for golf is a combination of various methods that stress muscular endurance, strength and power training.

- Rest periods should complement training goals, with a goal of muscular endurance requiring rest periods of 45 seconds or less; general strength goals requiring rest periods of 60 to 90 seconds; and maximum strength or power goals requiring rest periods of 120 or more seconds.

- Golf resistance training should be developed in components of off-season, pre-season and in-season training routines.

References

Burke, R.E., 1986. The Control of Muscle Force: Motor Unit Recruitment and Firing Patterns. In N.L. Jones., N. McCartney and A.J. McComas., eds., *Human Muscle Power.* Champaign, IL: Human Kinetics.

Byrnes, W. 1985. Muscle soreness following resistance exercise with and without eccentric contractions. *Research Quarterly for Exercise and Sport* 56:283.

Chu, D. 1996. *Explosive Power and Strength: Complex Training for Maximum Results.* Champaign, IL: Human Kinetics.

Costill, D.L. et al. 1979. Adaptations in skeletal muscle following strength training. *Journal of Applied Physiology* 46:96.

Harman, E. 1983. Resistive torque analysis of 5 Nautilus exercise machines. *Medicine and Science in Sports and Exercise* 15:113.

Hickson, R. 1980. Interference of strength development by simultaneously training for strength and endurance. *Journal of Applied Physiology* 45:255-263.

Hurley, B. 1994. Does strength training improve health status? *Strength and Conditioning Journal* 16:7-13.

Komi, P.V. 1979. Neuromuscular performance: Factors influencing force and speed production. *Scandinavian Journal of Sports Sciences* 1:2-15.
———. 1986. The stretch-shortening cycle in human power output. In N.L. Jones, N. McCartney and A.J. McComas, eds., *Human Muscle Power.* Champaign, IL: Human Kinetics.

Massey, B.A., and N.L. Clauhet. 1956. Effects of systematic, heavy resistance exercise on range of joint movement in young adults. *Research Quarterly for Exercise and Sport* 27(1):41-51.

Matveyev, L. 1981. *Fundamentals of Sports Training.* Moscow: Progress Publishers.

Melby, C. et al. 1993. Effect of acute resistance exercise on postexercise energy expenditure and resting metabolic rate. *Journal of Applied Physiology* 75(4):1847-1853.

Noth, J.B. 1992. Motor units. In P.V. Komi, ed., *Strength and Power in Sport.* Oxford: Blackwell Scientific Publications.

Porcari, J., and J. Curtis. 1996. Strength and aerobics at the same time? *Fitness Management* 12(7):26-29.

Radcliffe, J., and R. Farentinos. 1985. *Plyometrics: Explosive Power Training.* Champaign, IL: Human Kinetics.

Sale, D., and D. MacDougall. 1981. Specificity in strength training, a review for the coach and athlete. *Science Periodical on Research and Technology in Sport* (March).

Tarde, J. 1979. Easy ways to tone up your golf muscles. *Golf World* 18(3):57-59.

Tesh, P.A., and L. Larsson. 1982. Muscle hypertrophy in bodybuilders. *European Journal of Applied Physiology* 49:301-306.

Wilson, G.J. 1991. Stretch shortening cycle: Nature and implications for human muscle performance. *Journal of Human Muscle Performance* 1(3):11-31.

Wolkodoff, N. 1987. Mixing rest with workouts. *American Ski Coach* 10(5):
———. 1991. Plyometrics. *IDEA Today* 9(3):32-36.

Golf Flexibility

Flexibility is key to consistency, accuracy and power in your golf game. It aids coordination and in certain cases can reduce injuries. This is partly because muscular and joint stiffness can start for some golf athletes in their early 30s and will only get worse with each advancing year; thus, flexibility takes on more importance as one ages. And not only will you lose it if you don't use it, you have to work consistently and harder as you age to maintain flexibility. As with other fitness components, just playing golf is not enough to develop optimum flexibility for golf.

Tight joints and muscles are typically the result of inactivity — without regular exercise you lose flexibility and strength. Regular stretching helps reduce muscle tension, prevents muscle and joint injuries, increases range of motion, and improves circulation, balance and flexibility. Studies have shown that stretching after strenuous exercise will relieve both immediate and short-term discomfort. Stretching, staying physically active and training for strength loosens muscular "tightness," allowing you to work each muscle and joint through its full range of motion, or ROM. Range of motion is defined as the movement around a joint or set of joints and the connecting muscles, tendons, ligaments and bones. Research indicates that increasing ROM is essential for golfers, because if you lack adequate flexibility, you simply won't have tour-level mechanics.

Problems in your current swing patterns may not be the result of inadequate swing training or practice. They may stem from reduced ROM in the key joints and muscle groups that don't allow you to swing to your full potential. Improving this ROM means that you will be able to explore new swing patterns and movements. Statistics gathered from PGA touring pros show that the average shoulder turn is approximately 87 degrees at the top of the backswing, whereas the hips will have turned an average of 45 degrees. Flexibility is necessary to allow the body to coil in the turn like a spring and then effectively uncoil into the downswing.

The repetitive nature of the golf swing and the muscular imbalances it can cause heighten the need for the golf athlete to pay attention to flexibility levels. But staying flexible for golf is not an easy process. You can't just swing your

> **Research indicates that increasing ROM is essential for golfers, because if you lack adequate flexibility, you simply won't have tour-level mechanics.**

arms a couple of times on the first tee box and expect to be ready for optimal golf. Flexibility is a quality that must be built and maintained through training.

Flexibility and Golf Performance: Obvious and Hidden Relationships

As a golfer, you'll find that tight muscles are often associated with lack of strength, overuse injuries and muscular imbalances. The hamstrings are a perfect example — they're used constantly in the golf stance and also help to rotate the hips during the downswing. However, few golfers ever train or even consistently stretch this muscle group. Thus, it becomes a chronically inflexible area exacerbated by the repetitive demands of the golf swing.

Will your resistance training make you "muscle-bound" and will it interfere with flexibility? The answer is no, as long as you train with proper form and remember to maintain ROM. In fact, many resistance training regimes have been shown to improve flexibility. Olympic weightlifters, for example, have amazing flexibility because they're constantly pushing themselves through a full range of motion. It's the ROM in exercise that is key to simultaneously developing strength and flexibility.

It's the ROM in exercise that is key to simultaneously developing strength and flexibility.

Flexibility is important to create positions of mechanical power and efficiency.

Some golfers have extraordinary flexibility without engaging in a formal stretching program. This is because they combine golf with other activities, such as squash, tennis and resistance training. The more balanced your fitness program and the more emphasis you place on ROM activities, the less need you'll have for formal stretching. In fact, there are some golfers who, through a combination of genetics and their exercise patterns, don't need a formal stretching program at all.

So, will improving flexibility enhance your golf performance? The answer most likely is yes. Most golfers don't have enough overall ROM to develop a mechanically sound or efficient swing. Increasing flexibility will ameliorate the physical limitations of poor ROM. The result is a golf swing that can use all the important parts of the body for both power and consistency. Without adequate flexibility, a golfer can't fully or effectively use the hips, shoulders, back or arms in the golf swing. A lack of flexibility in the shoulders and trunk region means that the "X" factor — the difference between shoulder and hip turn at the top of the backswing — won't be optimal. And poor ROM in the hip region may contribute to a lack of power at impact.

Increasing range of motion is a particularly good idea for golfers over 40. The aging process causes loss of elasticity in support structures such as ligaments and tendons. By age 50 there is a drop in mobility in the hip joint that continues with age. It may be that the age-related drop in flexibility is due at least in part to lack of exercise and stretching. No matter the reason, the results of the research are clear: The older you become, the more you will need to train, especially in the area of flexibility, to maintain your physical abilities.

For the absolute best gains in golf flexibility, get more active physically and combine your activity with specific stretching exercises. Most golf athletes could explore new swing patterns and increase club-head speed by increasing their ROM — not to superhuman limits, but to levels of normal functioning achieved with a flexibility regimen. Want to swing like the pros? Stretch so you have the ROM of the pros!

Stretching Versus Warm-ups

A warm-up is different from a stretch, but it can include stretching. In most sports, stretching exercises have been included as part of a warm-up routine that includes substantial movement.

Active warm-ups can include stretching or may be based on other kinds of movement. An active warm-up will reduce injury, though not necessarily because it includes stretching. The active part of the warm-up, the more vigorous movement, is what really prepares the muscles for activity by increasing blood flow and temperature. The real benefit and application of stretching exercises for golf is in increasing and maintaining ROM: Optimal ROM is a physiological requirement for a consistent golf swing.

Stretching for golf can include a number of techniques, all of which are more or less effective for different muscle groups. Depending on your swing, you may combine calisthenic-type stretches for the hips while using slow reach-and-hold stretching for the trunk area and neurological relaxation methods for the upper body, especially the shoulders. All these activities qualify as

The age-related drop in flexibility is due at least in part to lack of exercise and stretching.

Stretching:
Any activity that singularly promotes flexibility by increasing range of motion through movement and formal stretching techniques such as static and ballistic stretches.

Warm-Up:
Any single activity or sequence of movement-based activities designed to increase blood flow and muscle temperature, and to prepare the athlete for more rigorous activity.

stretching, and all have a place in modern golf training. (Information on specific stretching systems and on how they are used for optimal golf follows later in this chapter.)

Example of a posture-specific static stretch for golf.

Can You Be *Too* Flexible for Golf?

Too much ROM can hamper rather than help your golf game. Over-stretching can force muscle groups into movements and positions that are potentially injurious. This is especially true in the relationship between the hip, back and hamstring muscle groups.

Avoid pushing your ROM too far beyond what golf requires in any of the key muscle areas. Otherwise, you probably will lose some of the force that can be activated by the "stretch reflex" at the top of the backswing. The stretch reflex is a protective mechanism designed to keep muscles and joints from overextending. When a muscle is stretched close to its maximum range, a set of sensors called *muscle spindles* sends a signal to the brain that the muscle is being over-stretched. The brain then sends a signal back to the muscle that activates a reflex response, thus heading off injury from over-extension. The speed and duration of a stretch helps determine how powerful any stretch reflex activation will be. For example, at the top of the backswing, if there is a slight amount of muscular tension from a stretch in the shoulders and hips, that tension activates the stretch reflex. This stretch reflex will help the muscles to fire or activate with greater force on the downswing.

Golfers with higher swing tempos are more likely to become over-stretched and lose power. The tendons, ligaments and muscles store "elastic" energy released in a golf swing in a way that is similar to propelling a rubber band by stretching and then releasing it. The combination of a high swing speed, short backswing and low total swing time is especially hurt by excessive ROM. Being

Too much ROM can hamper rather than help your golf game.

overly flexible for this kind of golf swing means the stretch reflex doesn't activate as powerfully, thus some force production is lost from the swing.

When combined, the stretch reflex and stored elastic energy can help increase the power of a golf swing. However, too much flexibility and you can't effectively use either of these power-generation mechanisms. If you have a short swing time, then a combination of active, dynamic and static flexibility training methods will work best. This combination will allow you to use the stretch reflex effectively. If your swing is relatively slow, then you should gear more of your training toward static stretching methods, which don't activate the stretch reflex in the opposite direction. This will allow you to precisely and slowly control backswing and downswing motion.

> **The stretch reflex and stored elastic energy can help increase the power of a golf swing.**

Types of Flexibility Training Methods Used in Sports

Static, or Reach-and-Hold: In this method you stretch to a specific position, then hold the stretch, normally for ten or more seconds.

Ballistic Stretching: In this method the muscle is pushed so far with active movement that it stretches back rapidly like a tight rubber band that has been released, utilizing the physical elasticity of the muscle and the activation of the nervous system (stretch reflex).

Proprioceptive Neuromuscular Facilitation (PNF): In this method, the nervous system in conjunction with various movements allows a muscle to relax while it is being stretched, therefore enhancing the training effects in a very short period of time. The most common method is where the muscle is alternately contracted then relaxed and stretched.

Active Flexibility: This type of flexibility is demonstrated in sport movements where one muscle group, when activated, forces the opposing muscle group to relax while it is pulled through a range of motion.

Passive Flexibility: In this method a training partner or external force is used to push a muscle or limb beyond its normal range of motion.

Dynamic Movement: This method relies on sets of exercises that gradually push the joints and muscles through greater range of movement over a period of time. It refers especially to the use of alternating muscle groups, as in swinging the arms forward to stretch the rear deltoid, then backward to stretch the chest muscles.

Golf: A Dynamic Game of Static Proportions

Flexibility for golf can be measured statically or dynamically. Static flexibility is related to your ability to move through a muscle's ROM regardless of speed and to hold it for at least a short period of time. Holding a split position in gymnastics is a good illustration of static flexibility. If you have a very low swing speed, static flexibility is more important at the top of the swing position. Dynamic flexibility is related to ROM during active movement, normally a fairly rapid movement. Examples are a very quick golf swing, the movements of a runner's legs during sprinting and a basketball guard making very rapid direction changes.

Golfers traditionally have approached golf from the static flexibility perspective — a natural result of the emphasis on static flexibility in general fitness programs. However, training for golf is really best approached by developing both forms of flexibility. There are times to use methods that promote static flexibility and times to use methods that promote dynamic flexibility. It all depends on the type of golf swing you have and the ultimate purpose of the stretching exercises.

Static methods are best at relieving muscle soreness and apply best to movements that occur very slowly. For some golfers with very slow swing speeds, increasing static flexibility is important in the shoulders. For golfers with moderate or faster swing speeds, dynamic or movement-based flexibility is important in the shoulders and the hips and will have a bigger effect on improving golf performance.

The movement-based stretching that builds these dynamic abilities can be as simple as general calisthenics. It can also be as complex as active and PNF stretching, in which a partner pushes you through a specific movement. However, for the purpose of improving your golf game, exercises that dynamically push a joint or set of joints and the accompanying muscle groups through a full ROM are the best movement-based stretching regime.

> **For some golfers with very slow swing speeds, increasing static flexibility is important in the shoulders.**

Active or Passive Flexibility: Which is More Important for Golf?

Active stretching is applicable to golf because it builds strength balance as well as flexibility. In this method, you use the muscle group or groups that oppose the ones you want to stretch in a motion that is opposite of the action of the target muscle group. Activating one muscle group means the opposite muscle group will relax (known as reciprocal inhibition) and can then be more effectively stretched. Because active stretching involves repeated contractions, the movement muscle group eventually gains strength from the repeated movements, further enhancing strength balance, a requirement of permanent flexibility.

For example, by lying on your back, extending one leg straight out by using the quadriceps and then attempting to pull the leg over your head with your hip flexor, or the front of your hip, your hamstring muscle group will relax. Repeatedly contracting the hip flexors while the quadriceps remain locked actively develops hamstring flexibility. This principle is used in other active stretching exercises found in the flexibility exercises chapter.

Active stretching, as in the exercise just described, will generally test as less effective for achieving static flexibility when measured scientifically than will static stretching. However, active flexibility has a higher correlation to sports performance, especially where the movement required is rapid and undergoes a direction change. The faster you swing and the more compact your swing, the greater your use of active flexibility. For example, as you actively stretch the target side rear deltoid by pulling your arm away from the target, as you would in a golf swing, you store elastic energy in the muscle. This can be combined with the stretch reflex to create a more powerful golf swing.

> **The faster you swing and the more compact your swing, the greater your use of active flexibility.**

Swing Patterns, Body Types and Physical Limitations

The key to optimal golf flexibility is to match your body type with your swing patterns, swing speed and physical training preferences. Not everyone is built the same way, so no two golfers should stretch the same way. There are individual differences in body types, support structures, past training patterns and musculature, so determining which kinds of flexibility training are right for you is something of an odyssey. Your goal is to discover which blend is most important to your golf game.

Stretching some muscle groups inappropriately can have disastrous consequences. For example, many gymnasts who stretched extensively as children find that their knee joints are loosened later in life, which can lead to premature wear and instability. Termed "joint laxity," this phenomenon also has been observed in football players and is considered to be a cause of such conditions as arthritis. In golf, as in any other sport, the goal is to gain range of motion from the muscles, not the support structures of the ligaments and tendons.

In picking the flexibility training methods best suited to your game, it's important to understand how muscles function and what contributes to and detracts from flexibility. In addition, there are factors that provide resistance to increasing ROM. During passive motion, in which a limb is slowly moved by an external force, the muscle itself accounts for around 40% of the resistance to ROM. The joint capsule, or surfaces of the joint, on average account for 47% of resistance to flexibility. Skin, tendons and ligaments combine for around 12% resistance.

Comparison of the relative contribution of structures to flexibility

Structure	Resistance to flexibility
Joint capsule	47%
Muscle (fascia)	41%
Tendon	10%
Skin	2%

In considering the resistance of various physical structures to flexibility, your goal in golf training should be to stretch the musculature, not damage the support structures.

One of the important principles of flexibility training is to stretch or elongate muscle without affecting support structures, which will prevent premature joint wear. Stretch the muscle, don't injure the joint! Some exercise experts have advocated that other methods besides static stretching can more effectively increase ROM without potential joint problems. This is because in other stretching methods the duration of the stretch is shorter, and particularly in PNF training, which produces gains through muscular contraction and relaxation, less stress is placed on the joints for a shorter period of time.

Research Conclusions: What Works the Best?

Flexibility training for golfers needs to be specific to golf and the different muscle groups and joints used in golf. Just as there are different club heads that impart different spin rates and distances to the ball, so too are there different flexibility methods. Most flexibility-training research centers on the static method and its effect on everything from relaxation to sports performance.

Testing of newer methods such as PNF (Proprioceptive Neuromuscular Facilitation, see page 83), which also actively involve the nervous system, may be less conclusive because scientists have not been able to gauge results over time on various populations of athletes. New flexibility-training combinations and applications are constantly being explored, and many have been successfully applied to sports with great short-term results. PNF holds great promise for golfers because of its high degree of effectiveness over short periods of time.

Why has static stretching been so popular with golfers? The original research on the benefits of flexibility was conducted in the 1960s by the noted physiologist Herbert de Vries, who observed that static stretching helps reduce muscular soreness. It is thought that muscular distress produces "microspasms" in affected muscle. The research demonstrated that static stretching definitely decreased electrical activity and spasms. This is why static stretching is recommended after resistance training: It helps reduce Delayed Onset Muscular Soreness (DOMS). This results when heavily exercised or stressed muscle responds by taking on fluid, temporarily decreasing spasms in order to repair itself. Stretch after heavy exercise and you won't get as sore later.

Should you bounce when you stretch? Ballistic movements, in which a muscle is rapidly pushed in one direction until the stretch reflex and stored elastic energy essentially pulls it back, have been blamed for causing injuries. But little empirical research proves that this is actually the case. Ballistic stretching is just as effective at developing flexibility as are static methods. In fact, there is a movement in sports training toward ballistic stretching, especially as the final component to a scientific warm-up. However, excessive use of ballistic stretching requires a better than average level of conditioning to begin with and no orthopedic problems.

There can be negative aspects to flexibility training. If you use inappropriate methods, stretching beyond what your sport requires, losing the dynamic tension connection, your golf game could get worse. Golf requires both static and dynamic flexibility, and it's important to understand the differences between the two in tailoring your stretching program to golf. As has been mentioned, research shows that active flexibility has a higher correlation to sports performance than does the ability to hold a stretch. Most athletes have higher static than dynamic flexibility scores, so static flexibility is not necessarily a good indicator of dynamic ability.

Dynamic flexibility training methods consistently produce the greatest gains in dynamic ROM, and static methods produce the greatest gains in static ROM. Some research indicates that there may be greater training effects on both ends of the flexibility spectrum rather than just one: You should combine both dynamic and static stretching methods to improve your golf game.

PNF holds great promise for golfers because of its high degree of effectiveness over short periods of time.

Ballistic stretching is just as effective as static methods at developing flexibility.

Active flexibility has a higher correlation to sports performance than does the ability to hold a stretch.

Flexibility and Injury: What's the Relationship for Golfers?

If you can't swing a club through a certain range of motion with your shoulders or hips, you run a higher risk of injury. Every golfer has an optimal range of flexibility, which, when combined with the demands of golf, contributes to or detracts from injury potential. For example, if you turn your shoulder 87 degrees in the swing when your shoulder's ROM is only 51 degrees, you risk injury. In addition, if you can't move properly in the golf swing, stress will be transferred to other parts of your body. For example, for many recreational golfers, shoulder inflexibility is the prime cause of low-back problems. Physical activity works in the body like a chain, and force is transmitted to the weakest link to accomplish the required movement.

In the relatively few studies that link stretching and injury, stretching in conjunction with warm-up exercises appears to decrease injury rates. Most athletes, including golf athletes, don't properly warm up or mentally prepare themselves for practice or performance. Calisthenic or movement-based exercises, which have been around since the first Olympic Games, help increase blood flow to muscles and reduce the risk of injury. Each year, roughly 70% of the golf related back and hip strains occur because of going directly to the driving range or first tee without adequately warming up. All it takes is 5 minutes for a minimal warm-up routine, which will increase performance and decrease injury potential.

Mind Your Muscle

Psychologically, regular stretching can be a mental cue that practice or competition is about to begin. Always warm up before golf, and your mind and body will begin to make the link between your warm-up and the mental focus required for your game.

Stretching strengthens the mind/body connection in other ways. Stretching — especially static stretching — combined with deep-breathing exercises has been demonstrated to decrease stress and tension. Relaxation is definitely important for golf. Some golfers have found that even though a pre-match stretching routine may do very little to increase flexibility that day, it can provide benefits in relaxation and focus. Staying loose, relaxed and focused in golf definitely leads to better performance.

If you want to reap full mental benefit from stretching, plan on developing a daily routine. Keep in mind that movement-based stretching does not appear to provide the same relaxation and tension-reduction benefits as static stretching. Practicing stretching exercises on a regular basis helps to establish a link between increasing focus and decreasing tension to the actual activity of stretching.

> **Psychologically, regular stretching can be a mental cue that practice or competition is about to begin.**

Guidelines for Stretching

So what is the best way to combine different flexibility-developing regimens with golf and exercise for golf? That depends on two things: your access to professional help and your time constraints. There is no doubt that most athletes, including golf athletes, need to perform regular, sometimes daily, flexibility training if they expect their flexibility to improve.

Before you start a flexibility program, there are some general guidelines and cautions you should observe. If you are in doubt about your fitness, or if you've had a joint or muscular injury, consult a sports medicine physician. You also can talk to other trained health and fitness professionals for advice. If you are fit to begin a stretching program, it is vital that you develop an individualized program that is part of a total conditioning program for golf. It's always a good idea to have a professional measure your flexibility before you start a stretching regimen.

Give your new flexibility training program the time it deserves. If you hurry through the stretching process, you'll lose your mental focus. You'll also lose the potential for increasing relaxation, and you could get an injury. Remember that stretching every day is preferable to a marathon session once a week, which will only increase your risk of injury and won't improve your flexibility. Like other forms of exercise, stretching should "overload" the system to force both permanent and short-term changes. In stretching, you have to push *slightly* beyond your limits if you expect those limits to change. Stretching, like resistance training, should stress proper mechanics and alignment. But don't quit resistance training to start stretching — the two work hand in hand for golf.

The methods you should use for increasing golf flexibility include static, dynamic, active and PNF methods. All are effective, and their combined use in golf works far better than just one method would.

Static stretching is excellent for relieving muscular soreness and for building static flexibility. In addition, joint systems susceptible to injury, such as the back, benefit more from static stretching because of its lower potential for causing injury. Movement-based stretching is good for the hips and upper body, especially in the last phase of a warm-up. Remember that the faster your swing, the more important movement-based and active stretching will be to your golf performance. Active flexibility, where one muscle group pulls as the opposing group relaxes, has a high correlation to improved facility of movement. PNF techniques are extremely effective if you can work with a trained professional.

Remember that stretching every day is preferable to a marathon session once a week.

Static stretching is most effective after exercise.

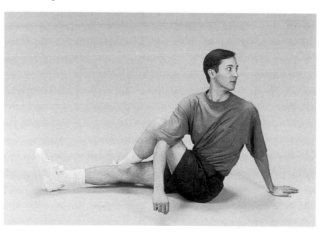

Stretching Before Golf: Only After a Warm-Up!

Incorporating stretching into an active warm-up is essential to consistent golf. In order for stretching and warming up to get you in the right frame of mind for your practice or game, you have to tell yourself why stretching and warm-ups are important. During the exercises, think of what you are going to practice, how you are going to go about it and the degree of success you expect. Professional teams in baseball and football that have combined warm-up programs of movement with flexibility training have found the combination improves practice performance.

A dynamic routine also can be used pre-match on the first tee box and as a warm-up for your aerobic or strength-training exercise routine. Emphasize progressively dynamic stretches for the shoulders and hips, and slower movements for the back. If you are short on time, a dynamic routine is more effective and safer than a static routine.

Before you stretch, get your muscles warm! If you are relatively new to exercise, you will need to perform light movements, such as calisthenics and aerobic activity, for at least 10 minutes before beginning a stretching routine. If you are relatively fit, 5 minutes of activity can be sufficient to get the muscles warm. Without that activity, a cold muscle may actually tear in a stretching routine.

In sports such as golf, where the stretch reflex and stored elastic energy is used to help accelerate movement, ballistic stretching used cautiously is the ideal last phase of a warm-up. Ballistic movements heighten sensitivity to the nervous system's firing of the stretch reflex, whereas static stretching diminishes that neurological sensitivity. The key to using ballistic methods successfully for golf is to gradually add range of motion through 10 to 15 repetitions — don't push for maximum ROM during the first few movements. For example, in arm circles, make small circles for the first few movements. After 10 repetitions, gradually and continually increase the range of motion.

As a golfer, you need and can benefit from static and active flexibility in your warm-up. For the shoulder area, it is traditional to use static stretches. Shoulders are turned relatively slowly in golf, which is one reason most golfers have used static methods to increase flexibility in that area. Movement and PNF-based stretching regimens have gained more popularity recently but are still not widely applied, especially to the shoulder area.

The ROM required to bring your arm from the shoulder to the other side of your body horizontally, as in a swing, is 130 degrees. Though static stretching methods will work to increase flexibility in this movement to some degree, movement-based stretching should be used also because of the loading/unloading component of the swing. In golf, ROM in the shoulder is more likely to be used dynamically. Though some players may pause slightly at the top of the swing, losing valuable stored elastic energy, at best the pause is brief. In most cases, the dynamic downswing movement starts almost instantaneously from the shoulder. Other muscle groups, such as the rotator cuff group, have a higher resistance to injury and make a greater contribution to golf if they have strength throughout the range of motion, not just a greater range of motion. Dynamic activity tends to build more strength than passive or static stretching does.

In sports such as golf, where the stretch reflex and stored elastic energy is used to help accelerate movement, ballistic stretching used cautiously is the ideal last phase of a warm-up.

Though static stretching methods will work to increase flexibility to some degree, movement-based stretching should be used also, because of the loading/unloading component of the swing.

Warming Up with Weighted Clubs

To a certain degree, swinging weighted clubs or 2 golf clubs together, and using other training aids, will improve dynamic flexibility in the shoulders. However, make the weighted club too heavy, and you will end up using other muscles either to protect the joint or to accomplish the movement. Golf is a blend of shoulder, hip and trunk rotation and movement, and adding weight to stretching movements may cause you to rotate more with the hips, for example, in order to protect the back.

Using a weighted club can be effective, yet it requires you to pay attention in order to discover just how far you can push to gradually increase ROM without engaging other muscle groups or joints. The momentum of swinging a heavy club most likely will take you past your normal stopping point, thus forcing additional muscles to engage. In addition, using a slightly different golf swing with a weighted club can confuse the brain: During the real swing, you don't know whether to use your normal swing or the heavy-club swing! If you train with a weighted club, always make sure you take plenty of normal swings afterward to reestablish the actual swing motor pattern with your improved flexibility. For these reasons, it is probably best to use your personal best flexibility methods combined with resistance training rather than a weighted warm-up club.

Strength Balance, Permanent Flexibility

Remember, golf is a sport that is extremely dependent on the external rotators and other muscles in the upper back and shoulder girdle. Most golf athletes traditionally have over-trained the internal rotators, or the pectoralis group, and anterior deltoids. This strength imbalance simply means the internal rotators are so strong they will never achieve full flexibility until the external rotators are developed to counter-balance their level of strength. A useful analogy is a suspension bridge, where function and structural integrity are dependent on each cable system exerting an equal amount of force. This same analogy is also why some golf athletes have chronic flexibility problems with their hamstrings and low backs: Those muscle groups are constantly overpowered by stronger quadriceps.

For flexibility to be permanent flexibility, it is important to get the system back in balance. In the case of the internal rotators, this means extra exercises with the external rotators, such as bent rows with external rotation, while aggressively stretching the chest. In the case of the hamstrings, it means extra sets of leg curls. Keep the system in muscular balance, and you can decrease your need for formal stretching exercises. Resistance training is the most efficient means for the golf athlete to assure this muscular balance.

Hip Specifics

The hip joint is a ball-and-socket joint and is best trained using dynamic movement because of the wide variety of movement patterns the hips undergo in golf. With your hips you can move your leg forward, backward, to the side and in a variety of diagonal patterns. Single leg circles followed by hip kicks as well as slide training are excellent methods for building dynamic flexibility in this region. Slide training, which forces different motions and stances,

Some golf athletes have chronic flexibility problems with their hamstrings and low backs. Those muscle groups are constantly overpowered by stronger quadriceps.

can also contribute to hip flexibility, especially if a strength deficit is a cause of hip inflexibility.

Back Specifics

Stretching the back is complex because of the multitude of ligaments and musculature that support the spine, as well as the movement limitations of each vertebra. The spine is more susceptible to injuries caused by rapid movements, which could cause damage to disks and ligaments. But golf is tough on the back, and, in most cases, gentle movement stretching and static stretching are preferred methods of increasing spine flexibility.

Other muscle groups, such as the hamstrings, rectus abdominis, obliques and hips, may be responsible for a lack of back and rotational flexibility. For example, tight hamstrings tilt the pelvis backward, which affects the erectors of the back. Without extensive testing by a trained health professional, the best means to insure back flexibility is to regularly strengthen the back's contributing and mediating muscle groups (hamstrings, hips, abdominals) and to regularly stretch the entire back system. Because of the stress golf can place on the back, a back-flexibility routine should be almost a daily regimen.

Without this kind of attention, most golfers will not have the strength or flexibility to maintain the best golf posture consistently through a round or a season. Regaining good posture should be a goal of both your strengthening and stretching programs. If posture is an issue for you, perform more back extensor exercises, such as back extensions; and rear deltoid and teres minor exercises, such as rear deltoid raises. Whenever possible, sit in back-friendly chairs.

> **Regaining good posture should be a goal of both your strengthening and stretching programs.**

Early-Morning Stretching for Golf

Like other forms of exercise, stretching is most effectively performed when you can devote adequate time to it and are free from distractions. For most golfers, this is first thing in the morning. However, during the early morning, the body is busy shifting fluids to the muscles and joints, as well as gradually increasing metabolism. Some golfers who have tried stretching statically within the first 60 minutes after waking in the morning have reported the results to be less than optimal. Until the muscles are adequately warm with good blood flow, and the proper amount of fluid has moved to the joint capsules, any attempt at stretching will be less than effective.

However, if you really want to stretch first thing in the morning, use the dynamic stretching routine outlined in the chapter titled "Flexibility Exercises." Wait at least 30 minutes after waking to go through the routine. Its rationale is two-fold: It allows you to use activity and ROM exercises to increase and maintain range of motion, and the exercises themselves serve as their own warm-up. Some sports scientists have found that a dynamic flexibility routine performed first thing in the day has positive transfer effects to sports where the athlete has little time to warm up. If you regularly get to the tee box after a 100-meter dash from the parking lot, then a dynamic early-morning routine will be a handicap reducer for you.

> **Some sports scientists have found that a dynamic flexibility routine performed first thing in the day has positive transfer effects to sports where the athlete has little time to warm up.**

> **Flexibility without strength is not permanent flexibility, nor is it flexibility that reaches its maximum potential.**

Stretching and Training Phases

Your training phase (off-season, pre-season and in-season) has a great deal to do with the flexibility training methods you employ — and when — to improve your golf game. In your off-season program, your goal should be to correct any strength imbalances and to make sure that strength in all directions of a movement is adequate to develop flexibility. Any weak points in a movement's range of motion should be addressed with resistance training or with the strength-development methods of PNF (for which you'll need a trained professional's help). Flexibility without strength is not permanent flexibility, nor is it flexibility that reaches its maximum potential. In the off-season, a few general stretches at the end of each workout should be sufficient to meet these needs.

During the pre-season phase of your training program, you should begin to get more specific and regimented in your flexibility training. For example, more emphasis on the rotator cuff and hip muscles on a daily basis is warranted during pre-season training. Flexibility training after aerobic or strength-building exercise is the best means to improve both your fitness and flexibility during training.

During the golf season you will need a separate flexibility routine, such as the early-morning dynamic routine, because of the time it takes to practice and play golf.

> **Dynamic stretching should receive more emphasis in pre-season and in-season programs.**

Stretching and Relaxation for Golf

If you choose to use static stretching as a means to relaxation as well as to developing flexibility, then it is essential to perform a light muscular warm-up before stretching. Five or more minutes of cycling or walking should be adequate to elevate muscle temperature for this purpose. If you have been training for more than 8 weeks, then as little as 2 to 4 minutes of dynamic exercise will be enough to raise muscle temperature and redirect blood flow. Even in this area golf athletes are individuals, and careful training records will help you adjust your warm-up time and the pace of your flexibility exercises.

Breathing is an important factor in stretching for relaxation. Make sure to take deeper breaths than normal and do not hold your breath during any stretch. Certain types of music, such as classical or light jazz, have been found to be very effective at helping athletes maintain a breathing rhythm during stretching.

Stretching in an Exercise Session

If you go through a formal exercise training session, such as resistance training or an aerobic workout, then static stretching after your routine will improve flexibility and alleviate muscle soreness. Stretch the muscles used in your training regimen as well as those that are your weak points in golf. Your progress should move from standing exercises, where you emphasize golf posture, to prone exercises for the back and hips. Shoulder, spine, hamstring and hip flexibility should be the focus of static stretching in this case. A key area to focus on in your stretching should be the pectoralis major and anterior deltoid, which limit motion in the opposing external rotator cuff muscles. Active stretching can be utilized at this time as well.

If you are exercising with a partner or use a trainer, then PNF and partner-assisted stretching methods will be beneficial. This is especially true if your needs include developing strength at weak points in a range of motion. Such PNF methods as repeated contractions, when directed by a knowledgeable trainer or other health professional, can significantly improve strength in extended positions and flexibility. However, unless you have professional help, PNF techniques should not be used.

Remember, in active exercises like resistance training, the best warm-up is using a lighter than normal resistance through a full range of motion. Your flexibility-development routine is best placed at the end of your lifting session, where it will do the most good.

Static stretching after your routine will improve flexibility and alleviate muscle soreness.

Stretching Before a Round or Practice Session

A major cause of inflexibility is not using muscles, so movement is the preferred method of stretching and warming up. The tee box presents special problems in that most courses don't have driving ranges or clubhouses with stretching mats or treadmills for active warm-ups. The best stretching regimen in this case is to actively stretch on the tee box in a standing position, simulating the movement requirements of the golf swing.

As illustrated in the photos on dynamic exercises (see "Flexibility Exercises" chapter), most of these exercises should resemble calisthenics. Then use the club in the final phase of the warm-up before striking the first ball. With limited time, active flexibility and dynamic movements will be the most effective. If you have time after your muscles are warm, static stretching can be added to the middle of the warm-up. If low-back or hip areas connected to low-back problems need attention, you should find a carpeted section somewhere in the clubhouse and go through some static and slow-movement stretches designed for these areas.

Posture-specific stretching encompasses the benefits of stretching multiple muscle groups.

Some observations and research support the idea that movement-based ROM stretching should be posture-specific. For example, if you want to stretch the hips for golf, then you should do so while standing. This will allow the body to activate other muscle groups to make the stretch more specific to a standing golf posture. You won't be able to stretch and activate posture stabilizers that need to be active during certain phases of the golf swing without performing standing stretches.

Stretching After Golf

For most golfers, this is the ounce of prevention! After a round of golf, you have moved your muscles on average more than 200 times in the golf swing, including practice swings, and your muscles are relatively warm. You'll be less sore, especially in your overworked muscles, if you stretch after your round. Concentrate on hamstrings, the lower back, the shoulders (both front and rear deltoids and the rotator cuff group), and the trapezius and teres major because of their relationship to posture and movement. Two to 3 minutes of static stretching in the clubhouse will decrease muscular soreness and allow you the added mental benefit of being able to focus on an analysis of your game or practice.

Individual Differences, Individual Situations

Your need for flexibility training and specific training methods change from day to day and are affected by other factors. Generally, colder or hotter weather increases your need to perform longer warm-ups. Stress causes more muscular tension, especially in the lower back and shoulders. These are two

Observations and research support the idea that movement-based ROM stretching should be posture-specific.

of the most common areas of injury on the driving range during warm-ups and require a longer warm-up routine with stretching of the key muscle groups, including the trapezius and latissimus dorsi.

It's better to start with a reasonable routine that you can then increase if it's too short than to hurry through your stretches at the same time you're trying to relax. If you feel pressure to hurry, you might get more tense than if you didn't stretch at all!

If you are new to training for golf, use more stretching exercises than you think you might need. As you gain fitness and pay more attention to proper warm-ups and resistance-training form and muscular balance, you will find that you can cut back on the amount of additional flexibility training you perform. Like other fitness factors, flexibility is much more difficult to build than to maintain. Try gradually reducing the number of flexibility exercises you perform, starting with 1 per week, and note the results. If your other training components are sound, you will be able to take out some of these exercises without sacrificing overall results.

Like other fitness factors, flexibility is much more difficult to build than to maintain.

Golf Flexibility KEY POINTS

- Muscular balance is a requirement for permanent flexibility.

- Always lift weights through a full range of motion because this promotes flexibility, especially when dumbbells are used.

- Stretch daily in some form, whether before your round, after your round or as part of a formal exercise session.

- Never stretch a cold muscle. During static stretching, always take time for movement that will prepare the muscle for optimal gains in flexibility.

- If you are going to stretch first thing in the morning, use a movement-based routine that will warm up the muscles as well as stretch them.

- When you perform movement-based stretching using either dynamic or ballistic stretches, start with a limited range of motion and gradually increase the range of motion through 10 to 15 repetitions, or until you become fatigued.

- A combination of methods, including static, dynamic and limited ballistic stretching, should be your training goal. Using all three of these methods in your workout will produce results superior to exclusive use of traditional static stretching.

- The faster your natural tempo in both backswing and downswing, the more your flexibility program should be geared toward active and dynamic stretching, which can help your body take advantage of the stretch reflex to generate more power.

- Every 3 to 4 weeks during the golf season, take a week or more and double your normal flexibility-training time for that period. By periodically increasing emphasis on strength, aerobic or flexibility training, you will keep each of these fitness components in peak form and also will rebuild key abilities throughout the golf season.

- Keep records of your stretching regimens and perform a mid-season analysis of the relationship between your stretching regularity and methods, other forms of training and your golf game.

- Effective stretching will require some degree of experimentation in the types and amounts you need to perform for optimal golf, so don't be afraid to try new regimens.

- Increasing your flexibility is an issue of training — not a contest. Don't allow another's expectations to make you think you don't have adequate flexibility. Focus on progressively reaching your individual goals, and don't compare yourself to others.

References

Asmussen, E., and F. Bonde-Petersen. 1974. Storage of elastic energy in skeletal muscles in man. *Acta Physiologica Scandinavica* 91(3):386-392.

Balaftsalis, H. 1982. Knee joint laxity contributing to footballers' injuries. *Physio Therapy in Sport* 5(3):26-27.

Bates, R.A. 1971. *Flexibility training: The optimal time period to spend in a position of maximal stretch.* Master's thesis, University of Alberta.

Bird, H. 1979. Joint laxity in sport. *Medisport: The Review of Sports Medicine* 1(5):30-31.

Broedelius, A. 1961. Osteoarthritis of the talar joints in footballers and ballet dancers. *Acta Orthopaedica Scandinavica* 30:309-314.

de Vries, H.A. 1961. Prevention of muscular distress after exercise. *Research Quarterly* 32(2):77-185.

Evans, M. 1996. *Instant Stretches for Stress Relief.* New York: Lorenz.

Fukashiro, S., M. Itoh, Y. Ichinose, Y. Kawakami, and T. Fukunaga. 1995. Ultrasonography gives directly but noninvasively elastic characteristic of human tendon in vivo. *European Journal of Applied Physiology and Occupational Physiology* 71(6): 555-557.

Hubley-Kozey, C.L., and W.D. Standish. 1984. Can stretching prevent athletic injuries? *Journal of Musculoskeletal Medicine* 1(9):25-32.

Iashvili, A.V. 1983. Active and passive flexibility in athletes specializing in different sports. *Soviet Sports Review* 18(1):30-32.

Jacobs, J. 1982. Loosen up those golf muscles. *Golf World* 21(3):30-31.

Jacobsen, E. 1938. *Progressive Relaxation.* Chicago: University of Chicago Press.

Johns, R.J., and V. Wright. 1962. The relative importance of various tissues in joint stiffness. *Journal of Applied Physiology* 17(5):824-828.

King, D. 1995. Glenohumeral joint impingement in swimmers. *Journal of Athletic Training* 30(4)333-337.

Knott, M., and D.E. Voss. 1968. *Proprioceptive Neuromuscular Facilitation.* New York: Harper and Row.

Lewandowski, P. 1995. To stretch or not to stretch? *Triathlete* 134 (June):106-108, 110.

Mallon, B. 1976. Stretch and strengthen your golf muscles. *Golf Digest* 27(3): 98-100.

Meckel, Y., H. Atterbom, A. Grodjinovsky, D. Ben-Sira, and A. Rotstein. 1995. Physiological characteristics of female 100 metre sprinters of different performance levels. *Journal of Sports Medicine and Physical Fitness* 35(3): 169-175.

Moore, M., and R. Hutton. 1980. Electromyographic evaluation of muscle-stretching techniques. *Medicine and Science in Sports and Exercise* 12:322.

Richardson, B. 1990. Flexibility. *Australian Golf Digest* (August):84-89.

Vuori, I. 1995. Exercise and physical health: musculoskeletal health and functional capabilities. *Research Quarterly for Exercise and Sport* 66(4):276-285.

Wilson, G.J. 1991. Stretch shortening cycle: Nature and implications for human muscle performance. *Journal of Human Muscle Performance* 1(3):11-31.

Resistance Training Exercises

In resistance training, details make a difference in ultimate results. Use the right techniques with the correct numbers of sets and repetitions, and the chances are good that you will meet your training goals.

Training Principles

Safety

Safety is important with any form of exercise, and this is especially true in resistance training. The best means to ensure safe and effective exercise is to stress form before resistance level and to make sure you are familiar with the exercise, the equipment, and your own limitations. It's important at first to use a resistance lighter than you feel you can handle simply to gain an understanding of exercise mechanics and your limitations. Remember, what feels right for one set will become much heavier as your workout progresses and you use multiple sets.

Form Equals Function

Form is not only a key to safety but is paramount to improvement. For example, if in a bicep curl you are constantly using the back in a "throwing" or bending motion, the biceps will never be properly stressed, and you won't get as much out of training. Don't be tempted to use improper form to advance resistance too quickly. Though your results may appear great in the short term, you risk injury and poor long-term progress.

Progression

No matter what the resistance or repetition maximum (RM) level, the first few sets of exercise should be done with lighter resistance. Even after you have performed a dynamic warm-up, the first set of exercise should be performed using lighter resistance. In general, the first set of exercise should be done with 70% of the weight you would normally use, adding a few more repetitions. This is especially important in power loads with less than 6 repetitions, where the major muscle group may be able to take the physiological stress yet the supporting or secondary muscle groups risk significant injury.

Record Keeping

You'll be more successful and more motivated if you keep records of your workouts. Include the date, exercise, resistance level and number of repetitions accomplished. You also should keep miscellaneous notes and comments.

Number of Sets

> As a beginner or novice golf exerciser, the total amount of work you accomplish is the most important factor, at least for the first three to four weeks.

How many sets of an exercise should you perform? That depends on the time you have available, your level of fitness, and your training experience, to name a few of the most important factors.

As a novice golf exerciser, the total amount of work you accomplish is the most important factor, at least for the first 3 to 4 weeks. You could perform 25 repetitions at one time or 5 sets of 5 repetitions and attain almost the same results. After training for 3 to 4 weeks, as you gain a composite of muscular endurance and strength and can add more resistance, the number of sets and repetitions — and the choice of exercise — become far more important. The rules governing sets can be summarized in the following:

- Performing 1 set of an exercise is better than no exercise and will produce a significant training effect if the intensity is high enough. This can include gains in strength and strength maintenance.
- Performing 1 set of an exercise is not as effective at building or maintaining strength, power or muscular endurance as performing multiple sets.
- Performing 2 sets of resistance exercise is not significantly better than performing 1 set except in building muscular endurance.
- Performing 3 sets of resistance exercise is generally superior to 1 or 2 sets.
- Performing 4 sets of resistance exercise is generally superior to 3 sets.
- If you have limited time, perform at least 1 set; if you have more time, perform 3 or 4 sets.

Rest Periods Between Sets

Remember that proper rest periods should be incorporated into your resistance training routine for optimum results. You can use the right exercise and the right number of repetitions, but if your rest periods aren't sufficient, you won't get optimum results. For strength and power, you need enough rest between sets so that your short-term energy supply (ATP-PC) can resynthesize. Without adequate levels of that compound you won't be able to work hard enough to gain strength or power. In building muscular endurance, however, recovery of this compound is not particularly important. The best general guidelines for rest periods are:

- To build muscular endurance, or when performing sets of over 15 repetitions, use rest periods of 45 seconds or less.
- To build general strength or strength/endurance, or when performing sets of between 8 and 15 repetitions, use rest periods of 60 to 90 seconds.
- To build maximal strength or power, or when performing sets of less than 8 repetitions, then at least 120 seconds are necessary for full recovery of muscular energy.

Breath to Tempo

Many athletes forget to breathe regularly during resistance training, and this can shorten a training session; you simply won't recover between sets as effectively. In addition, holding the breath during exertion can cause a buildup of pressure in the chest. In general, concentric or lifting motions should be accompanied by exhaling, and eccentric, or lowering motions should be accompanied by inhaling.

Maintaining proper speed is important to training results. Lift too slowly, and you'll run out of fuel before you complete the set. Lift too quickly, and the muscle won't be stressed or worked through the full range of motion, which means less desirable results and a higher chance of injury. The best speed for most exercises is 1 second or slightly longer on the concentric (lifting) phase and 1 to 1.5 seconds on the eccentric (lowering) phase. Maintain a smooth, constant motion in both lifting and lowering.

Effective Resistance Training

• Stress form and resistance level.

• Always perform a general dynamic warm-up of treadmill walking or other aerobic exercise for 3 to 5 minutes before resistance training.

• Exercise or train large muscle groups or multi-joint exercises first, such as bent rows, chest press and leg extensions.

• When performing a new exercise, use lighter than anticipated resistance to learn the correct mechanics.

• Keep records: It will motivate you and let you discover which training regimens have had the most benefit for golf.

• Continue resistance training through the golf season to maintain power, strength and muscular endurance.

• Vary sets, repetitions, exercises and exercise order periodically.

• Every 8 weeks of resistance training, take a 1 week break, which will heighten results through recovery.

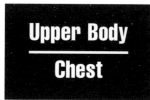

Upper Body
—
Chest

Dumbbell Chest Press

Major muscle groups: Pectoralis major, anterior deltoid, triceps

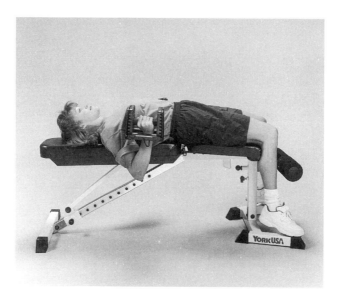

Starting position:
Supine on bench with feet flat on floor; approximately 85-degree knee angle; thumbs pointing at shoulders.

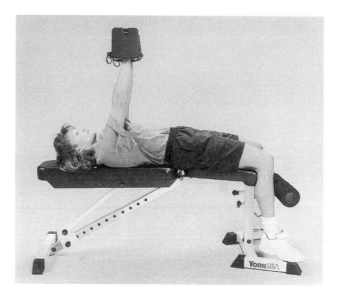

Motion:
Push dumbbells upward, rotating wrists when just above the shoulder level so that thumbs are pointing at each other and dumbbells are parallel with shoulders. Reverse the motion to lower. Repeat.

Dumbbell Incline Press

Major muscle groups: Upper portion of pectoralis major, anterior deltoid, triceps

Starting position:
Supine on bench, hips firmly on seat; feet flat on floor, helping to hold hips on the bench; bench set at 35 to 60 degrees in relation to floor; thumbs pointed at shoulders.

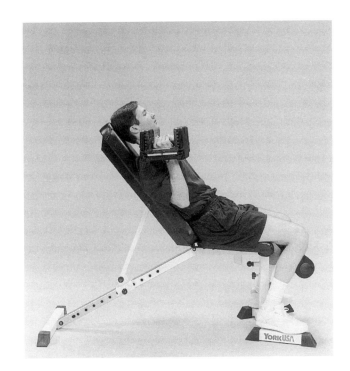

Motion:
Dumbbells move upward and rotate inward so that at the top of the press dumbbells are over the shoulders and in line with the shoulders with thumbs pointing at each other. Reverse the motion to lower. Repeat.

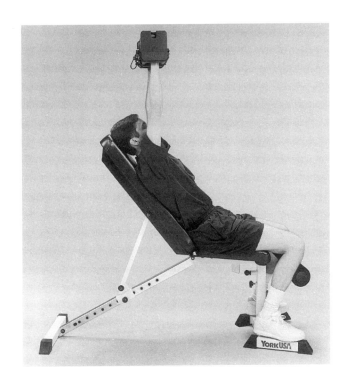

Upper Body

Chest

Dumbbell Butterfly

Major muscle groups: Pectoralis major

Starting position:
Supine on bench with feet flat on floor or bench at approximately 85-degree knee angle. Dumbbells start at position just below chest with elbows bent at a 25- to 40-degree angle.

Motion:
Press upward, bringing dumbbells together just below the shoulders and keeping arms bent in same position until the end of the motion, when elbows straighten to get full muscle activation, then lower and repeat.

Dumbbell Decline Butterfly

Major muscle groups: Lower portion of pectoralis major

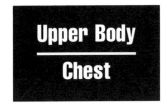

Starting position:
Supine on bench, which should be declined downward at 15 to 20 degrees; feet locked into support on bench. Dumbbells start at position just below chest with elbows bent at a 25- to 40-degree angle.

Motion:
Press upward, bringing dumbbells together just below the shoulders and keeping arms bent in same position, then lower and repeat.

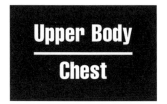

Upper Body
_____
Chest

Dumbbell Decline Press

Major muscle groups: Lower portion of pectoralis major, anterior deltoid, triceps

Starting position:
Supine on bench, which should be declined downward at 15 to 20 degrees; feet locked into support. Dumbbells start at approximately shoulder height, parallel to bench.

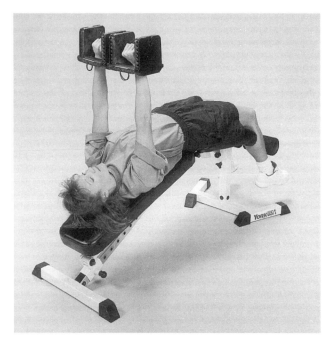

Motion:
Press dumbbells upward directly over shoulders with arms fully extended rotating dumbbells to position parallel with shoulders. Lower and repeat.

Low Row with Pulley

Major muscle groups: Latissimus dorsi, trapezius, biceps

Upper Body
Back

Starting position:
Seated with knees comfortably bent and slight upper-body forward lean with natural arch in lower back; firm grip on handles 2/3 of the way below the knees. During the motion, strive to keep the shoulders and elbows in a low position.

Motion:
Pull backward toward abdominal section, keeping the handles fairly low; pull to just below the rib cage, extending the back slightly while inhaling. Lower and repeat.

Upper Body
Back

Bent Row, Dumbbell with External Rotation

Major muscle groups: Latissimus dorsi, trapezius, biceps, posterior deltoid, infraspinatus, teres minor

Starting position:
On flat bench, use the hand and knee on one side for support, keeping the back flat or parallel to the bench or floor. Dumbbell should be firmly grasped with thumb pointing inward to midline and dumbbell parallel to plane of shoulder.

Motion:
Pull dumbbell to a point just below the shoulder joint, keeping the elbow as high as possible while rotating the arm and wrists outward so that in the finish position the thumb is facing forward. Lower and repeat.

Bent Row, Dumbbell

Major muscle groups: Latissimus dorsi, trapezius, biceps, posterior deltoid

Starting position:
On flat bench, use the hand and knee on one side for support, keeping the back flat or parallel to the bench or floor. Dumbbell should be firmly grasped with thumb pointing forward.

Motion:
Pull the dumbbell to a point just below the shoulder joint, keeping the elbow as high as possible. Lower and repeat.

Lat Pull-Down, Pull to Neck

Major muscle groups: Latissimus dorsi, biceps

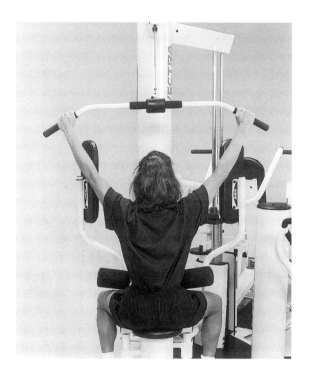

Starting position:
Feet on floor, thighs under knee brace; use wide overhand grip; look ahead and slightly downward.

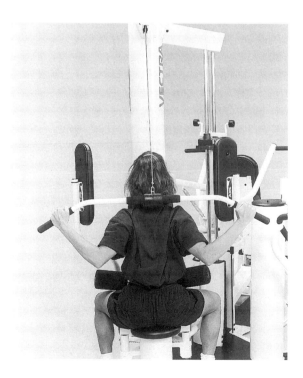

Motion:
Pull the bar to the base of the neck in a smooth motion while maintaining back and neck position, then lower the resistance and repeat.

Lat Pull-Down, Pull to Upper Chest

Major muscle groups: Latissimus dorsi, biceps

Upper Body
Back

Starting position:
Feet on floor, thighs on knee brace; use wide overhand grip; look ahead and upward while leaning back at approximately 25 to 35 degrees.

Motion:
Pull the bar to the sternum, making sure the elbows and hands are pulling straight down while maintaining back and neck position, then lower the resistance and repeat.

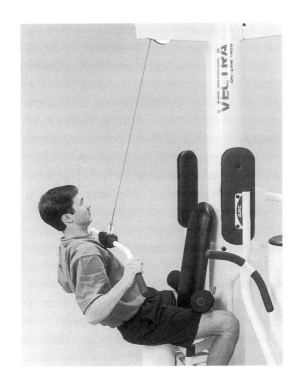

Upper Body
Back

Lat Pull-Down, Bicep Pull

Major muscle groups: Latissimus dorsi, biceps

Starting position:
Feet on floor, thighs on knee brace; use shoulder width underhand grip; look ahead and upward while leaning back at approximately 25 degrees.

Motion:
Pull the bar to the sternum, making sure the elbows and hands are pulling straight down while maintaining back and neck position, then lower the resistance and repeat.

Dumbbell Trapezius Row, 30 Degrees

Major muscle groups: Trapezius, biceps, posterior deltoid

Starting position:
Place bench at approximately 30 degrees, with feet behind hips and chest on bench. Dumbbells start directly below shoulders with thumbs facing inward.

Motion:
Dumbbells should be pressed upward while arms and elbows rotate externally so that the shoulder girdle is elevated at the end of the motion. Lower and repeat.

Dumbbell 20-Degree Upright Row

Major muscle groups: Trapezius, biceps, posterior deltoid

Starting position:
Athletic stance; knees bent 15 to 20 degrees; hip or pelvic tilt forward so shoulders are just over toes. Dumbbells should be grasped so that thumbs point to each other.

Motion:
Maintaining athletic stance, pull dumbbells upward to a point in line with the sternum, elbows higher than dumbbells in finish, then lower and repeat.

Military Dumbbell Press

Major muscle groups: Anterior and medial deltoid, triceps

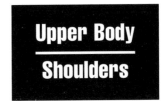

Upper Body
___
Shoulders

Starting position:
Sit on bench, which should be set at 90 degrees; if shoulder flexibility is low, set the bench at 80 degrees for a slightly inclined back. Feet should be flat on the floor, dumbbells at shoulder level.

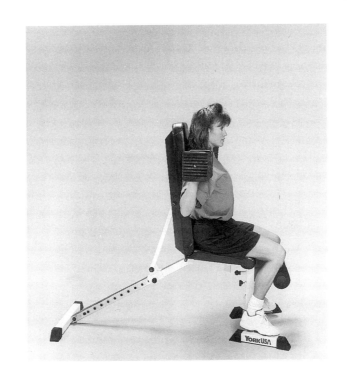

Motion:
Dumbbells travel upward in line or parallel with shoulders just above shoulders, keeping the dumbbells at the sides or as far back as possible. Lower and repeat.

Dumbbell Side-Lying Flye

Major muscle groups: Posterior deltoid, infraspinatus, teres minor

Starting position:
Lie on a flat bench with legs slightly bent for support and the non-working arm providing additional support. Grasp a light dumbbell with the working arm fully extended and just below the level of the bench, with thumb parallel to the plane of the body.

Motion:
Raise the dumbbell in line with the plane of the shoulder until it is directly over the shoulder, then lower to starting position and repeat.

Dumbbell Lying L Flye

Major muscle groups: Infraspinatus, teres minor

Upper Body
Shoulders

Starting position:
Lie on a flat bench with legs slightly bent for support and the non-working arm providing additional support. Grasp a light dumbbell with arm bent at 90 degrees, elbow tucked into side, weight starting at bench level next to torso, with thumb parallel to the plane of the body.

Motion:
Keeping elbow tucked in, raise the weight upward with a rotating movement until it is almost directly over the shoulder. Lower and repeat.

Dumbbell Rear Deltoid Raise

Major muscle groups: Posterior deltoid

Starting position:
Sit on bench with feet flat on the floor and the back at a 30- to 45-degree angle. Grasp the dumbbells parallel to the bench, with thumbs facing forward, and a slight bend in the elbows.

Motion:
Maintaining the bend in the elbows, raise the weight so that it is parallel with the shoulders while holding the upper-body position. Lower and repeat.

Dumbbell Lateral/Medial Deltoid Raise

Major muscle groups: Medial deltoid

Starting position:
Athletic stance, slight
bend to knees, very
slight bend to back.
Grasp dumbbells
or cable handle with
slightly bent elbows and
thumbs rotated to face
outward.

Note:
This exercise can be
done with cables or
dumbbells.

Motion:
Raise dumbbells or
cable handle, maintain-
ing slight elbow bend,
to a position slightly
higher than the shoul-
ders. Lower and repeat.

Upper Body

Arms

Standing Bicep Curl, Dumbbells

Major muscle groups: Biceps brachii, flexor carpi radialis

Starting position:
Athletic stance, slight bend to knees, very slight bend to back. Grasp the dumbbells with arms fully extended, wrists and thumbs facing forward.

Motion:
Raise the dumbbells from the elbows in one smooth motion, keeping the elbows locked to your side. Finish at approximately shoulder level, with palms facing shoulders. Lower and repeat.

Bicep Curl with Dumbbells, "Preacher" Version

Major muscle groups: Biceps brachii, flexor carpi radialis

Upper Body
—
Arms

Starting position:
Sit on bench, with preacher attachment firmly anchored so top of attachment is just below shoulders. Grasp one dumbbell with arms fully extended, thumbs facing upward, working arm fully extended along the pad.

Motion:
Raise the dumbbell keeping shoulder and chest firmly positioned on the pad, with the dumbbell finishing in full vertical. Lower and repeat.

Upper Body
––––––
Arms

Triceps Press-Down

Major muscle groups: Triceps, flexor carpi radialis, carpi ulnaris

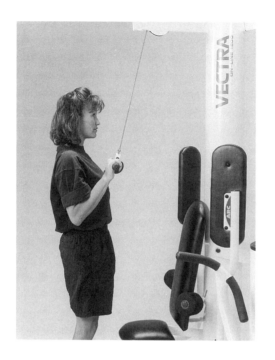

Starting position:
Athletic stance, slight bend to knees, very slight bend to back. Grasp the bar at shoulder height with elbows tucked into the sides, palms facing downward.

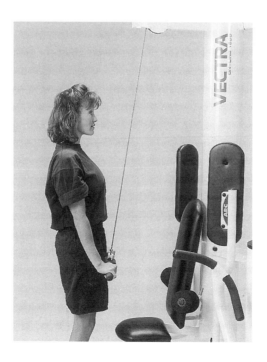

Motion:
Push the bar downward while keeping the elbows tucked into the sides, finishing at full extension at thigh level. Lower the weight, return to starting position and repeat.

Reverse Triceps Press-Down

Major muscle groups: Triceps, extensors carpi radialis longus, carpi radialis brevis, carpi ulnaris

Starting position:
Athletic stance, slight bend to knees. Grasp the bar at less than shoulder height with elbows tucked into the sides, palms facing upward.

Motion:
Push the bar downward while keeping the elbows tucked into the sides, finishing at full extension at thigh level. Lower the weight, return to starting position and repeat.

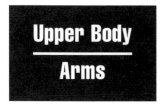

Upper Body
Arms

Dumbbell Supine Triceps Press

Major muscle groups: Triceps

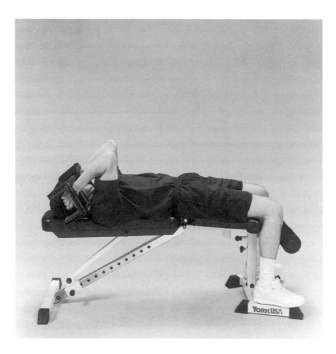

Starting position:
Lie flat on bench, feet on the floor. Grasp dumbbells, point elbows at the ceiling, upper arm vertical, keep hands and dumbbells next to the ears/shoulders area.

Motion:
Press dumbbells upward, fully extending arms using only the triceps while maintaining vertical position of upper arm. Lower and repeat.

Wrist Curl

Major muscle groups: Flexor carpi radialis, carpi ulnaris

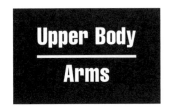

Upper Body
—————
Arms

Starting position:
Sit on bench, place one forearm on thigh with wrist and dumbbell just over the knees, palms up using the other arm to secure the working arm.

Motion:
Allow the dumbbell to roll down the extended fingers and then pull dumbbell back up, making sure the lower arm remains stable and in contact with the thighs. Repeat for desired repetitions, then repeat with other arm.

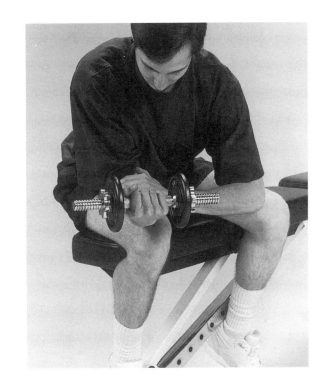

Upper Body
___
Arms

Reverse Wrist Curl

Major muscle groups: Extensors carpi radialis longus, carpi radialis brevis, carpi ulnaris

Note:
When starting a resistance program, most golf athletes will only be able to perform the reverse wrist curl with 50% of the weight used in the wrist curl.

Starting position:
Sit on bench, place one forearm on thigh with wrist and dumbbell just over knee, palm down, secured with other hand over forearm.

Motion:
Extend the wrist upward, making sure the lower arm remains stable and in contact with the thigh. Lower and repeat.

Radial Flexion or "Thor's Hammer"

Major muscle groups: Extensor carpi radialis longus, flexor carpi radialis, abductor pollicis longus

Starting position:
Seated on a bench with feet secure, with thumb up, grab the handle end of the spin-lock dumbbell while using the other hand as a brace under the elbow.

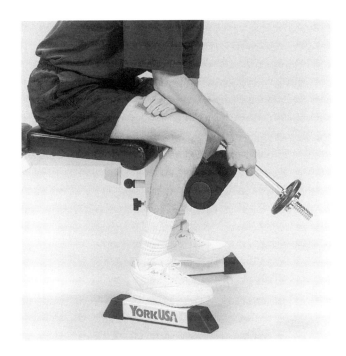

Motion:
While maintaining contact with the thigh and other hand, raise the dumbbell upward until it is at almost a right angle to the forearm. Lower and repeat.

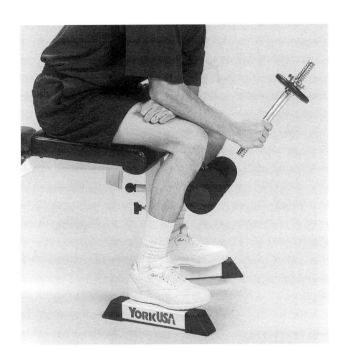

Ulnar Flexion

Major muscle groups: Flexor carpi ulnaris, extensor carpi ulnaris

Starting position:
Seated on a bench, with feet secure, arm fully extended to floor, dumbbell grasped so weighted end is pointing downward.

Motion:
While maintaining a vertical arm position, raise the heavy end of the dumbbell upward until it almost touches the arm. Lower and repeat.

Basic Crunch

Major muscle groups: Rectus abdominis

Starting position:
Lie supine on floor, keeping feet flat on floor and knees at an angle. Hold hands behind the neck and head for support, or place them across the chest if you have significant neck strength.

Note:
This and other abdominal exercises can be performed relatively effectively with one of many commercial ab-roller devices.

Motion:
Maintaining support of the head and neck, focus the eyes directly overhead. Pull with the abdominals in a smooth motion so that the shoulder blades roll off the floor and the lower back is kept pressed to the floor. Lower and repeat.

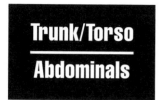

Trunk/Torso
Abdominals

Rotary Crunch

Major muscle groups: External oblique, internal oblique, erector spinae

Starting position:
Lie supine on floor, keeping feet flat on floor and knees at an angle. Hold hands behind the neck and head for support, or place them across the chest if you have significant neck strength.

Motion:
Maintaining support of the head and neck, pull with the abdominals/obliques so that the shoulder blades roll off the floor and to one side in a smooth upward motion. Keep the lower back pressed to the floor. Lower and repeat to the other side.

Side Bends with Dumbbell

Major muscle groups: External oblique

Starting position:
Athletic stance, knees slightly bent. Hold light dumbbell in one hand with palm in toward side, arm fully extended.

Note:
Because of the potential sheer force to the spine with heavy weights, only light dumbbells are recommended for this exercise.

Motion:
In a lateral, not forward, motion, lower the dumbbell along the side of the body to the knee, then pull the dumbbell up using side flexion in the other direction until the dumbbell reaches the hip and arm is straight. Lower and repeat, then repeat set on other side.

Trunk/Torso
—————
Abdominals

Arm/Leg Crunch

Major muscle groups: Rectus abdominis, external obliques, hip flexors

Starting position:
Lie supine on floor, keeping feet flat on floor and knees at an angle. Hold hands behind the neck and head for support, or place them across the chest if you have significant neck strength.

Motion:
Maintaining support of the head and neck, pull with the abdominals/ obliques so that the shoulder blades roll off the floor and to one side in a smooth upward motion, at the same time pulling the bent leg on the opposing side toward the curling or crunching side (e.g. if you are curling to the left, then pull the right shoulder to the left leg). Keep the lower back pressed to the floor. Lower and repeat to the other side.

Back Extension

Major muscle groups: Erector spinae

Trunk/Torso
Back

Starting position:
Lie face down on floor, carpet or exercise mat with arms extended forward and palms down.

Motion:
Using the back muscles, arch upward so the chest comes off the floor, using arms and hands for balance and support, not for pushing up. Focus your gaze directly ahead. Hold, lower and repeat. For advanced version, arch legs off floor as well as the chest.

Trunk/Torso
———
Back

Opposite Back Raises

Major muscle groups: Erector spinae, hamstring group

Starting position:
Crouch on hands and knees with back flat and parallel to the floor. Keep your weight evenly divided between hands and feet.

Motion:
While balancing on one hand and the leg on the opposing side (e.g., right hand, left leg), simultaneously raise the other arm to shoulder level while also raising its opposing leg (e.g., left arm, right leg) to hip level, fully extending both. On the eccentric, or lowering, motion, bring the arm and leg down at the same time without allowing them to touch the floor. Repeat for the desired number of repetitions on one side before switching to the other side.

Side Medicine Ball Throws (Advanced Exercise)

Major muscle groups: Erector spinae, rectus abdominis,
external obliques, internal obliques

Starting position:
Athletic stance with
knees bent, slight for-
ward pelvic tilt. Facing
a partner who throws
a medicine ball to you,
catch the ball to one
side, and keep the ball
close to the side.

Motion:
The force of the ball
should cause the spine,
hips, and shoulders to
twist to the side. At the
point of muscular ten-
sion, simply uncoil and
allow the ball to go back
in the other direction to
your partner. Complete
all repetitions on one
side before moving to
the other side.

Trunk/Torso
Combination

Swing Plane Medicine Ball Throws
(Advanced Exercise)

Major muscle groups: Erector spinae, rectus abdominis,
external obliques, internal obliques

Starting position:
Athletic stance with knees bent, slight forward pelvic tilt. Facing a partner who throws a very light and small medicine ball to you, catch the ball with both hands and, extending from the left shoulder, take it in an arc through a lessened range of motion compared to your golf swing.

Motion:
Go back nearly to the top of your backswing, then come down in the other direction, ending by throwing the ball back to your partner.

Dumbbell Squat

Major muscle groups: Quadriceps group, hamstring group, gluteus maximus, erector spinae

Starting position:
Dumbbells resting at close to top of shoulder, held securely with hands. Feet are shoulder width apart, with toes/knees pointing outward from 15 to 25 degrees.

Note:
Leg press can be substituted for the squat.

Motion:
Lower the weight slowly, allowing the knees to bend forward while the hips move backward, as if about to sit. Maintain the curve in the back by keeping the chest and head elevated. As you progress downward, maintain a good back position by looking slightly up, then return to the starting position with the opposite motion and repeat.

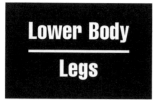

Lower Body
—————
Legs

Leg Extension

Major muscle groups: Quadriceps group, rectus femoris

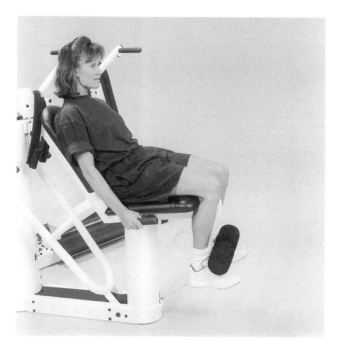

Starting position:
Determine the proper seat-back position by placing the middle of the knee joint as close as possible to the axis point of the machine. If there is a pad adjustment for the shin, it should be placed just above the ankle. Grip the handlebars or seat pad securely.

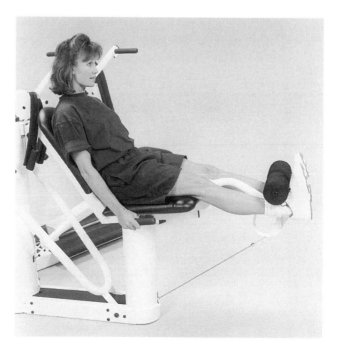

Motion:
Extend the lower leg upward until there is full extension of the knee, where the leg is almost straight. Lower the resistance and repeat.

Leg Extension, Toes Out

Major muscle groups: Quadriceps group, rectus femoris

Lower Body
___
Legs

Starting position:
Determine the proper position by placing the middle of the knee joint as close as possible to the axis point of the machine. If there is a pad adjustment for the shin, it should be placed just above the ankle. Grip the seat pad securely, starting with toes pointed outward approximately 15 to 20 degrees.

Note:
Performing this exercise by keeping the toes pointing outward during the movement will activate the vastus medialis, which tends to be weak in most golf athletes.

Motion:
Extend the lower leg upward until there is full extension of the knee, where the leg is almost straight. Lower the resistance and repeat.

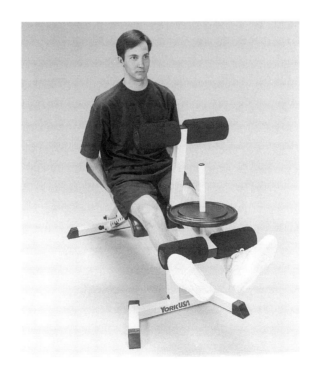

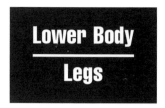

Lower Body
Legs

Leg Curl, Prone

Major muscle groups: Hamstring group

Starting position:
Using a leg-curl bench with a bend in the middle or a free-weight bench with decline adjustment, align the knee joint with the axis of the machine. If the pad adjusts, place it just above the ankle joint and grip either the bottom of the bench or the hand grips.

Motion:
Pull the pad upward, making sure the abdominals do not contract and "jackknife" during the exercise. Pull almost to the buttocks, then lower the resistance and repeat.

Leg Curl, Standing

Major muscle groups: Hamstring group

Lower Body
—
Legs

Starting position:
With the non-exercising leg firmly on the floor, align the knee joint with the axis of the machine. If the pad adjusts, place it just above the ankle joint and grip seat pad and/or handles for upper body support, ensuring the hips are stable during the movement.

Motion:
Pull the pad upward in a curl motion, making sure the upper body stays vertical during the exercise. Pull almost to the buttocks, then lower the resistance and repeat, then repeat with other leg.

Standing Calf Raise

Major muscle groups: Gastrocnemius, soleus

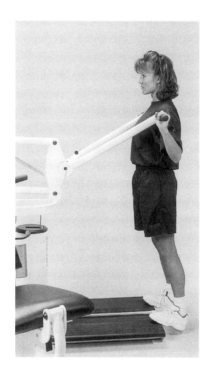

Starting position:
Using a leg press or standing calf machine, place the toes and balls of the feet on the platform, keeping feet about shoulder width apart. Make sure the resistance pad is placed firmly on the shoulders or handles held at shoulder height.

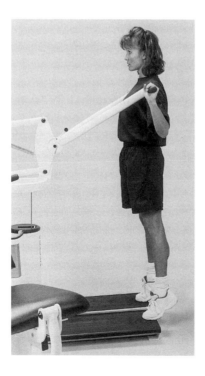

Motion:
Flex the ankle on the platform, or raise upwards on the balls of the feet, until full movement is reached, then lower and repeat.

Cable Adduction

Major muscle groups: Adductors of the hips, including adductor longus, brevis, magnus, gracilis

Lower Body
Legs

Starting position:
In a position slightly away from the machine, support foot flat, cable attached just above the ankle on inside leg, slightly away from midline of body.

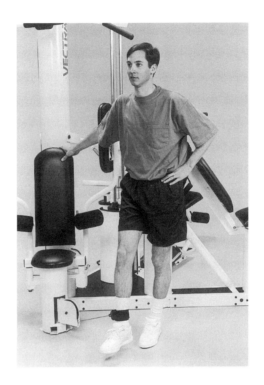

Motion:
While maintaining upper body support and posture, move the cabled leg, while straight, to the other side of the body in a lateral movement, crossing over the midline of the body. Lower, repeat, then repeat with other leg.

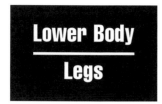

Lower Body
———
Legs

Cable Abduction

Major muscle groups: Abductors of the hips, including gluteus medius, gluteus minimus

Note:
If this machine is not available, using a slide board in conjunction with interval training may be substituted for a similar training effect.

Starting position:
In a position slightly away from the machine, support foot flat, cable attached just above the ankle on outside leg.

Motion:
While maintaining upper body support and posture, move the cabled leg, while straight or locked at knee, outward in lateral movement. Lower, repeat, then repeat with other leg.

References

Allerheiligen, B. 1994. Program design: Beginning weight training. *Strength and Conditioning* 16(2):26-29.

Allerheiligen, B., and R. Rogers. 1995. Plyometrics program design: Part 2. *Strength and Conditioning* 17(5):33-39.

Baker, G. 1996. Shoulder shrugs: Glute-ham raise. *Strength and Conditioning* 18(2):56-57.

Bompa, T.O. 1993. *Periodization of Strength: The New Wave in Strength Training*. Toronto: Veritas Publishing.

Clippinger, K. 1996. In a slump? Carry yourself a little taller. *Shape* 15(4):74.

Ellison, D. 1989. Exercise technique: Adductor exercises. *Australian Fitness and Training* 4(6):36-37.

Elrick, H. 1996. Exercise is medicine. *The Physician and Sportsmedicine* 24(2):72-76,78.

Ferguson, M. 1995. The seated row: Exercise technique. *Network* 7(6):12-13, 15.

Harris, N. 1992. Preventing golf injuries through exercise. *Sideline View* 13(10):1-4.

Hyatt, G. 1990. Exercise technique: Quadriceps quartet. *Australian Fitness and Training* 5(4):36-38.

King, I. 1990. Exercise technique: Bench press. *Sports Specific* 6:12-13.

Kraemer, W.J. 1983. Exercise prescription in weight training: A needs analysis. *National Strength and Conditioning Association Journal* 5:64-65.

Larkin, A.F., W.F. Larkin, W.F. Larkin II, and S.L. Larkin. 1990. Annual torso specific conditioning program for golfers. In A.J. Cochran, ed., Science and Golf: *Proceedings of the First World Scientific Congress of Golf*. London: E & FN Spon.

Pink, M.M., F.W. Jobe, L.A. Yocum, and R. Mottram. 1996. Preventative exercises in golf: Arm, leg, and back. *Clinics in Sports Medicine* 15(1):147-162.

Sprague, K. 1996. *More Muscle*. Champaign, IL: Human Kinetics.

Sutherland, M. 1995. The cable crossover: Exercise technique. *Network* 8(1):12-14.
———. 1995. The shoulder press: Exercise technique. *Network* 8(2):18-20.

Wilson, G.J. 1996. Weight training program design: Importance of muscular recovery and prevention of over-training. *Network* 8(6):30-32.

Wolkodoff, N. 1994. *Resistance Training Exercises For Better Golf*. Denver, CO: ExerTrends.

Flexibility Exercises

The Big Picture

One of your goals as a golf athlete is to maintain the kind of strength and muscular balance that promotes adequate flexibility. Without that strength balance from development and maintenance using resistance training, you will need more time for flexibility training.

Thus, the first place to address flexibility is in the weight room to make sure your resistance program maintains strength and muscular balance. This will decrease your need for formal flexibility training. In addition, the following exercises represent the most important areas for flexibility development or maintenance. With a balanced conditioning program, many golf athletes have found the use of the following stretches on a regular basis more than sufficient to build and maintain flexibility.

Physiological Prerogative

Every golf athlete is different in their need for flexibility training. This includes type, quantity and timing, or placement before and after exercise. You will have to do some experimentation to find out which combinations work best for your game and physical-training program.

Dynamic: Before the Swing, Upon Awakening

If you are going to stretch on the tee box or driving range, then dynamic exercise, which improves range of motion (ROM), is best. Use the combination of these dynamic exercises on the tee box and range to not only stretch the muscles but warm up key areas as well. The important feature to dynamic and active stretching is that it occurs gradually. Each repetition should increase or add ROM, with the beginning repetitions moving slower as well as having less ROM.

Static: After Exercise or Golf

The best time to do reach and hold exercises for golf is when they do the most good — when the muscle is warm. After golf and exercise are the best time for static stretches for this reason, and they have the best chance at reducing muscular soreness. The key to static stretches are to get to a point where you feel muscular tension, then hold the stretch for at least 10 seconds.

You Should Stretch More When...

Like any other fitness factor, your need for flexibility training, both in type and amount, changes with how much golf you play and how much other physical training you are performing at the time.

In general, when you add more golf or are starting at the early part of the season, you should add more flexibility training, especially after playing or practicing. This will help alleviate muscular soreness. If you play golf 2 or more consecutive days, your need for additional flexibility training increases, especially in the trunk region and hamstrings, which are utilized both in the golf stance and swing. Even though you may not feel the need for more flexibility training after 2 days of golf, it is a sound prevention strategy for alleviating muscular soreness during the 48 hours after golf. On consecutive golf days, you also should add more dynamic exercises as part of your warm-up.

Adding physical training in either frequency or intensity will generally increase your need for flexibility training. Stretching exercises should be placed at the end of each training session before you have cooled down to pre-exercise levels for optimum effectiveness.

Arm Circles to Wings

Muscle groups: Pectorals, deltoids, internal/external rotators

Dynamic Exercises

Starting position:
Athletic stance, feet shoulder width, slight bend to knees, slight bend to back.

Notes:
Activates the external rotators, which helps the golf athlete to be cognizant of these muscle groups during the warm-up and enables them to fully function during the first few swings.

Motion/stretching technique:
Start with small arm circles, 15-20, gradually gaining ROM both clockwise and counter-clockwise. Then use a light contraction of the pectorals, followed by a strong contraction of the rear deltoids in a swinging motion parallel to the ground or floor.

Dynamic Exercises

Active External Rotation

Muscle groups: Pectorals, internal rotators, anterior deltoids

Notes:

Tempo and muscular activation are key to getting the pectorals and anterior deltoids to relax through a strong contraction of the rear deltoids and external rotators. Also an excellent warm-up exercise on the first tee box or range. Like other dynamic stretches, always begin with less than full ROM for the first 5 to 10 repetitions, gradually building ROM and intensity.

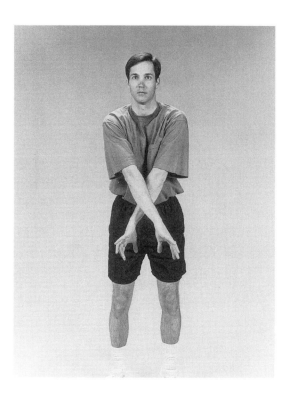

Starting position:

Athletic stance, feet shoulder width, slight bend to knees. With arms starting at the sides, cross arms over at elbows, arms straight, pectorals contracted.

Motion/stretching technique:

Move arms backward and up into military press position with full, active external rotation pulling the arms back as far as possible, repeat.

Torso Turret

Muscle groups: Rectus abdominis, erector spinae, external obliques, internal obliques

Dynamic Exercises

Starting position:
Athletic stance, feet shoulder width, slight bend to knees and back, arms in military press/ externally rotated position.

Notes:
Also a great dynamic stretch before practice or on the first tee box.

Motion/stretching technique:
Begin to twist along the axis of the spine both directions gradually increasing the ROM while keeping the arms, shoulders, head and neck locked as a unit. Use bend in knees and back to stabilize the hips, and isolate the torso in the movement.

Dynamic Exercises

Standing Single Leg Kicks

Muscle groups: Hamstring group, gluteus maximus, hip flexors

Notes:
Great active stretch while waiting with the cart. If you lack hip flexibility, begin with the target leg, then non-target leg, and a repeated sequence again with the target leg.

Starting position:
Standing, one hand braced on golf cart, door or weight bench, slight lean to non-working side. Begin to gradually kick forward and back while maintaining posture and back support.

Motion/stretching technique:
Increase ROM over 10-15 kicks. Change support arm and reverse position, and repeat with other leg. For advanced exercisers, with same leg, begin small circles after completing the forward and backward movements, gradually increasing ROM over 10 repetitions.

Standing Circular Swings

Muscle groups: Pectorals, anterior deltoid, external rotators

**Dynamic
Exercises**

Starting position:
Standing, athletic stance,
slight bend to both
knees and back.

Notes:
Excellent tee box
stretch with limited
space since it is
accomplished with
arms without a club.

**Motion/stretching
technique:**
While keeping shoulders
fairly stationary, swing
arms from side to side
with both arms going
in the same direction.
Gradually increase ROM
over 10 repetitions, then
add 5+ repetitions at full
range of motion.

Static or Reach and Hold Stretches

Standing Chest Stretch

Muscle groups: Pectorals, anterior deltoid

Notes:
Most appropriate after formal exercise or golf.

Starting position:
Face wall or weight machine, athletic stance. Place arm closest to support, palm against support, arm flat at side.

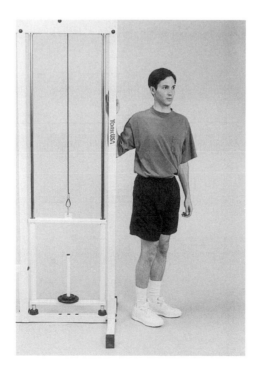

Motion/stretching technique:
Slightly turn diagonally away from support, with feet, torso and hips as a unit, until you feel the stretch in the area. Hold for at least 20 seconds.

Supine Hip/Back Rotation

Muscle groups: Erector spinae, hamstrings, obliques, gluteus maximus

**Static or
Reach and
Hold Stretches**

Starting position:
Lying on floor, arms
outstretched, legs flat.

Notes:
Golfers generally
have one side weaker/
tighter than the other,
so this side should
be stretched first, then
the other side, then
once more on the
weak/tight side. This
stretch is best after
exercise or golf.

**Motion/stretching
technique:**
Take the first leg, fully
extended and, while
keeping shoulders flat,
roll over to the opposite
side. Reach until the
point of muscular
tension, hold for 20+
seconds. Slowly go back
to the starting position
and repeat with the
other leg.

Static or Reach and Hold Stretches

Supine Hamstring

Muscle groups: Hamstrings

Notes:
Best use is after exercise or golf.

Starting position:
Lying on floor, arms outstretched at sides, knees at angle with feet flat on floor.

Motion/stretching technique:
Extend one leg, and with leg completely straight, pull with arms until tension is felt, hold for 20+ seconds. Lower leg and repeat with other leg.

Standing Hamstring

Muscle groups: Hamstrings

Static or Reach and Hold Stretches

Starting position:
Athletic stance with knees, back slightly bent.

Notes:
While static stretches are best after exercise, this one can be done on the first tee because it doesn't require much space, and after hitting balls the muscles should be warm enough for there to be benefit.

Motion/stretching technique:
With one leg bent 25 to 35 degrees, and supporting the body, extend the other leg straight with heel touching the ground until tension is felt. Hold for 20+ seconds and repeat with other leg.

Static or Reach and Hold Stretches

Seated Trunk Twist

Muscle groups: Rectus abdominis, erector spinae, external obliques, internal obliques

Notes:
Best done after golf or exercise.

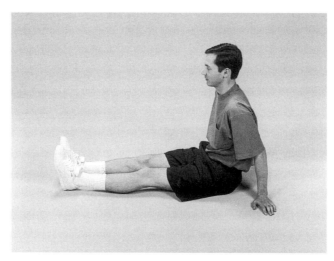

Starting position:
Seated on floor with both legs extended.

Motion/stretching technique:
Place one ankle on the outside of the opposite knee, reach around with the other hand and place elbow on the side of the raised knee. Use that elbow to help you twist around the axis of the spine. Hold for 30+ seconds, release and repeat with the other side.

Prone Active Extension

Muscle groups: Erector spinae, rectus abdominis

Static or Reach and Hold Stretches

Starting position:
Prone on floor, with hands slightly ahead of shoulders.

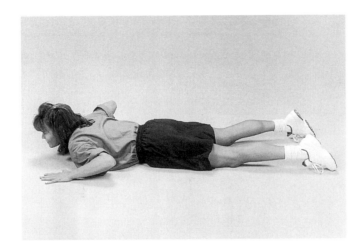

Notes:
This exercise uses the activation of the erector spinae to stretch the rectus abdominis.

Motion/stretching technique:
Arch up with upper body slightly, using hands for support, and repeat.

Static or Reach and Hold Stretches

Standing Calf Stretch

Muscle groups: Gastrocnemius, soleus

Notes:
Best after exercise, especially resistance training for the legs.

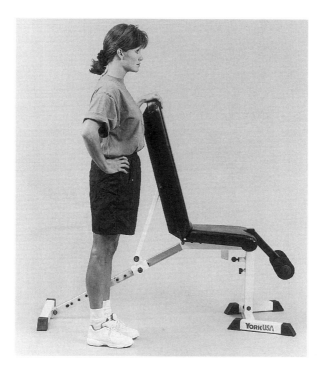

Starting position:
Using bench or chair for support, athletic stance with one foot ahead of the other.

Motion/stretching technique:
Move forward slightly, pressing knees and hips forward while maintaining foot contact until stretch is felt in both legs and hold. Repeat with the other side.

Bench Hip Flexor

Muscle Groups: Hip flexors, gastrocnemius, soleus

Starting position:
Athletic stance, 2
to 3 feet in front
of bench, which is
horizontal, approximately knee height.

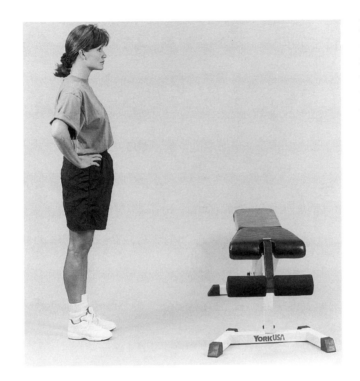

Notes:
Stretching the hip
flexor on the non-
target side is essential
to developing hip
turn at impact.

Motion:
While keeping the back
foot facing forward and
flat on the floor, place
the other foot firmly on
the bench, facing
directly forward. Keeping the back foot on the
floor, push forward with
upper body upright,
until the hip flexor of
the back leg is stretched.
Hold, repeat with target
leg, then repeat again
with non-target leg.

Static or Reach and Hold Stretches

Side Bend Stretch

Muscle groups: Obliques

Notes:
This stretch can be performed statically or with a rhythm as a dynamic stretch, yet because of the potential stress on the spine, speed should be limited.

Starting position:
Athletic stance, preferably against a wall

Motion/stretching technique:
Side flexion to one side without bending forward, hold for 2 to 3 seconds, then slowly go the other direction and repeat.

Active Wrist Flexion

Muscle groups: Forearms, flexor carpi ulnaris, palmaris longus, extensor carpi radialis brevis

Active Stretches

Starting position:
Seated or standing, athletic position, one hand in neutral position with other palm over hand.

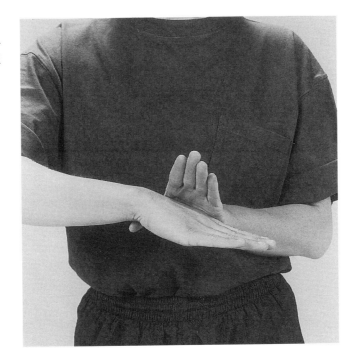

Notes:
Can be done after exercise, especially reverse wrist curls, or between 9's and on the practice tee after a few active exercises.

Motion/stretching technique:
Flex the wrist as far as possible, then use the other hand to assist the movement. Hold for 10+ seconds. Repeat with the other hand.

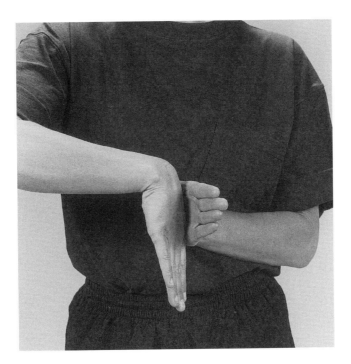

Active Stretches

Active Wrist Extension

Muscle groups: Forearms, flexor carpi ulnaris, palmaris longus, extensor carpi radialis brevis

Notes:
Can be done after exercise, especially wrist curls, or between 9's and on the practice tee after a few active exercises.

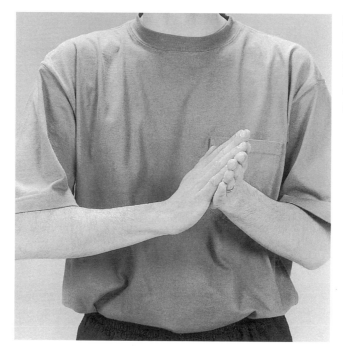

Starting position:
Seated or standing, athletic position, one hand with moderate extension, palm against palm.

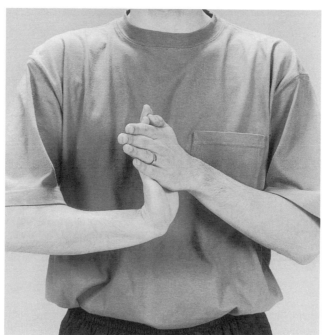

Motion/stretching technique:
Actively extend the wrist as far as possible, then use the other hand to assist the movement. Hold for 10+ seconds. Repeat with the other hand.

Upper Back/Shoulder

Muscle groups: Supraspinatus, rear deltoids, latissimus dorsi, infraspinatus, trapezius

Posture Specific Stretches

Starting position:
Face the stretching device with feet approximately 4 inches from the base with hands at shoulder height or above and slightly less than chest width grasping the cords firmly, thumbs upward.

Motion:
Unlocking knees, and with a pelvic tilt of trying to tuck the tail bone under the stomach, lean back into a semi-standing/sitting position, with one hip farther back than the other, until the stretch is felt. Hold and return to starting position; repeat to other side.

Frontal Chest/Shoulder

Muscle groups: Pectorals, anterior deltoid

Starting position:
Face away from the stretching device with left foot approximately 6 inches from the base, right hand on cord below shoulder height, left hand on cord at shoulder height or slightly above the shoulder for advanced exercisers.

Motion:
Unlocking knees, move forward until stretch is felt. Hold for 10+ seconds and repeat with other side.

Golf Turn Stretch

Muscle groups: Middle and posterior deltoids, infraspinatus, teres minor, teres major, latissimus dorsi

Starting position:
Stand at a 90-degree angle to the middle line of the platform, right foot 6 inches from the middle column of apparatus, with right hand on cord at chest level and left hand on cord at shoulder height at approximately 45-degree angle to plane of shoulders. Athletic/golf stance with feet 8 to 12 inches wider than hips.

Motion:
Unlock knees and waist, and lean whole body to left while maintaining firm grasp on cords until stretch is felt. Hold; repeat with other side.

Posture Specific Stretches

Combination Stretch

Muscles: Pectorals, anterior deltoid, hip flexors, gastrocnemius, soleus

Notes:
This stretch is very time efficient because of the combination effect on the chest, shoulders, hips and lower legs. If performing this movement correctly, you should not feel this stretch in your lower back.

Starting position:
Facing forward on the platform, place right foot directly in front of column, left foot approximately 12 to 14 inches ahead of the right foot. Grasp cords at slightly above waist height, with overhand grip.

Motion:
Step forward with front foot 12 to 14 inches, pressing forward with knees and hips, maintaining upright body position, with both feet flat on floor. Hold stretch; repeat with other leg.

Standing Hamstring

Muscles: Hamstring group, erector spinae

Posture Specific Stretches

Starting position: Right foot facing forward, just right of center of platform, middle or farther back, facing to the left side of the platform, placing left foot or ankle on cord at height between knee and hip depending upon current flexibility level, grasping a cord with right hand for support close to center column of apparatus.

Notes: To increase stretch if you have higher levels of hamstring flexibility, place leg one cord higher.

Motion: While maintaining a straight leg, lean forward at the hip/waist grasping a cord just above the left foot with the left hand until stretch is felt. Hold and repeat with other side.

References

Beaulieu, R.A. 1981. Developing a stretching program. *The Physician and Sportsmedicine* 9(11):59-69.

Burkett, L.N. 1971. Cause and prevention of hamstring pulls. *Athletic Journal* 51(6):34.

Chappuis, J.L. and G.D. Johnson. 1995. The "super six" stretches for golfers. *The Physician and Sportsmedicine* 23(4):87-88.

Harrison, D. 1996. Conditioning programs for hurdlers. *Modern Athlete and Coach* 34(2):37-39.

Hatfield, F.C. 1982. Learning to stretch for strength and safety. *Muscle Fitness* 43(12):24-25, 193-194.

Kravitz, L., and D. Kosich. 1993. Flexibility: a comprehensive research review and program design guide. *IDEA Today* 11(6):42-49.

Kosich, D. 1991. Exercise technique: Stretching the "Hot Spots." *IDEA Today* 9(3):37-39.

Massara, G., and F. Scoppa. 1995. Proprioceptive muscle stretching. *Journal of the International Council for Health, Physical Education, Recreation, Sport, and Dance* 31(2):38-43.

McFarlane, B. 1987. Warm-up Design Patterns. *National Strength and Conditioning Association Journal* 9(4):22-29.

Ninos, J. 1996. Stretching the quadriceps. *Strength and Conditioning* 18(1):68-69.

Ninos, J. 1995. Stretching the inner thigh. *Strength and Conditioning* 17(6):72-73.

Poux, D., and R. Laurens. 1993. Stretching et golf. Dans, Poux, D. (ed.), *Medecine et traumatologie du golf* Paris, Masson: 37-49.

Roozen, M.M., and T.A. Herbert. 1995. Enhancing flexibility: stretching past the norm. *Strength and Conditioning* 17(6):18-25.

Ross, M.D. 1995. Stretching the hamstrings. *Strength and Conditioning* 17(6): 35-36.

Roundtable. 1984. Flexibility, *National Strength and Conditioning Association Journal* 10:73.

Vermeil, A., and L. Dennis. 1985. Get stronger, get better. Four easy-to-do exercises that will increase your power and control on the course. *Golf Digest* 36(4):57-60.

Whelan, K. 1996. Stretching — shoulder and arm. *Triathlon Sports* 12(1):32,34.

Wolkodoff, N. 1995. *Flexibility Exercises For Better Golf.* Denver, CO: ExerTrends.

Training Programs

Because of the demands golf places on a schedule, it is essential to consider carefully which physical capabilities you want to address with your training time. Planning helps ensure that you will get maximum benefit from your training sessions.

Planning physical training for sports has become a science over the last 20 years. Originally, this field focused very specifically on the needs of a particular sport. Therefore, it was both difficult and inappropriate to use a football training model for a marathon runner. Some of the exercises and principles might have applied, yet the differences in application were much greater than were the similarities in any particular exercise.

Compared to other sports, there's been a lack of research on applying various sports training models to golf. However, by dissecting the physiological, psychological, and even coordination requirements of golf, a model can be developed to guide training. Remember, a sports training model is only a starting point, and the best conditioning coaches in every sport make individual variations to any model or system based on individual needs.

Although you can use principles and programs from this book, it will take some experimentation on your part to fine-tune training approaches to your golf game and needs. Not everyone responds the same way to a given training program. For example, you may find that resistance training through a full range of motion decreases your need for additional flexibility training. In addition, no two athletes will devote the same amount of time to physical training, which influences results.

Strength is uniquely utilized in golf because the golf swing uses primarily power and muscular endurance.

Physical Requirements for Golf

Golf is a unique sport in that it requires the use of a number of physical abilities over a period of 4 or more hours. In terms of energy system fitness, aerobic endurance isn't directly involved in each golf shot, yet it does contribute to reducing overall fatigue and maintaining energy, focus and concentration. Strength is uniquely utilized in golf because the golf swing uses primarily power and muscular endurance. Club-head speed is a function of power and speed generation, and repeating the swing during practice and a round is a function of muscular endurance. The key to resistance training for golf is to identify which muscle groups function in the swing with power and which function with muscular endurance. Strength is also important in certain muscle groups, such as the forearms, triceps and wrists, where positions tend to be held during the swing.

On the surface, flexibility is the most obvious fitness factor in golf. However, the type of flexibility needed varies. The faster and shorter your swing, the more you rely on dynamic and active flexibility. **The slower and longer your swing, the more dependent you are on static flexibility.** Every golf athlete is genetically different in his or her need for and response to flexibility training. Flexibility is the one fitness component that is dependent on other fitness factors, such as strength, for optimum development and maintenance.

Golf also has another unique feature: A golfer's skills need to be as good as his or her conditioning. Golf requires a good deal of practice time, so additional physical conditioning has to be time-efficient. Some sports, such as running or basketball, are fitness builders in themselves — just participating in them has a substantial fitness effect. But because golf relies on fitness yet doesn't build fitness, a golf athlete needs physical training aside from golf. The planning of a golf athlete's physical training is key to maximizing results and ensuring that there is enough time for golf practice and play.

Designing Fitness Programs: Balancing Variation and Consistency

Exercise scientists have coined a term to describe how to best train for sports: "periodization." The original principles for high-level training programs were developed from training for Olympic sports. Key to these principles is dividing training into phases to meet specific goals. By doing this, training is focused and there is an increased likelihood that higher levels of sport fitness will be developed. Each training phase becomes more specific to sport and individual needs.

Although you may have heard a good deal about "sport-specific training," too much specificity without first developing basic physical abilities doesn't produce optimal results. For example, always training the shoulder rotator cuff muscle groups with isolation exercises for muscular endurance will result in the muscle groups becoming "stale" and potentially losing strength over time. The best sport-training models use such specificity as the final training stage after basic fitness components such as strength and general aerobic conditioning have been established.

Therefore, the first phase of your training program should be focused on developing general fitness, then transisiton to higher levels of general fitness. The last training phase, which takes place before any sport's season begins, is where basic qualities of fitness are tailored to the specific requirements of the sport. However, for golf, remember that sport-specific doesn't necessarily mean training with weighted clubs or swing simulators. It simply means training the appropriate muscles to develop the quantities of strength, muscular endurance, power and flexibility that are needed for the sport.

Sport-specific doesn't necessarily mean training with weighted clubs or swing simulators. It means training the appropriate muscles to develop the quantities of strength, muscular endurance, power and flexibility that are needed for the sport.

One of the greatest observations of training science is that the best training program works well for only so long. Use a training stimulus (the amount of resistance, particular exercise, ordering of workout components) to stress the system, then give it time to adapt and grow, then change the variables. Without changing your program periodically your muscles become stale from lack of variation and overemphasis on one component. This observation has led to the recent boom in cross-training, engaging in different activities at different intensities. Variation in any fitness component generally produces better results than does always using the same regimen and intensity. This is equally true for resistance, energy system and flexibility training. In golf, the more fitness equipment and techniques you can incorporate into your conditioning program at different times, the better your long-term results will be.

Training *Phases* — Not Just Training

The science of periodization divides training into various phases. Each phase has a specific progression that is designed to bring the athlete to increasingly higher states of physical readiness. A golf athlete trains in each phase more specifically for his or her golf program by moving to exercises and training intensities that are closer to the actual demands of the sport. For example, you might perform a general stretching routine of three or more stretches in the off-season, with in-season work focusing on the internal rotators and hip flexors, which will then gain flexibility the more golf is played. Dividing a golf conditioning program into training phases not only improves training progress but also reduces the chances of over-training and the risk of injury from performing one exercise for too long.

A successful golf conditioning program should progress from general to specific, and from relatively easy to relatively difficult. For example, when you first begin aerobic exercise for golf, your sessions of treadmill exercise should be relatively easy, at 60% of your maximum heart rate (MHR). As you progress in your training and get closer to golf season, you might use walking sprints or intervals at 85% of your MHR, with less total time spent per exercise session. Essentially, you will be doing what Olympic athletes do — starting off with a high volume of low-intensity exercise and then progressing to less time spent on exercise that is performed at a higher intensity.

Should training for golf be the same every year? This isn't really a yes or no question but a matter of residual fitness. Most athletes who adopt year-round training find that the residual fitness value increases from year to year. Certain qualities, such as basic strength, flexibility and aerobic endurance are maintained with both a specific and a general program. The formal program in which you try to increase basic fitness can be shortened with each successive training year, assuming you stay active.

Training Phases in Golf

There are universal training phases that, even though you aren't training for the Olympics, can help your golf training. Each training phase has specific goals that are best attained in a specific order. Because strength is a prerequi-

> A successful golf conditioning program should progress from general to specific, and from relatively easy to relatively difficult.

> Most athletes who adopt year-round training find that the residual fitness value increases from year to year.

site for power, your pre-season golf program should initially focus on strength then move toward using heavier weights and fewer repetitions for power.

Although resistance training has been the focus of most modern training planning, aerobic conditioning and flexibility should follow the same planning approaches for maximum results. Those 2 areas can benefit just as much from dividing training into manageable phases with specific physiological objectives.

Three training phases apply to golf: off-season, pre-season, and in-season. Each training phase has a specific set of qualities to be developed for optimal conditioning for golf. The phase outlines that follow will give you the minimum or basic exercises for the key muscle groups you should focus on in your program. In addition, each suggests a set of exercises for advanced golf athletes or for those with extra time to spend on physical conditioning.

In the off-season, your goal is to improve your general physical condition, or basic fitness.

Off-season

This is the period that follows the end of a golf season and lasts until 8 to 15 weeks before the next season starts. It is the preparatory physical training period for the pre-season program. For most golfers the off-season covers January, February, and March. In this phase your goal is to improve your general physical condition, or basic fitness. Variety is important in improving general conditioning. Starting too soon to focus on specific muscle groups and exercises will only result in an inadequate basic fitness level, with the consequence that your later specific training will not be satisfactory.

Training Phase Goals

Off-season:

General physical conditioning, variety, balanced training, non-specific emphasis, use of cross training.

Pre-season:

Build each fitness component to its maximum needed for golf, transfer high-level fitness to specific qualities.

In-season:

Maintain key abilities, periodic rebuilding of basic fitness, peak for key tournaments.

Energy System Training Component

Training Focus: Non-golf-specific general aerobic training, development of general aerobic fitness.

Training Modes: Variety of treadmill walking, stair climbing, slide board and other training modes on a rotating, or cross-training, basis.

Training Duration and Intensity: 60 to 75% of MHR, 20 to 30 minutes per session, three to four times per week.

Resistance Training Component

Training Focus: General overall body strength and muscular endurance. Correction of any strength imbalances from previous season — for example, weak hamstrings or external rotators in the shoulders.

Training Modes: Use of multi-joint exercises for most muscle groups and single-joint exercises such as triceps extensions and side-lying flyes for specific weak areas, in addition to body-weight-resistance exercises such as pull-ups and push-ups.

Sets, Repetitions, Progressions: Major exercises starting with 3 sets of 15 to 20 repetitions, then progressing to 3 or more sets of 8 to 10 repetitions, then back to 3 or more sets of 15 repetitions.

Flexibility Training Component

Training Focus: Focus on strength balance and full range of motion, general stretching exercises.

Training Modes: Dynamic stretches and movement before exercise, key static stretches after exercise.

Novice Off-season or Beginning Program

Note: If you are new to exercise or haven't exercised regularly for 2 or 3 months, then use the following program for 2 to 4 weeks. This will allow you to become familiar with the exercises, techniques, your current abilities and your equipment while gradually increasing your fitness. After mastering the form of the exercises, you can then go on to the regular off-season training program. It is based on the same major muscle group exercises to develop strength and muscular endurance.

Warm-up

Frequency: Daily before each exercise session.

Exercises:
    Arm circles to wings
    Standing circular swings
    Active external rotation
    Torso turret
    Standing single-leg kicks

Resistance Training

Frequency: 2 to 3 days per week.

Upper-body exercises (followed by sets and repetitions):
    Dumbbell chest press: 2 x 15
    Bent row: 2 x 15
    Side-lying flye: 1 x 20
    Bicep curl: 2 x 15
    Triceps press-down: 2, 15

Basic trunk/torso and leg exercises
Note: Perform the sets to muscular failure (MF) unless otherwise noted. Muscular failure means that you must quit the exercise because you are fatigued to the point that the exercise is very difficult.
    Basic crunch: 2, MF
    Back extension: 2, MF
    Side bends with dumbbell: 1 x 20
    Leg exercises:
    Leg press: 3 x 15
    Leg extension: 2 x 15
    Leg curl: 3 x 15

Aerobic Training

Frequency: 2 to 3 times a week at an intensity of 60 to 75% MHR for 15 to 20 minutes.

Mode: Vary your aerobic training mode each time you work out. Choose from these modes: treadmill walking/running, stationary cycling, stair climbing or aerobic riding.

Flexibility Training

Frequency: Use the following exercises at each workout, using dynamic movement routine before exercise as a warm-up (see warm-up section for beginning program, above) and static stretching after exercise as a cool-down.

After-exercise static stretches:
    Supine hip/back rotation
    Supine hamstring
    Seated trunk twist

Regular Off-season Training Program

Warm-up

Practice daily before each exercise session
    Arm circles to wings
    Standing circular swings
    Active external rotation
    Torso turret
    Standing single-leg kicks

Resistance Training

Frequency: 2 to 3 days per week.

Basic upper-body exercises for schedules with limited time
(followed by sets and repetitions):

Dumbbell chest press: 3-4 x 12-15
Bent row: 3-4 x 12-15
Military press: 3 x 12-15
20-degree upright row: 3 x 12-15

Advanced upper-body exercises for schedules with extra time
(followed by sets and repetitions):

Lateral/medial deltoid raise: 2 x 20 once a week
Rear deltoid raise at 45-degrees: 2 x 20 once a week
Side-lying flye: 2 x 25 once a week

Basic trunk/torso exercises for schedules with limited time
Note: Perform sets to muscular failure (MF) unless otherwise noted.

Basic crunch: 2, MF
Back extension: 2, MF
Opposite back raises: 2 x 15 each leg-arm
Side bends with dumbbell: 2 x 25 *or*
Rotary abdominal machine: 2 x 25 *or*
Rotary crunches: 2 x 25

Advanced trunk/torso exercises for schedules with extra time
(followed by sets and repetitions):

Arm-leg crunch: 2 x 20 once a week
Rotary crunch: 2 x 20 once a week

Basic leg exercises for schedules with limited time
(followed by sets and repetitions):

Squat or leg press: 3-4 x 15
Leg extension: 3 x 12-15
Leg curl: 3 x 10-15
Standing calf raise: 2 x 15-20
Adduction/abduction: 1 x 15-20 once a week

Advanced leg exercises for schedules with extra time
(followed by sets and repetitions):

Leg extension, toes out: 1 x 15-20 once a week
Standing calf raise: 1 x 15-20 twice a week

Aerobic Training

Frequency: 3 sessions a week at an intensity of 65 to 75% MHR for 20 minutes.

Mode: Vary the mode each time you work out. Choose from treadmill walking/running, stationary cycling, stair climbing or aerobic riding.

> Because golf relies on fitness yet doesn't build fitness, a golf athlete needs physical training aside from golf.

Flexibility Training

Frequency: Use these exercises daily at each exercise session, using dynamic movement routine before exercise as a warm-up (see warm-up section for regular program, page 176) and static stretching after exercise as a cool-down.

After-exercise static stretches:
Supine hip/back rotation
Supine hamstring
Seated trunk twist

Pre-season

The pre-season is the period beginning 8 weeks before your golf season starts. For golfers starting seriously in June, the pre-season would be April and May. The overall goal in this training phase is to build each fitness quality to its maximum, then to begin the transfer of general fitness to specific fitness components. Performing the golf-specific exercises and routines at the end of this training phase is the goal.

Energy System Training Component

Training Focus: Continue general aerobic training, move to more golf-specific exercises with increasing intensity.

Training Modes: Decrease variety of exercise modes, moving toward the dominant or prime exercise mode, such as treadmill walking with incline.

Training Duration and Intensity: 70 to 80% MHR, 30 minutes per session, 1 to 2 times per week; 75 to 90% MHR, 20 to 30 minutes per session with interval programs, 1 to 2 times per week.

Note: Using the higher intensity range requires higher fitness levels and medical clearance.

Resistance Training Component

Training Focus: Develop maximal strength, then transfer that strength into power and muscular endurance in specific muscle groups.

Training Modes: Use of multi-joint exercises initially, with selected single-joint and single-muscle groups to be increasingly emphasized. The end of this training phase will look similar to the exercises and regimes for in-season maintenance.

Sets, Repetitions, Progressions: Exercises should start with multiple sets of 12 repetitions and progress to more intense sets of 6 to 8 repetitions for maximal strength. After 1 to 2 weeks of maximal strength work with 6 to 8 repetitions, muscular-endurance muscle groups, such as the rotator cuff group, should be trained primarily with 15 to 20 repetitions. Meanwhile, power muscle groups, such as the pectoralis major, should be trained with sets of less than 6 to 8 repetitions.

> The pre-season is the period beginning 8 weeks before your golf season starts. The overall goal in this training phase is to build each fitness quality to its maximum, then to begin the transfer of general fitness to specific fitness components.

Flexibility Training Component

Training Focus: To develop golf-specific flexibility and to counter the effects of increased and more intense physical training. In this phase, the golf athlete should begin to match specific flexibility exercises for the rotator cuff, hamstrings and low back to desired training effects. Because each golfer will respond differently to full-ROM exercise, there are different needs in maintaining flexibility.

Training Modes: Dynamic movement before exercise, dynamic routine early in the morning, dynamic-static mix of stretching after exercise, development of dynamic routine as part of a golf warm-up, posture-specific exercises.

> Because each golfer will respond differently to full-ROM exercise, there are different needs in maintaining flexibility.

Pre-season Training Program

Warm-up
Daily before any physical activity:
Arm circles to wings
Active external rotation
Torso turret
Standing single-leg kicks
Standing circular swings

Resistance Training
Frequency: 2 to 4 days per week.

Basic upper-body exercises for schedules with limited time
(followed by sets and repetitions):
Dumbbell chest press: 3 x 6-15 once a week
Dumbbell decline butterfly: 3 x 12-15 once a week
Dumbbell incline press: 3 x 6-15 once a week
Dumbbell decline press: 3 x 6-16 once a week
Bent row: 3-4 x 6-15 twice a week *or*
    Low row with pulley: 3 x 6-15 twice a week *or*
    Bent row/external rotation: 3-4 x 8-15 twice a week
Lat pull-down, variety: 3-4 x 6-15 twice a week
Military press: 3 x 6-15 twice a week
20-degree upright row: 3-4 x 6-15 twice a week
Side-lying flye: 2 x 25 once a week
Lying L flye: 2 x 25 once a week
Bicep curl: 3-4 x 8-15 twice a week
Triceps press-down: 3-4 x 8-15 twice a week
Wrist curls: 3 x 12-20 twice a week
Reverse wrist curls: 3 x 12-20 twice a week

Advanced upper-body exercises for schedules with extra time
(followed by sets and repetitions):
     Lateral/medial deltoid raise: 2 x 20 once a week
     Rear deltoid raise: 2 x 20 once a week
     Bent row/external rotation: 2 x 6-15 twice a week
     Trapezius row, 30-degree: 2 x 8-15 twice a week
     Thor's Hammer: 1 x 20 once a week
     Ulnar flexion: 1 x 20 once a week

Basic trunk/torso exercises for schedules with limited time
Note: Perform sets to muscular failure (MF) unless otherwise noted.
     Basic crunch: 2, MF twice a week
     Back extension: 2, MF twice a week
     Arm/leg crunch: 2, MF once a week
     Opposite back raises: 3 x 15 each leg/arm, once a week
     Side bends with dumbbell: 2 x 15 once a week

Advanced trunk/torso exercises for schedules with extra time
(including sets and repetitions):
     Side medicine ball throws: 2 x 15 once to twice a week
     Swing-plane medicine ball throws: 2 x 15 once to twice a week

Basic leg exercises for schedules with limited time
(followed by sets and repetitions):
     Squat or leg press: 3 x 6-15 twice a week
     Leg extension: 3 x 6-15 twice a week
     Leg curl: 4+ x 6-15, three times a week
     Adduction/abduction: 3+ x 8-15 three times a week
     Standing calf raise: 2+ x 12-20 twice a week

Advanced leg exercises for schedules with extra time
(followed by sets and repetitions):
     Leg extension, toes out: 2+ x 15-20 once a week

Aerobic Training

Frequency: 3 times a week at an intensity of 65 to 85% MHR for 20 to 40 minutes.

Mode: Vary the mode at each workout.

Note: Every aerobic segment should be followed by 3 to 5 minutes of substantially lower intensity activity to serve as a cool-down, lowering heart rate to 55 to 60% MHR.

Weeks 1 through 4:

Twice a week:
     Treadmill walk at grade, 20+ minutes, 65 to 80% MHR

Once a week:
     Slide board, stair machine, bicycle, or rider; 20+ minutes, 65 to 75% MHR

Weeks 4 through 8:

Once a week:

Treadmill intervals, 35+ minutes; alternate 1 minute of low-level walking at 60 to 70% MHR with 2 minutes of faster speeds with significant elevation to reach 75 to 85% MHR (for example, recovery periods of 2.5 mph at 1% grade with intervals of 3.4 mph at 8% grade).

Once a week:

Treadmill aerobic workout, 30 minutes; after warm-up, increase grade and speed and maintain 75% MHR for 30 minutes, followed by cool-down.

Once a week:

Aerobic workout on slide board, stair machine, bicycle or rider, 20 to 40 minutes; after warm-up, increase resistance or speed to maintain 70% MHR for duration, followed by cool-down.

Flexibility Training

Frequency: Daily, using dynamic movement routine before exercise as a warm-up (see warm-up section for pre-season training program, p. 179) and static stretching after exercise as a cool-down.

After-exercise static stretches
Supine hip/back rotation
Bench hip flexor
Supine hamstring or standing hamstring
Seated trunk twist
Prone active extension
Active wrist extension
Active wrist flexion
Posture-specific stretches

In-season

This is the period of the golf season. For most golfers it runs from June through September or October. The major training goal at this time is to maintain the fitness level developed in the pre-season with a minimum of time spent away from the course. However, because the golf season is so long, it is virtually impossible to maintain "peak" conditioning.

Every 3 to 4 weeks, golf athletes should spend more time rebuilding basic fitness, then re-tailor it to golf. This is easily accomplished by adding 1 extra resistance training session a week and increasing the repetitions to 15 to 20 per exercise to reestablish muscular endurance. Aerobic fitness is rebuilt by adding 1 extra session as well, or by increasing the intensity of the existing training schedule.

Because most recreational golfers play golf on the weekend, it is important to distribute training time throughout the week to enhance rather than detract from golf. For example, Monday should be the heavy resistance training day, stressing strength and power. Wednesday or Thursday should stress muscular endurance. In this way, golf on the weekend will be enhanced rather than compromised, because using heavy weights just before competi-

> Because the golf season is so long, it is virtually impossible to maintain "peak" conditioning... it is important to distribute training time throughout the week to enhance rather than detract from golf.

Walk the course less than three times a week, and three aerobic sessions will be necessary.

tion may throw off your game, whereas muscular endurance training a few days before will have almost no negative effects.

Energy System Training Component

Training Focus: Maintaining aerobic fitness in conjunction with walking the course.

Training Modes: Use of treadmill walking/running at inclines to simulate the course as the dominant mode.

Training Duration and Intensity: 70 to 80% MHR, 30 minutes per session, 1 to 2 times per week; 75 to 90% MHR, 20 to 30 minutes per session with interval programs, 1 to 2 times per week.

Note: The actual number of extra sessions per week depends on how many golf holes are walked during the week. If you walk the course more than 3 times a week, then 2 aerobic sessions probably will be adequate. But walk the course less than 3 times a week, and 3 aerobic sessions will be necessary.

Resistance Training Component

Training Focus: Maintain balance between muscular endurance and power, with some strength.

Training Modes: Perform as many multi-joint exercises as possible to save time, with single-joint-isolation exercises for key muscle groups such as the forearms, rotator cuff and hamstring groups. Place more emphasis on back and abdominal strength to compensate for the stresses of golf.

Sets, Repetitions, Progressions: Power muscle groups like the pectoralis major should use sets of less than 6 to 8 repetitions, strength groups like the hamstrings should use 10 to 12 repetitions, and muscular endurance groups like the rotator cuff should use 12 to 20 repetitions.

Flexibility Training Component

Training Focus: Maintain specific flexibility developed to this point, and counter the effects of increased golf play. For example, the hip flexors and extensors tend to get progressively tighter during the season because of the lateral movement required by golf.

Training Modes: Dynamic movement before exercise; dynamic routine early in the morning; mix of dynamic and static stretching after exercise, especially golf; use of dynamic routine as part of a golf warm-up, posture-specific stretching after exercise.

In-season Training Program

Warm-up

Frequency: Daily before any physical activity.

Exercises:
    Arm circles to wings
    Active external rotation
    Torso turret
    Standing single-leg kicks
    Standing circular swings

Resistance Training

Frequency: 2 to 3 days per week.

Day 1: Strength and Power

Basic upper-body exercises for schedules with limited time
(followed by sets and repetitions):
    Dumbbell chest press: 2 x 6-10
    Dumbbell decline press: 1 x 6-10
    Bent row: 1 x 12
    Bent row, external rotation: 2 x 8-10
    Lat pull-down, behind neck: 2 x 6-10
    Military press: 1 x 10
    20-degree upright row: 3 x 10
    Wrist curls: 2 x 15
    Reverse wrist curls: 2 x 15

Advanced upper-body exercises for schedules with extra time
(followed by sets and repetitions):
    Trapezius row, 30-degree: 2 x 8-10
    Thor's Hammer: 1 x 20
    Ulnar flexion: 1 x 20

Basic trunk/torso exercises for schedules with limited time
Note: Perform sets to muscular failure (MF) unless otherwise noted.
    Basic crunch: 2, MF
    Back extension: 2, MF
    Side bends with dumbbell: 2 x 15

Advanced trunk/torso exercises for schedules with extra time
(including sets and repetitions):
    Side medicine ball throws: 1 x 15
    Swing-plane medicine ball throws: 1 x 15

Basic leg exercises for schedules with limited time
(including sets and repetitions):
    Squat or leg press: 3 x 6-10
    Leg extension: 2 x 10-15
    Leg curl: 4 x 6-10
    Standing calf raise: 2 x 15-20

Advanced leg exercises for schedules with extra time
(including sets and repetitions):
    Adduction/abduction: 2+ x 15-20

Day 2: Strength and Muscular Endurance

Basic upper-body exercises for schedules with limited time
(including sets and repetitions):
    Dumbbell chest press: 1 x 20
    Incline chest press: 2 x 15
    Bent row, external rotation: 2 x 15
    Lat pull-down: 2 x 20
    Side-lying flye: 2 x 25
    Side-lying L flye: 2 x 20
    Bicep curl: 2 x 15
    Triceps press-down: 2 x 12-15
    Wrist curls: 1 x 20
    Reverse wrist curls: 1 x 20

Advanced upper-body exercises for schedules with extra time
(including sets and repetitions):
    Lateral/medial deltoid raise: 1 x 20
    Rear deltoid raise: 1 x 20
    Bent row, external rotation: 2 x 15
    Bicep curl, preacher version: 2 x 15
    Trapezius row on bench, 30-degree: 1 x 15
    Thor's Hammer: 2 x 15
    Ulnar flexion: 2 x 15

Basic trunk/torso exercises for schedules with limited time
Note: Perform the sets to muscular failure (MF) unless otherwise noted.
    Basic crunch: 1, MF
    Arm/leg crunch: 2, MF
    Opposite back raises: 2 x 15 each leg/arm
    Side bends with dumbbell: 1 x 15

Advanced trunk/torso exercises for schedules with extra time
(including sets and repetitions):
    Side medicine ball throws: 1 x 15
    Swing-plane medicine ball throws: 1 x 15

Basic leg exercises for schedules with limited time
(including sets and repetitions):
    Squat or leg press: 1 x 20
    Leg curl: 2 x 20
    Adduction/abduction: 2 x 15
    Standing calf raise: 1 x 25

Advanced leg exercises for schedules with extra time
(including sets and repetitions):
    Leg extension: 2+ x 15-20

Aerobic Training

Frequency: 2 to 3 times a week at an intensity of 65 to 85% MHR for 20 to 40 minutes.

Once a week:

Treadmill intervals, 35+ minutes; alternate 1 minute of low-level walking at 60 to 70% MHR with 2 minutes of faster speeds and significant elevation where heart rate reaches 75 to 85% MHR. Use different speed and grade combinations to raise heart rate to the desired level.

Once a week:

Treadmill aerobic workout, 20 minutes; after warm-up, increase grade and speed and maintain 75% MHR for 20 minutes followed by cool-down.

Once a week:

Note: The 3rd aerobic training session is determined by how much you walk the course. If you walk the course 3 or more times per week, then 2 training sessions are adequate. If you walk the course 2 times or less, then add the 3rd aerobic workout.

Aerobic workout on slide board, stair machine, bicycle or rider, 20 minutes; after warm-up, increase resistance or speed to maintain 70% MHR for duration, followed by cool-down.

Flexibility Training

Frequency: Daily, using dynamic movement routine before exercise as a warm-up (see warm-up section for in-season training program, above) and static stretching after exercise as a cool-down.

After-exercise static stretches:
    Bench hip flexor
    Supine hip/back rotation
    Supine hamstring or standing hamstring
    Standing chest stretch
    Prone active extension
    Seated trunk twist
    Active wrist flexion
    Active wrist extension
    Posture-specific stretches

Training Programs KEY POINTS

- Successful physical training for golf requires planning, which will help the golf athlete train more effectively.

- Golf training requires the year be divided into off-season, pre-season and in-season training phases.

- Goals of the off-season phase are to maintain fitness and correct any strength or flexibility imbalances.

- Goals of the pre-season phase are to develop maximal strength, aerobic fitness, and flexibility and then tailor these qualities to golf performance.

- The in-season program is necessary to maintain conditioning and performance through the golf season because golf by itself is not enough to maintain conditioning levels.

References

Allerheilegen, B., and R. Rogers. 1995. Plyometrics program design. *Strength and Conditioning* 17(4):26-31.

Bloomfield, J. 1979. Modifying human physical capacities and technique to improve performance. *Sports Coach* 3:19-25.

Benson, H. 1980. *The Relaxation Response*. New York: Avon Books.

Bompa, T.O. 1983. *Theory and Methodology of Training*. Dubuque, IA: Kendall/Hunt.

———. 1993. *Periodization of Strength: The New Wave in Resistance Training*. Toronto: Veritas Publishing.

Dintiman, G., and R. Ward. 1988. *Sportspeed*. Champaign, IL: Human Kinetics.

Doulillard, J. 1994. *Body, Mind and Sport*. New York: Crown.

Egoscue, P. 1992. *The Egoscue Method of Health Through Motion*. New York: HarperCollins Publishers.

Elam, R. 1994. Avoiding back injuries from the squat or leg press: Part 2. *Performance Conditioning for Volleyball* 1(7):1-2.

Fleck, S., and W. Kraemer. 1997. *Designing Resistance Training Programs*. 2d ed. Champaign, IL: Human Kinetics.

Fleck, S., and W. Kraemer. 1996. *Periodization Breakthrough!* Ronkonkoma, NY: Advanced Research Press, Inc.

Gilliam. G.M. 1981. Effects of frequency of weight training on muscle strength enhancement. *Journal of Sports Medicine* 21:432-436.

Hahn, A.G. 1992. Physiology of training. In J. Bloomfield, P.A. Fricker, and K.D. Fitch, eds., *Textbook of Science and Medicine in Sport*. Victoria, Australia: Blackwell Scientific Publications.

Hakkinen, K. 1985. Factors influencing trainability of muscular strength during short term and prolonged training. *National Strength and Conditioning Association Journal* 7:32-37.

Horrigan, J., and J. Robinson. 1991. *The 7-Minute Rotator Cuff Solution.* Los Angeles: Health For Life.

Israel, S. 1972. *The acute syndrome of detraining.* Berlin: GDR National Olympic Committee. 2:30-35.

Koutedakis, Y. 1995. Seasonal variation in fitness parameters in competitive athletes. *Sports Medicine* 19(6):373-392.

Kraemer, W.J. 1983. Exercise prescription in weight training: A needs analysis. *National Strength and Conditioning Association Journal* 5:64-65.

Kurtz, T. 1991. *Science of Sports Training.* Island Pond, VT: Stadion Press.

Larkin, A.F., W.F. Larkin, W.F. Larkin II, and S.L. Larkin. 1990. Annual torso-specific conditioning program for golfers. In A.J. Cochran, ed., Science and Golf: *Proceedings of the First World Scientific Congress of Golf.* London: E. & F.N Spon.

McLaughlin, T. 1995. Resistance training programme. *Thrower* 67:19-22.

O'Bryant, H., and M. Stone. 1987. *Weight Training: A Scientific Approach.* Edina, MN: Burgess Press.

Pauletto, B. 1986. Intensity. *NSCA Journal* 8(1):33-37.

————. 1987. Resistance training versus weight lifting. *National Strength and Conditioning Association Journal* 9(4):65-67.

Poliquin, C., and P. Patterson. 1989. Classification of strength qualities. *National Strength and Conditioning Association Journal* 11(6):48-50.

Porcari, J., and J. Curtis. 1996. Strength and aerobics at the same time? *Fitness Management* 12(7):26-29.

Schweigert, D. 1996. NDSU women's track and field strength program: Power events. *Strength and Conditioning* 18(1):52-60.

Sleamaker, R. 1989. *Serious Training for Serious Athletes.* Champaign, IL: Human Kinetics.

Selye, H. 1956. *The Stress of Life.* New York: McGraw-Hill.

Spassov, A. 1988. Constructing training programs: Part II. *National Strength and Conditioning Association Journal* 10(5):65-70.

Starting a resistance training program. 1996. *Olympic Coach* 6(1):14-15.

Steinberg, J. 1996. Women and weightlifting. *First Aider* 66(2):9.

Stone, M.H. 1993. Literature review: Explosive exercises and training. *National Strength and Conditioning Association Journal* 15(3):7-15.

Stone, M.H. et al. 1982. A theoretical model of resistance training. *National Strength and Conditioning Association Journal* 3(5):36-39.

Syster, B., and G. Stull. 1970. Muscular endurance retention as a function of length of detraining. *Research Quarterly Exercise and Sport* 41:105.

Vermeil, A., and L. Dennis. 1985. Get stronger, get better. Four easy-to-do exercises that will increase your power and control on the course. *Golf Digest* 36(4):57-60.

Wathen, D. 1987. Flexibility: Its place in warm-up activities. *NSCA Journal* 9(5):26-27.

Westcott, W. 1991. *Strength Fitness*. Boston: Allyn & Bacon.

Wilson, G.J. 1996. Weight training program design: Importance of muscular recovery and prevention of over-training. *Network* 8(6)30-32.

Wolkodoff, N. 1987. Resistance training for endurance athletes. *American Ski Coach* 10(5):31.

————. 1990. In-season plyometrics: Maintaining and developing functional strength. *American Ski Coach* 13(5):10-11.

Young, W. 1993. Training for speed/strength: Heavy vs. light loads. *National Strength and Conditioning Association Journal* 15(5):46-57.

Zatsiorsky, V.M. 1992. Intensity of resistance training facts and theory: Russian and European approach. *National Strength and Conditioning Association Journal* 14(5):34.

Fuel for Golf

Although it's not like running a marathon, playing golf requires a sound nutritional foundation for training and performance. You are what you eat, and your game will reflect the long-term effects of what you eat every day as well as what you eat on the course.

Your food intake determines how effectively you train, the benefits you derive from training, and your ability to play consistently for 18 holes. Optimal nutrition for golf will also have a positive effect on your health by potentially increasing your resistance to heart disease and stress.

Golf is a sport of short bursts of high-intensity activity (the actual golf swing) interspersed with low-level exercise (walking). Your body needs certain types of fuel to maintain high energy levels during practice and play. It's tempting to believe that nutrition doesn't matter in golf, and in one area it doesn't — for the duration of a single golf swing. In fact, to fuel one golf swing you could probably consume a diet of pretzels and beer and still be

With the recognition that golf is a sport, the principles of modern sports nutrition mean the old food choices aren't optimal for performance.

successful. However, if you want to boost your overall performance both physically and mentally, or even just the coordination and timing of your swing, nutrition is a big deal. Add the psychological stress of golf to the potentially extreme weather conditions in which it is played, and nutrition becomes even more important for your best performance.

Terms and Definitions

To understand how nutrition ties into golf performance, it's essential to understand the basic terms of nutrition. They will give you a framework on which to apply the principles of sports nutrition in order to improve your physical training and golf game.

Essential Nutrients: Elements the body must have to survive, which include fats, proteins, water, vitamins and minerals.

Non-Essential Nutrients: Those food or food-related compounds the body can manufacture and does not need to ingest in order to survive.

Carbohydrates: Sources of fuel containing no fat and made up of molecular chains of carbon and hydrogen.

Complex Carbohydrates: Sources of high-starch food energy that are digested slowly and steadily: for example, potatoes and grain products.

Simple Carbohydrates: Sources of high-sugar food energy that are absorbed quickly into the digestive system, e.g., fruit juice or honey.

Glycemic Index: The speed at which carbohydrates are converted to blood sugar influenced by fiber and sugar factors.

Fats: A concentrated energy source, which burns slowly and is slowly digested, including such foods as butter, cheese, nuts and olive oil. Some fats, primarily animal fats, increase cholesterol levels, where some plant fats, such as olive oil, either have no effect on cholesterol or decrease cholesterol levels.

Proteins: Nutrients essential to health that form bones and muscles and that are a relatively poor source of energy.

Vitamins and Minerals: Compounds (enzymes and catalysts) that, in conjunction with food energy, help to build, repair and maintain the body.

Water: A liquid composed of two parts hydrogen, one part oxygen. It is essential to life.

Kilocalorie: The basic unit used to measure the energy-producing value of food, commonly expressed as kcal, Calorie or C.

Metabolism: Physiological activity fueled by food energy; the rate at which calories are burned by a person during exercise (exercise metabolism) and rest (resting metabolism), generally expressed in kcal per hour or minute.

BMR: Basal metabolic rate, or the number of calories a person uses during an hour or day at complete rest.

RMR: Resting metabolic rate, or the number of calories used during everyday tasks such as reading and typing.

EMR: Exercise metabolic rate, or the number of calories used during moderate to strenuous exercise.

RDA: U.S. Recommended Daily Allowances, minimal intake levels of essential and nonessential nutrients necessary for the nutritional needs of most healthy people.

Understanding Nutrition

Your body uses food like a car uses gas. Especially important for the car is the octane rating, or quality of the fuel. However, the nutritional picture of the human body as it relates to training and golf performance is more complicated than simply fuel. Human nutrition involves energy, growth, regulation and repair. Your body undergoes a constant process of rebuilding cells in bones, ligaments, muscle and skin. Although most golf athletes think of sports nutrition in terms of fuel, it is useful to evaluate other nutritional processes and how they relate to sports and golf training. It is important to recognize which nutrients play the greatest roles in physical training and golf performance. You may also find this information useful in improving your general health.

Fuels for human energy come from two primary sources: fats and carbohydrates. Protein is a poor short-term fuel source. Essential nutrients are needed both for energy and for system rebuilding during rest or exercise. Proteins, fats and water are considered "macro" nutrients essential for human survival and growth. Micro nutrients include vitamins and minerals, which are essential for growth and enhance the function and usability of macro nutrients.

Calories are the units by which the energy potential of food is measured. It is important for you as a golf athlete to know what nutrients are in the calories you consume. Scientifically, the calorie unit used as a measure of energy potential in food is equivalent to the amount of energy needed to raise the temperature of one gram of water 1 degree Celsius. However, this measurement is too small to be of any use in planning nutritional intake or exercise programs. A better measurement is the kilocalorie, or kcal, which is the amount of energy needed to raise the temperature of one kilogram of water 1 degree Celsius. Whenever you see "Calories" spelled with a capital C, the word is actually representative of kilocalories.

Understanding the caloric needs of various activities, how tissues are rebuilt each day, and the values of macro-nutrients, such as proteins, fats and carbohydrates, will help you eat right for golf performance. If you monitor the actual kcals you need accurately, you won't gain weight or feel as tired, and your physical training and golf performance will be at its peak.

Fuels for human energy come from two primary sources: fats and carbohydrates.

While all the major nutrients can be used as fuel, the human system prefers carbohydrates and fats for energy.

Functions and Fuel Energy

Nutrients	Uses	Energy/Kcal per gram
Carbohydrates	Fuel-rapid, nutrients	4
Fats	Fuel-slow, nutrients, vitamin transfer, insulation	9
Proteins	Tissue growth maintenance	4

Foods that appeal to you may contain more or less kcals than you think. It's difficult to tell the energy value of a food just by looking at it on the plate. Which foods provide the most food energy? Carbohydrates and proteins provide 4 kcals of energy per gram, alcohol provides 7 kcals per gram, and fat provides a whopping 9 kcals per gram. This is why 2 teaspoons of butter (a pure fat) on a medium-sized baked potato (a complex carbohydrate) have more calories than the entire potato. The octane rating of the food energy is not always relative to the physical size of the food; it is more a matter of fuel type.

Metabolism, Exercise and Diet

Every golfer has heard, "So-and-so has a slow metabolism and can't lose weight." Metabolism refers both to the physiological processing of various macro-nutrients and to the direct and indirect physiological effects of food and exercise. In order to stay at your best weight for golf, your food intake should match the needs of your metabolism and activity levels. Exceed your nutritional needs in calories and you gain weight; dip below those needs and you lose weight.

Basal metabolic rate, or BMR, can vary greatly from one individual to another and is a function of activity level, genetics, muscle mass, fitness level and training type and frequency, just to name a few factors. Exercise or activity-based metabolism, or EMR, also can vary greatly from one person to another based on fitness level, familiarity with the exercise activity, intensity of the exercise activity, and even environmental factors, such as heat, cold and extreme altitude. This is why two golfers of the same apparent age, size and activity levels can have different energy needs and experience different effects from the same activity.

Most human energy needs are determined by movement and constant physiological activity. During exercise or a game of golf, the number of calories expended is determined by the exercise level or actual work output. But there is also a post-exercise effect, in which more calories are expended when the body is at rest, and this is a key feature in successful weight loss. The higher the intensity or difficulty of the exercise and the longer the exercise session, then the higher the post-exercise metabolism. Exercise contributes to weight loss not only by the direct expenditure of calories during the exercise but also in the indirect expenditure of calories after the exercise is finished.

Basic Fuels and Building Blocks: Carbohydrates, Fats and Proteins

Carbohydrates: Rocket Fuel

Carbohydrates are foods whose molecules form into simple or complex chains of sugars. Simple sugars include single and double sugar molecules known as monosaccharides and disaccharides. The key thing to remember about simple sugars is that whatever their form (fruit juice, milk sugar, corn syrup, honey, fructose or simple table sugar), they are readily accessible for the energy needs of the body. Need a boost on the 17th hole? Then a sport beverage with simple sugars as the main ingredient may be the ticket. However, if simple sugars are not used for energy needs within a short period of time, they will be converted to storage compounds, including muscle glycogen (stored sugar), liver glycogen or fat. Your body does rely on a fairly constant supply of blood glucose (a form of sugar in the blood) to fuel the brain and to some degree the muscles, depending on activity. Most people have found that restricting simple sugars in the diet heightens athletic performance and reduces excess weight.

Complex carbohydrates, such as the starches found in plant foods like rice, whole grains and potatoes, have become a hot topic over the last ten years. They have been touted as the preferred fuel for athletic performance. These long chains of sugar molecules provide a longer fuel "burn" during activity and have more vitamins and minerals than simple sugars.

Nutrient Density: The Key to Choosing Carbohydrates

Nutrient density is a term that describes how many calories a food contains along with the number of other nutrients it has, such as essential vitamins and minerals. In general, the simpler the sugar, the less nutrient-dense it is. For example, although honey is considered by many to be a "natural food," its effect on the body is almost the same as that of processed table sugar, and it has almost the same nutrient density. A soft drink slugged down on the golf course, for instance, does not provide the nutrients of a fortified sports drink, which isn't as nutrient-dense as a potato. However, since a baked potato is not a convenient snack on the 10th tee box — there is a practical side to sports nutrition!

Carbohydrates can help you recover from training or other physical activity. In fact, some carbohydrates taken immediately after a hard training bout will be readily absorbed by the muscles and used to replenish energy. Though golf is rarely taxing enough to provoke the need for this kind of replenishment, the rigors of training are a different story. After a difficult resistance training workout or long aerobic session, a sport drink or fruit juice with some water will help replenish energy reserves if it is taken within 30 minutes.

Carbohydrates should also be chosen for their glycemic index, or how fast they are converted to blood sugar. Because golf is a game of endurance, carbohydrates and food combinations that lower the glycemic response of insulin production, which helps regulate blood sugar, will result in better maintenance of blood sugar and energy levels. Factors that influence this index are the amount of fiber and sugar/carbohydrate profile of the food. For example, bread, even though a complex carbohydrate, has a high glycemic index. Vegetables, some fruits and legumes (dried peas and beans), because of their fiber content, have a low glycemic index. Adding some fat and protein will dull the glycemic response of high-carbohydrate/high-sugar foods. Balance in combining foods is recommended for this reason.

Fats: Tortoise Fuel

Fats serve a number of important functions in the body, including carrying the fat-soluble vitamins A, D, E and K, and insulating and cushioning the organs. Fats are the most energy-rich macronutrient at 9 kcal per gram, which means fats require a long time to metabolize. Fats burn slow, steady and long,

Some carbohydrates taken immediately after a hard training bout will be readily absorbed by the muscles and used to replenish energy.

whereas carbohydrates burn fast and hot — a kind of metabolic tortoise-and-hare scenario.

Fats have a number of components, including triglycerides, cholesterol and lecithin. Triglycerides are found in all fatty foods and supply energy. They are also the form in which fat is stored in the body, in fat cells. Fats can be further divided into saturated and unsaturated fats. (If you have a cholesterol problem, this section may help you understand how you can improve your health as well as your golf game!) Saturated fat is found in animal products

Golf is a sport that relies on both fats and carbohydrates for aerobic fuel.

such as meat, whole dairy products and eggs. These fats are solid at room temperature. Plant foods are the primary sources of unsaturated fats, which include vegetable oils, avocados, olives, soybeans and nuts. Unsaturated fat is liquid at room temperature.

In general, most golf athletes eat too much animal fat and not enough unsaturated fat, thus their dietary profiles are heavy in saturated fats. Current studies indicate that Americans on the average get more than 44% of their total calories from fat. This dietary profile has been linked to elevated blood cholesterol levels, which is a major factor in coronary heart disease. American Heart Association guidelines state that saturated or animal fats should make up no more than 10% of total calories, and only 30% of total calories should come from all fats.

Most golfers would like to lose weight, improve athletic performance and reduce the risk of lifestyle-related diseases such as heart disease. This requires lowering fat intake to the level recommended by the American Heart Association and making sure that total fat intake occurs over the course of the day rather than all at one meal. Going to the other extreme, of very little or no dietary fat, can lead to low energy levels, poor absorption of nutrients and poor tissue constitution, especially in the skin and hair. Balance is the key, with the proper proportions of carbohydrates, fats and proteins being maintained in all meals.

Your body uses fat for essential functions. It can make or synthesize much of the fat it needs, except for essential fatty acids. Linoleic acid, a polyunsaturated fat found in nuts, vegetable oils and wheat germ, can't be made by the body and must be eaten in your diet. Linolenic acid, another fatty acid, is also important for hormonal production and regulation. This is why consuming a wide variety of vegetables, nuts or nut products (taken sparingly because of their high calorie content) and fish is important to nutritional health.

Good Fats versus Bad Fats

Bad fat	*Good fat*
Saturated fats	Monounsaturated fats
Hydrogenated oils	Polyunsaturated fats
Beef lard, butter	Olive oil
Hydrogenated oils	Peanut oil
Coconut & palm oils	Canola oil

Golf athletes should attempt to limit fat consumption to fats that have a neutral or positive effect on health and performance.

Proteins: Raw Materials

Proteins are used by the body for energy and for building and maintaining tissue. Although proteins are not the primary source of energy during golf, they can and will be used as energy by the body when there is not enough carbohydrate and fat present. However, extra protein in the diet is not easily converted to energy because the process of converting it is chemically complex.

Amino acids are known as the "building blocks of protein" and are of two types: essential and nonessential. Of the 22 total amino acids, 9 cannot be synthesized by the human body and must be taken from food. The quality of the protein you eat will affect your training results, especially in resistance training. Generally, animal products provide a better balance of the 9 essential amino acids, yet they generally have a higher fat content than plant sources such as beans or tofu, and they contain cholesterol, which plant foods do not. Plant sources of protein need to be combined in order to assure that the balance of the 9 essential amino acids is met because no single plant source contains all the essential amino acids. Eating a wide variety of plant-based proteins every day will ensure that the proper combinations are made if your diet leans toward being vegetarian.

Protein Needs and Golf

During golf's competitive season, you may need more protein than you realize. Even though you're not tearing down and rebuilding tissue like a bodybuilder, you still undergo the normal processes of tissue repair. In addition, if you continue to exercise during the golf season, you'll definitely need extra protein. This is especially true during the off-season, when your aerobic training and resistance training should be at higher levels than normal. In general, most people need a minimum of .6 grams of protein per pound of body weight to function well. Some research suggests that some athletes require more protein than this minimal level. Many weightlifting-based sports, where building strength and muscle is important, require a minimum level of 2+ grams of protein per pound of body weight.

Maintenance and Growth Determine Protein Needs

It's important for golfers to distinguish between two physiological needs: maintenance and growth. During in-season maintenance, one is not usually involved in exercises that substantially increase the need for protein beyond normal levels. If, however, you exercise strenuously each week with both aerobic training and resistance training, then your protein needs climb. Your body will be building and rebuilding more muscle and using a small amount of protein as fuel. In golf, this will affect your protein needs in different ways.

During the off-season, your training likely will include resistance training and aerobic training in addition to swing practice, all of which will increase slightly your need for protein. The exact amount will depend on the intensity of your exercise sessions, the number of sessions, the training phase and your overall physical condition. If you're in a resistance training phase to build muscular size and strength and are in moderate physical condition, your body will probably need additional protein.

During the golf season, your need for extra protein will depend on how much you play, how you play (riding in a cart rather than walking, for instance) and your personal maintenance exercise routine. Even a maintenance physical conditioning program could increase protein need beyond the minimum RDA. If you lift weights three times a week during the season, plan on adding extra protein to your diet.

Resistance training generally increases the need for more protein.

Older golf athletes need to be concerned about protein intake to ensure that muscle mass, or lean tissue, stays constant as age increases. Maintaining lean tissue leads to a stable metabolism, a key component in weight control. Resistance training and protein intake go hand in hand: The more resistance training you do to build strength, the more protein you need for growth and rebuilding tissue, even when you are older.

Water, the Coordination Connection

If you are a golfer, you can't drink too much water.

Water serves a number of physiological functions, including transportation of nutrients, hormones, antibodies and waste products. In addition, water helps to regulate body temperature, which is key to optimal training and to maintaining golf-game consistency in hot and humid conditions. The adult human body is roughly 55 to 60% water, depending on muscle mass and fat, and that water volume must be replaced approximately every 12 days.

Muscle is approximately 78% water, so without adequate hydration, muscle can't be built, maintained or kept functioning properly. If you eat properly and train hard yet don't take in adequate water, your training results will be minimal. Increase the amount of exercise, add the variables of temperature — high altitude, low or high humidity — and the need for water significantly increases beyond basic levels. Most adults need at least 2.5 quarts a day for basic functioning. Heat, exercise and varying humidity conditions can increase this need

Older golf athletes need to be concerned about protein intake to ensure that muscle mass, or lean tissue, stays constant as age increases.

to over 7 quarts per day in extreme circumstances for golfers. Just about any activity performed in the heat will increase regular water needs for both metabolic and heat-regulatory functioning. The length of a golf round combined with high temperature means that water is more important in golf than in most other sports.

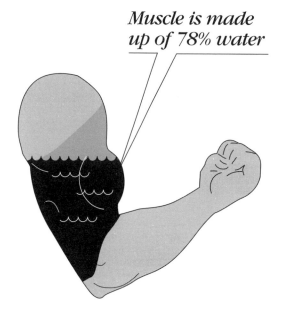

Muscle is made up of 78% water

Muscle is 78% water, so adequate water in physical training and golf performance will ensure functioning to full capabilities.

Water is also vital to golf performance because as little as a 2% water loss in the body is enough to impair physical and cognitive functioning. You can't pay attention or focus correctly without an adequate amount of water. Golf is tough enough without losing concentration or weakening your swing because you haven't had enough water to drink.

Vitamins and Minerals

Vitamins and minerals are often believed to contain energy. In reality, only carbohydrates, fats, proteins and alcohol contain food energy. Vitamins and minerals only aid in physiological functions such as metabolism — they provide no energy in themselves.

Complex chemicals known as enzymes are necessary to help the body control metabolism and growth. Enzymes are catalysts for the release of energy and nutrients. Vitamins are important components in the work of enzymes and are either fat- or water-soluble. Thirteen vitamins are needed for energy, growth and tissue repair. For example, some of the B vitamins are responsible in part for metabolism and are therefore useful in exercise and golf. But just how many vitamins a person gets from the diet is the subject of debate. Eating a varied, regular and balanced diet, including a wide variety of fruits and vegetables, is the best first step toward making sure your diet is adequate in vitamins and minerals.

Minerals have similar functions to vitamins but are inorganic. These substances, such as calcium, copper and manganese, have diverse functions in

Thirteen vitamins are needed for energy, growth and tissue repair.

the human body. Minerals are necessary for growth, especially of the bones and teeth. In addition, minerals aid certain functions, such as muscular contraction and nerve impulses. Minerals are generally taken into the body with foods, especially plant foods. Twenty-five of the 106 elements are considered essential minerals in human nutrition.

Training for golf and playing golf don't normally warrant massive dietary supplementation of vitamins and minerals. But if you have poor nutritional habits, and most people do, your need for supplementation grows. Because of substantial research documenting the toxic affects of megadoses of certain vitamins and minerals, massive oversupplementation is not recommended. In other words, taking a multiple vitamin/mineral preparation with approximately 100% of each vitamin's and mineral's RDA is considered safe and even prudent if you have less than the best nutritional habits.

Dietary Pitfalls and Golf Performance

In the golf swing, a small deviation can have disastrous results. Nutrition for golf athletes is no different. Small changes can have negative effects. Avoid these pitfalls, and the quality of your physical training will improve as your handicap goes down.

Don't Go for Carbohydrates Only

Because carbohydrates are the preferred fuel for exercise, some golfers eat carbohydrates to the exclusion of fat and protein. Although this may provide some short-term energy, the long-term effects are a lack of protein for rebuilding tissues and to use as fuel, and a lack of fat to use as fuel. Remember that although carbohydrates may be the most readily used fuel in the body, they aren't the only fuel. During most exercise, the body uses a combination of fats, carbohydrates and even a small amount of protein as fuel.

Simple sugars are not the same nutritionally as complex carbohydrates — vegetables and grains, for instance. Most of the time golfers would do best to steer their carbohydrate consumption toward complex rather than simple carbohydrates. Complex carbohydrates have a higher nutrient density per unit of energy. In addition, look for carbohydrates that have a low glycemic index and can be combined with some fats and proteins.

Balanced Protein

Most golfers eat all their protein in one meal. They might order a large steak or extra meat, especially for dinner. But the human body functions best with a constant supply of protein that is evenly distributed among meals and snacks. Consuming all your protein in one sitting means you're probably getting a moderate to high amount of fat and calories at one time as well. Since the human body can't use or metabolize a large amount of fat or protein at one time, this is the reason many people gain weight. And because big meals usually occur in the evening, you get up in the morning sluggish and find it's tough to kick your metabolism into high gear. Make sure you have a complete protein source, in moderate amounts, at breakfast, lunch and dinner.

During most exercise, the body uses a combination of fats, carbohydrates and even a small amount of protein as fuel.

Make sure you have a complete protein source, in moderate amounts, at breakfast, lunch and dinner.

Thirst always lags behind need, so using thirst as a water-regulation device means you'll be shortchanging your body's water needs....Drink 12 ounces of water before a round and then at least 6 ounces every 2 to 3 holes thereafter.

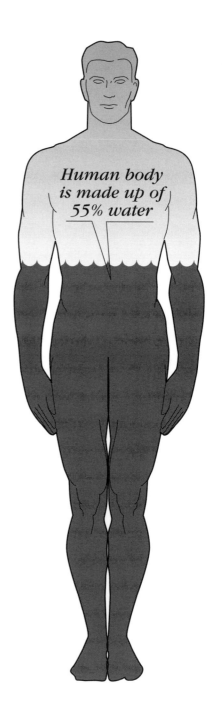

Human body is made up of 55% water

Spread out the Fat

If you are trying to lose weight, boost your health and improve your golf game, then be concerned about your fat intake and when it occurs. As with protein, most golfers with poor nutritional habits take in a large amount of fat all in one meal. This results in weight gain and low energy levels. But keep some fat in your diet. Fats are essential to health and have received what some would consider a bum rap lately. It's not that fat by itself is bad for you, but too much fat (an intake higher than 30% of total dietary calories) at the wrong time (all at once) and of the wrong kind (animal fat) can lead to obesity and myriad problems, including heart disease, liver disease and certain cancers.

Drink Before You Become Thirsty

A common mistake many golfers make is to wait until they are thirsty before drinking water. Thirst always lags behind need, so using thirst as a water-regulation device means you'll be shortchanging your body's water needs. Because golf is a sport of concentration, golfers are often so focused on the game that they tend to ignore the small thirst signals their bodies give. A good rule of thumb is to drink 12 ounces of water before a round and then at least 6 ounces every 2 or 3 holes thereafter.

During golf, avoid drinks with caffeine, including soft drinks, caffeinated tea and coffee, as well as alcohol. Caffeine and alcohol act as diuretics, enhancing the body's normal water loss and contributing to dehydration on the course. This effect is heightened frequently because of high temperatures during the golf season as well as the fact that most golfers are already dehydrated before the middle of their rounds. Water or sports drinks are a far better choice for replacing fluids than caffeinated drinks or alcohol.

> **Because most people don't drink enough water, they rely too heavily on food to replace water in their bodies.**

Don't Skip Breakfast

Most golfers skip breakfast and eat heavy dinners. (As previously mentioned, if you've eaten a heavy dinner, you are more likely to skip the morning meal.) This pattern causes both weight gain and low energy levels. And when breakfast *is* eaten, often inappropriate and incomplete foods, such as a bagel (all carbohydrates, very little protein or fat) and a large cup of coffee (giving a boost from caffeine, not nutrients) are chosen. Instead, if time is short for you in the morning, try eating a low-fat muffin or other low-sugar carbohydrate with 6+ ounces of low-fat yogurt or milk. Most commercial muffins are high in fat and sugar, so check before chomping. Some of the nutritional shake products on the market can be excellent choices for breakfast because they pack a nutritional punch and add water to your diet.

Having two breakfast patterns, one for rushed days and another for days when you have more time, will make it easier and simpler for you to shift gears and use Plan B when necessary.

The Value of TEF

Some of the energy you expend comes from simply digesting your food. Called the thermogenic effect of food (TEF), this process generally accounts for approximately 10% of the total calories you take in at any given meal. However, if you eat smaller meals throughout the day, this rate goes up slightly. So if you are trying to lose weight for golf, eat four or five smaller meals to burn more calories.

A bonus strategy to boost TEF is to take a short walk after dinner, which will lower the levels of triglycerides in your blood as well as introduce extra physical activity. If you are hungry late at night, try eating air-popped popcorn or a high-water fruit such as melons or an apple.

Don't Eat Past 8 p.m.

This can be a problem with business dinners and social occasions, because the next morning you will tend to skip or eat a nutritionally inadequate breakfast. Your goal should be to have dinner started no later than

> **Eating at least one serving of fruits, vegetables, or whole grains will add significant fiber to each meal, reducing the effects of the fat you eat.**

6 P.M. and concluded no later than 7 P.M. If you *do* eat later, eat lightly. Make sure you have breakfast before 9 A.M. and lunch no later than 1 P.M.

Don't Use Food to Replace Body Water

Because most people don't drink enough water, they rely too heavily on food to replace water in their bodies. One easy trick to boost your water intake is to drink a full glass of water before each meal — it will get you closer to the necessary water intake levels and help keep you from overeating.

Counting Fat Grams and Calories

Because golf athletes count strokes, they are more likely to count calories and grams of fat. Unfortunately, counting fat grams or calories for single meals rarely accomplishes anything and may wreak psychological havoc. For instance, if you allow 8 grams of fat at breakfast but eat 12, you might just go for the ice cream later, thinking that, since you've already blown it, why bother worrying. Counting the grams of fat in your breakfast yogurt and then eating a burger and fries on the course negates any of the benefits of the low-fat yogurt.

The best alternative is to think in terms of balance at each meal. Balance your proteins, carbohydrates and fats in both health-savvy and golf-smart ways. Each half-cup of protein you consume should be accompanied by an equal or greater amount of complex carbohydrate, which contains fiber to help inhibit fat absorption. Eating at least one serving of fruits, vegetables or whole grains will add significant fiber to each meal, reducing the effects of the fat you eat.

The Ideal Golf Diet

So what is the ideal diet, and how different is it from the ideal golfer's diet? The answer is that the two are similar. Both diets should contain a balance of carbohydrate, protein and fat at each meal. The exact amount of protein and carbohydrates you need depends on your training schedule. If you're exercising during the pre-season and performing more than four resistance training sessions per week, you'll need slightly more protein for muscular growth and rebuilding.

The ideal balance of nutrients for golf would be:
Pre-season: 20-30% fat; 40-55% carbohydrate; 15-35% protein
In-season: 20-30% fat; 40-55% carbohydrate; 15-30% protein

In-season nutritional requirements for protein can be lower if you are performing less supplemental exercise, especially resistance training. With fewer resistance training sessions, you don't need quite as much protein to help build muscle.

Although three squares a day is a good start toward optimum nutrition, three smaller meals, together with well-balanced snacks or supplements, is even better. Remember that the thermogenic effect of food (TEF) is enhanced if you eat six smaller meals, which will help you lose weight. Just think of the extra energy your body must expend just to digest those additional smaller meals or snacks. It's a fallacy that skipping meals or eating one large meal each day aids in weight loss.

What are some good foods for golfers to eat in these smaller meals or snacks? It's definitely easier to plan a balanced meal if you are preparing a large amount of food. It becomes more difficult to combine carbohydrate, protein and fat when preparing a smaller meal. Many golfers turn to products such as protein shakes and meal replacement bars for their light meals or snacks.

Shake up to the Bar

Golfers, beware of the nutritional imbalance of some commercially available protein shakes and protein bars. Although these snacks are convenient, in eating them you may overindulge in one nutrient at the expense of another. Some of the popular energy bars on the market are almost too high in carbohydrates and too low in fat and protein. The result is an energy low right after the carbohydrate metabolizes. The solution is to find a bar with a higher fat content, 20 to 30%, and a reasonable amount of protein, 8+ grams, as well as more complex rather than simple carbohydrates with a low glycemic index.

Although they are heavily advertised, many protein drinks are too high in protein and too low in carbohydrates and fats for golfers. Though these products may be useful for athletes in extremely strenuous resistance training programs, such as off-season training for football or bodybuilding, they probably contain far more protein than a golf athlete needs while training for golf. With the proper nutrient distribution, a golf athlete probably will get more protein in his or her diet than is needed when the three major meals and three snacks contain protein. A major protein supplement is therefore probably not necessary. With an increasing awareness of differing nutritional needs, some companies have developed drinks that are more balanced, with less protein and higher complex carbohydrate balances; and these products make good snacks or occasional meal replacements.

Many protein drinks are too high in protein and too low in carbohydrates and fats for golfers.

Products with higher complex carbohydrate balances and lower protein make good snacks or occasional meal replacements.

Pre-training Guidelines

What should you eat just before you exercise? That depends on your exercise program. Although some people can exercise right after a meal, this is the time when the body is moving blood to the digestive organs. This causes a conflict between the working muscles, which need blood, and the digestive

Additional carbohydrates are not necessary after only 30 minutes of exercise because you won't have reached a point where you have depleted the carbohydrates stores in your body. Water is the most important nutrient to replace after exercise.

organs. For most people, unless the meal is light, waiting 30 to 60 minutes to begin exercise is a good idea. If it has been 2 or 3 hours since your last meal, then try drinking 6 to 8 ounces of a non-citrus juice with 12 ounces of water or one of the balanced meal-replacement bars with 12 ounces of water before you exercise. Before exercise, your goal is to be properly hydrated, with just enough fuel for the exercise session.

Post-exercise Guidelines

If your exercise session was strenuous enough, then some post-exercise recovery foods may be in order. Generally, if you work out continuously for one-and-a-half hours or more, then some carbohydrates taken right after exercise will greatly enhance your recovery. Remember that this is best done within four hours after exercise, and preferably within 30 minutes, to have the best replenishment effect.

In general, your goal after strenuous exercise is to replace lost carbohydrates and, in the case of extensive sweat loss, some electrolytes (dissolved salts and minerals present in the blood and body fluids). Additional carbohydrates are not necessary after only 30 minutes of exercise because you won't have reached a point where you have depleted the carbohydrates stores in your body. Water is the most important nutrient to replace after exercise. Even resistance training causes significant water losses. The easiest way to tell how much water you have lost is to weigh yourself before and after exercise and then to replace that much fluid. Because water loss and metabolic rates differ from individual to individual, no two people need to replace the same amount of water after exercise.

During heavy exercise your body can use more water just to keep your metabolism going. Approximately 2.7 grams of water are stored with every gram of glycogen (muscular carbohydrate), both of which are metabolized in heavy exercise. As you expend this energy you have to cool your body, which may require an additional quart or more of water per exercise session.

The need to replace electrolytes after exercise has fueled an entire industry of sport drinks with added electrolytes. The depletion of these compounds, which include sodium, potassium and chloride, are a problem only in endurance events lasting over 2 hours. During golf or after normal exercise, the need for these compounds is minimal, unless you are literally running between each shot.

If you're hungry on the course, try eating a balanced energy bar followed by 8 to 12 ounces of water.

With a well-balanced diet, a golf athlete will easily replace any lost electrolytes in his or her next couple of meals. If your exercise session lasts less than an hour, drink water. If the workout was intense, eat fruits or drink fruit juice or one of the sport drinks. Some nutritionists believe that fruits and fruit juices are superior to sport drinks because they contain substantial vitamins and other minerals. For this reason, apple juice has become a popular and effective post-exercise recovery drink. After your next exercise session, assuming it lasts more than an hour, try 6 to 8 ounces of juice and water. Be aware that citrus-based juices have been reported to cause stomach upsets in some individuals after exercise. If this happens to you, try apple or some other non-citrus juice.

The need for post-exercise food will be stronger if you don't have enough fuel in your body when you begin the exercise session. If you exercise after work, then take in some fuel prior to exercising. You can try juice and water, or try one of the balanced energy bars.

What to Eat Before and During Golf

Before playing a round of golf, make sure you are adequately fueled. Don't skip any meals or deviate from your normal meal patterns, which could affect both your energy level and your concentration. Because most golf courses don't make nutritious food available, it's essential for you to take some portable food to the course with you. Golf courses are generally not supportive of good nutritional habits, and a hot dog eaten before the back nine is far from providing the kind of fuel a golfer needs to play at his or her best. When in doubt about a food choice at a club, it's better to have a balanced energy bar that fits the nutritional requirements previously outlined. If you play a variety of courses, always carry two or three balanced bars with you. These bars should be 20 to 30% protein, 40 to 55% carbohydrate (complex and low-glycemic) and 20 to 30% fat.

Energy bars for golf performance should have a balance of protein, carbohydrate and fat.

When in doubt about a food choice at a club, it's better to have a balanced energy bar.

Another important requirement is to be properly hydrated. Drink at least 12 ounces of water (not a caffeinated drink like coffee or tea!) right before your round. During your round, make sure you consume 3 to 6 ounces of water every 2 holes. This will help you metabolize your fuel and keep you from overheating. The best strategy is to take a water bottle with you and take a drink every time you walk to the next tee box.

If you're hungry on the course, try eating a balanced energy bar followed by 8 to 12 ounces of water. Even though a sport beverage will give you an immediate boost from simple carbohydrates and possibly some electrolytes, an energy bar will better fulfill the nutritional requirements necessary to play optimal golf and maintain even blood sugar levels. However, if you want to take fluid energy that will give you a boost for an hour or less, a sport beverage may be just the ticket. Remember that an energy bar that is too low in fat and protein may give you an immediate energy boost only to leave you somewhat flat in a short period of time. Here's a pretty good rule of thumb: If it will be more than an hour until your next meal, eat a well-balanced energy bar; it if will be less than an hour, drink a sport beverage.

Fuel for Golf KEY POINTS

- Nutrition is important for golf, just as in any other sport. Nutrition has a big impact both on your physical training and your golf performance.

- Eating a balanced diet with a regular meal and snack schedule is the first step to improving golf performance and to realizing the benefits of physical training.

- Carbohydrates are the main sources of fuel for the body, and complex carbohydrates burn longer than simple sugars.

- Golfers should eat more complex than simple carbohydrates to improve training and golf performance.

- Glycemic index, or the speed at which a carbohydrate is converted to blood sugar should be a consideration in choosing carbohydrates.

- Fats provide long-term energy and are important in stabilizing energy levels during a round of golf.

- Spread your fat intake evenly throughout the day to lessen your chances of weight gain and to improve health.

- Proteins are the raw materials your body uses to build muscle and repair tissue.

- Golf itself requires minimal extra protein, yet heavy exercise, especially resistance training, increases the need for protein.

- Most golfers will get adequate protein, even during periods of resistance training, by making sure to consume at least one protein source at each meal.

- Water is the most neglected golf nutrient.

- On days of practice and actual play, stick to your regular meal and snack pattern.

- Carry at least 3 balanced energy bars with you in case your round occurs during your regular mealtime or there are less than optimal food choices at the course.

- If you hit an energy low and have 60 minutes or less to the end of the round, drink a sport drink to keep your energy up. If there is 61+ minutes to go, eat a balanced energy bar.

- Drink water often and before you are thirsty; on the course plan on routinely drinking 3 to 6 ounces of water every two holes.

References

Arnot, R. 1995. *Dr. Bob Arnot's Guide to Turning Back the Clock.* Boston: Little, Brown.

Atallah, A. 1995. L'eau dans l'alimentation du sportif. (Place of water in the nutrition of the athlete.) *Medecine du sport* 69(5):260-263, 265-267.

Berning, J.R., and S.N. Steen, eds. 1991. *Sports Nutrition for The '90s:* The Health Professional's Handbook. Gaithersburg, MD: Aspen Publishers.

Clark, N. 1996. 40-30-30 or 60-15-25? Which percentage of calories from carbohydrates, proteins and fats is healthiest? *Coaching Volleyball* (December 1995/January 1996):16-17.

——. 1996. The power of protein. *The Physician and Sportsmedicine* 24(4):11-12.

——. 1996. Sports bars: The powerfood of the '90s? *Coaching Volleyball* (April/May):16-17.

Coleman, E. 1995. The BioZone Nutrition System — dietary panacea or myth? *Sports Medicine Digest* 17(12):6-7.

Colgan, M. 1993. *Optimum Sports Nutrition.* Ronkonkoma, NY: Advanced Research Press.

Cooper, K.H. 1994. *Dr. Kenneth Cooper's Antioxidant Revolution.* Nashville, TN: Thomas Nelson.

Dunne, L.J. 1990. *Nutrition Almanac.* 3rd ed. New York: McGraw-Hill.

Frail, H. 1995. Overview of training nutrition. *Masters Athlete* 1:3.

Grundy, M. 1996. Eating through pre-season. *Sport Health* 14(1):22-23.

Jackson, P. 1996. Snack attack. *Women in Sport* 1(5):36-37.

Kleiner, S.M. 1995. The role of meat in an athlete's diet: Its effect on key macro- and micronutrients. *Sports Science Exchange* 8(5):1-5.

LeClair, P. 1997. 40/30/30: The nutritional program that may dramatically improve your athletic performance. *Martial Arts Magazine* (July 1997):68-73.

Mermel, V.L. 1995. A review of contemporary sports nutrition. *Athletic training: Sports Health Care Perspectives* 1(3):228-244.

O'Neill, M. 1996. Functional foods: Eating beyond 2000. *Network* 9(1):40-41.

Parker, S. 1996. Ironing out your troubles. *Women in Sport* 2(1):54-55.

Pelly, F. 1996. Sports fatigue: Is your diet to blame? *Network* 9(2):21-22.

Plotkin, M.J. 1993. *Tales of a Shaman's Apprentice.* New York: Viking.

Pritikin, N. 1979. *The Pritikin Program for Diet and Exercise.* New York: Bantam.

Sears, B. 1995. *The Zone.* New York: HarperCollins Publishers.

Zuti, W.B., and L. Golding. 1976. Comparing diet and exercise as weight reduction tools. *The Physician and Sportsmedicine* 4:59-62.

Ergonomics

Improving your fitness can definitely make golf easier on your body. Golf is tough on the system because of the repetitive coiling and uncoiling motions of the golf swing. There are ways to minimize the debilitating impact of golf on your body besides increasing fitness levels. These concepts can substantially reduce the impact on your body and improve both performance and your golf comfort. Injuries in golf that are equipment-related can come from a wide variety of causes including repetitive motion injuries to impacting a root with the club head.

Clubs

Clubs are essential to golf. They are the tool, period. While much of the attention on club design has centered on performance improvement, the resulting designs also eased the force transmitted back up the shaft to your body. Even a scratch golfer has an occasional "fat" shot or just hits a hard piece of ground or imbedded object. That singular blow causes or contributes to a golfer's elbow and wrist injuries. These are the types of injuries that could keep you away from golf for months.

Some of the principles of club design can help you gain an edge in body comfort, while still increasing your performance. Golf club companies in general have designed clubs that have attempted to increase distance and accuracy while being more forgiving. Many golfers will try a new club before adding additional practice time to hone technique or add physical conditioning.

Materials from the space program and other industries are constantly being applied to golf. New materials in club heads can make the club significantly lighter and stronger. They have created a cavernous cavity where mis-hits require almost deliberate skill.

No discussion about materials of golf clubs would be complete without addressing knock-offs, or copies, of major brands and models. If you think that a knock-off will give you the same performance improvement and decrease injury potential, think again. Because knock-offs have to look like the original to sell, they seldom have the same technical features and quality of construction. What

A 2- or 3- degree change in spine angle can translate to a similar change in how the club approaches the ground during ball contact.

looks good probably doesn't perform the same. The brand-name manufacturer and major custom club maker have made a commitment to golf as a sport and as an industry, as well as to the individual golfer. Weights, loft and lie are subject to strict specifications, and knock-offs rarely offer the original manufacturer's attention to functional detail and performance.

Physical conditioning levels definitely affect swing consistency and therefore equipment fit. For example, most golfers lack strength and flexibility in their hamstrings and trunk region, so their golf stance changes during the round as they fatigue. A 2- or 3- degree change in spine angle can translate to a similar change in how the club approaches the ground during ball contact. Conditioning levels affect both the initial fit of clubs, and the consistency of that fit during the round or practice session.

Physical Swing Changes and Custom Clubs

In some cases, the fat or thin shot can be caused by the postural shift resulting from the lack of muscular strength or endurance to make a consistent swing. In other cases, it's simply a lack of practice that translates into a lack of consistency. If the golfer would have been sufficiently conditioned, many of those shots and injuries would have been significantly lessened both in impact and recuperation time. If your equipment doesn't fit, it will increase the chances of injury and definitely decrease your performance.

Most golfers are going to hit some fat or thin shots based on their lack of practice, less-than-optimum lies, and lack of consistent golf swings. A good first step is having clubs specifically built for your loft, lie and swing specifications. A key decision point is how much conditioning you will regularly pursue to improve your golf game, and then take that into account during club fitting. For example, if you haven't exercised for years and start a conditioning program based on this book, which you will maintain the rest of your life, you should wait 4 to 8 weeks until the conditioning program has had an impact in order to fit clubs more accurately. For example, a sound and scientific conditioning program will result in increased levels of power and flexibility, both of which tend to increase club-head speed and change equipment dynamics and fit.

Basic club design also can influence injury and scoring potential. Not all club heads are equal in their playability and results for all golfers. Custom club options should offer a variety of club head styles, as not all golfers need or can benefit from the same club head.

Men and women generally have significantly different needs in club fitting. In general, women's clubs should be different in lower overall weight, and should have more torque or less resistance to twisting, and a lower actual flex point in the shaft. Grip size and length of shaft also varies greatly from men's to women's clubs.

Obviously, if the club is not designed to do some of the work in the shot, a golfer will be tempted to swing harder than normal. Some of the golf injuries come from swinging the club too hard in difficult situations. The advantage of the ever-mutating club designs is not only performance improvement but the injury reduction potential from the psychological variable of

A key decision point is how much conditioning you will regularly pursue to improve your golf game, and then take that into account during club fitting.

confidence. When you are more confident, you tend to relax, and the golf swing is more effortless.

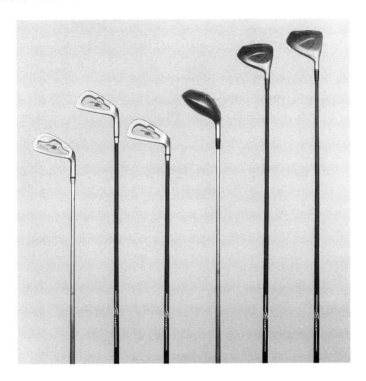

Custom clubs will allow the golf athlete to enhance performance by utilizing individual physiological abilities and characteristics in their swing.

Custom clubs are essential in obtaining your best golf swing. Without properly fitted equipment, conditioning benefits will not be optimally realized because, in part, they will be used to compensate for ill-fitted equipment. A

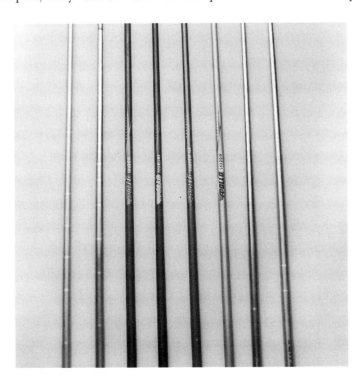

Shafts should fit your game and physiological abilities.

Properly fitted equipment will maximize results with the least amount of physical effort.

good fit makes the bad shots better and less frequent, while your percentage of relatively good shots increases. Unless you are measured and then matched to the clubs, there is little guarantee that clubs right out of the box are right for your swing and physical ability. Custom clubs add substantially to the ability to make a consistent swing in tune with your physical make-up.

Shafts often are deemed the engine of the club. The most important characteristic of a golf shaft should be the fit to your game. Shafts should be fitted for material type, kick point and overall flex, or bending. Torque, or the resistance to twisting, also should be considered based on the golf swing and conditioning factors. Fit to your game means you will use your capabilities in power, endurance and flexibility.

As you increase your physiological capabilities, you may need to change your club and shaft system. As you get stronger, more flexible and build your abilities to turn your hips into the ball, the shaft that once fit you may not any more.

Remember, if your equipment doesn't fit, you will make some type of swing compensation to adjust for improper equipment. While conditioning will prevent some injuries, the constant physical stress of less than optimum mechanics from trying to swing improperly fitted clubs will contribute to or result in some type of injury. Properly fitted equipment will maximize results with the least amount of physical effort. Clubs should be fitted for your personal specifications.

Factors that should be considered are:

- club head type
- swing weight
- offset versus non-offset
- loft
- lie
- shaft material
- shaft flex
- kick point
- overall weight
- grip size/grip type
- clubhead speed
- physical strength, power, muscular endurance and flexibility
- grip strength

Fitting systems can be static or dynamic. Static fitting systems use measurements that don't involve ball flight. Measuring the distance of your fingertips to the floor or measuring lie angle at setup are examples of static measurement. Dynamic fitting systems stress lie angle at impact and use ball flight to help determine club specifications. Some systems use both static and dynamic information combined.

Dynamic fitting will allow the golf athlete to measure the suitability of various components to physiological abilities.

Golfers should pursue a conditioning program they will maintain; develop a sound fundamental swing through a PGA or LPGA instructor; and then get fit for clubs. Fitting without lessons, good fundamentals and improved physical abilities means new clubs may result in a marginal improvement in golf performance compared to optimizing all the factors.

Spike Systems: Grip Not Rip

Historically, a golf spike has been a long protrusion from the shoe meant to provide grip. Enter the world of spikes which aren't spikes in the conventional sense. These use patterns, swirls and even retraction with spring-like pressure to give grip while diminishing damage to the green. These different systems mutated from the groundskeepers, who were worried that the increased level of golf play was leading to the greens' destruction.

The other benefit of these systems, and one that is closer to the physiological nature of golf, is what these systems do for your body. In short, wearing them makes golf easier on the body.

With conventional steel spikes of 8 millimeters, there are a number of mechanical problems that occur when walking on hard surfaces such as cart paths. Besides the obvious problem of slippage, traditional golf spikes on hard surfaces can change the mechanics of how you walk. The normal gait of the foot absorbing shock through pronation (inward rolling of the foot), then rolling to the outside of the foot for support, is harder in spikes. Alternative spikes provide a more normal walking pattern on hard surfaces allowing a more natural gait. Also, if you have significant knee or hip problems, non-conventional spike systems are a good idea. Conventional spikes may provide too much grip and result in significant torque to the knees and hips.

Alternative spikes provide a more normal walking pattern on hard surfaces allowing a more natural gait.

Another advantage of these alternative gripping systems is they provide less foot stress and make shoes last longer. Because spikes push up from a hard surface, unless you're wearing a totally rigid golf shoe, you get pressure points from spike pressure. If you run or generally have "bad" feet, this can be one more source of foot irritation. This is especially true with the soft-soled shoes, which tend to pass along more of this pressure through the shoe sole. There is no doubt that these spike systems can provide less wear to the green, and more comfort for the feet.

Not all gripping systems work equally well on wet surfaces. Some of the shorter spikes can have disastrous results in walking up or down hills and in wet conditions. This may be an area where the retractable spike has an advantage in giving extra traction on wet surfaces while providing for a normal or near-normal walking motion on cart paths.

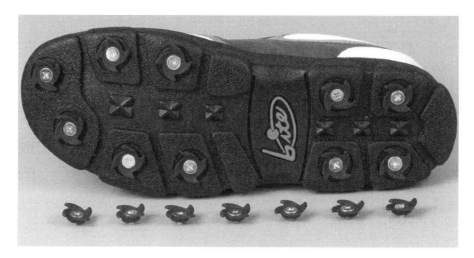

Sport Footbeds

Your feet provide the link for force transmission during the swing. Without proper support and contact, the golf swing will be inefficient and inconsistent. In addition, the lack of foot support in a walking game means less comfort and enjoyment.

The golf shoe supports the foot and provides a system of "spikes" to grip the ground during the transfer of force. However, the movement of the foot inside the shoe, both during the golf swing and walking, is important to both performance and comfort. The foot must maintain a supported, neutral position which allows for the normal function of the foot rolling inward (pronation) then outward (supination) in walking. In the golf swing, this neutral position allows the best weight transfer mechanics.

While orthotics and footbeds inside the shoe correct foot problems such as excessive pronation, they provide other golf benefits as well. They also improve performance and substantially increase comfort. Remember, the insoles inside most golf shoes will not give enough support for either walking or the weight transfer during the golf swing.

Good footbeds should possess certain characteristics. While heel and arch support are important, the front of the foot can benefit from support as well. This is why many other athletes, such as tennis players and skiers, favor full-foot support. In addition, the footbed should be placed in the shoe so the fit of the shoe is essentially the same as when the original sock-liner was used. You should be able to remove the old foam sockliner, and replace it with a sport footbed without any noticeable change in the way the shoe fits.

Another essential characteristic of a full-foot support is flexibility in the forefoot. As you walk the course, the shoe has to flex, and the footbed should flex at this same point without breaking down. Not all footbeds share this characteristic.

> **Footbeds, which replace the sock liners in most golf shoes, will increase golf performance and comfort.**

Carrying Systems: It's Not Just a Bag

Golf is a walking sport. However, with heavier bags, more clubs and making sure you are stocked for a three-day survival course, carrying the golf bag is not easy. This is especially true considering that the modern golf swing and work/sitting postures place tremendous stress on the back.

Carrying a traditional golf bag can aggravate an existing back condition, and in some cases cause back pain and injury. The reasons are simple: the stress of carrying a traditional golf bag (22+ pounds on average), combined with the lateral and twisting motions of golf, causes back stress. In the modern golf swing, during the takeaway and downswing, much of the stress on the back is placed laterally, or in sideways movements. This is termed "shear force." In carrying a traditional golf bag on one shoulder, the opposite side muscles — in this case the obliques, have to activate to keep you from falling over with the weight of the golf bag. Unfortunately, the axis point for this lever system is the spine.

These lateral shear forces in themselves can be minor for a well-conditioned athlete, yet when adding the golf movement stress of 200+ swings per round, this can cause anything from premature fatigue to serious injury.

Part of the evaluation of how to carry clubs comes from understanding the kinesiology and mechanics of carrying loads with the spine. In general, the more evenly the weight is distributed between the shoulders, the better. This is part of the reason that backpacks use both shoulders equally: the force is distributed

> **The stress of carrying a traditional golf bag (22+ pounds on average), combined with the lateral and twisting motions of golf, causes back stress.**

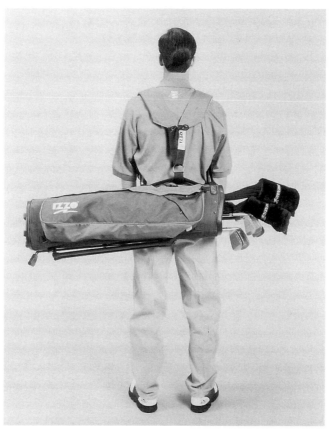

Carrying systems to be effective should allow for symmetrical load distribution.

so there is no lateral shear force from favoring one shoulder or side. The closer the load to the center of gravity and the spine, the better. The shorter the lever arm, or distance from the spine to the load, the less force transmitted with injury potential.

In male golfers, the center of gravity is approximately 57% of height, while in female golfers it is about 55% of height. With the normal spine angles, the human system is more able to bear the stress on the back in the small of the back than on the abdominal side. Thus a carrying system should fit both of these requirements: equal weight distribution between the shoulders, and as close as possible to the center of the small of the back.

The clubs and walking movement should occur with the least amount of muscular effort or activation. Traditional golf bags activate the opposite side from the bag, which fires the obliques, a muscle group used in the golf swing. Needless to say, one does not want to expend any extra energy on carrying the clubs, when this muscle group is used in pulling and stabilizing the spine in each golf swing. This is also part of the reason that traditional golf bags can contribute to fatigue and injury. You are using a muscle group that is probably not adequately trained to start with, and between the golf swing and carrying the clubs, the back is severely over-stressed.

Carrying the clubs on one shoulder, and then swinging the bottom of the bag around to the other shoulder, does not meet these criteria for easing back stress. Also, using asymmetrical add-on straps which are not like a backpack only partially solve the problem. Without equal weight distribution in the right spot, you change your natural gait. This places further stress on the back and causes even more fatigue from muscles you aren't used to exercising.

If you want to ease your load while walking, use a carrying system where the weight is evenly distributed from right to left and placed directly in the small of the back, as close as possible to the body's center of gravity. The strap system has to be symmetrical, which allows for walking without holding the bag, a necessity to a normal walking gait.

The Eyes Have It

Golf is a visual game and over the last 10 years, sports eyewear has been recognized to have major benefits both in health and increasing golf performance. Even in hazy or cloudy conditions, your eyes are subject to damaging ultraviolet (UV) rays. Most good sport performance eyewear will protect your eyes from these harmful rays, and the wraparound models offer the best protection from both UV rays and wind.

Some golfers have reported that "rimless" designs also are better for putting because of the lessened visual distractions without a frame. The option to change lens colors for varying light conditions is also a plus at reducing eye strain and increasing golf performance.

Sport eyewear that wraps around the eye area is a plus for golfers in reducing glare and wind.

Ergonomics KEY POINTS

• Custom clubs, fitted for loft, lie, shaft flex and design will substantially increase performance and decrease swing-related stress.

• Alternative spike systems will make walking easier and will decrease joint torque in the areas of the back, knees and hips.

• While orthotics have been used medically to improve foot function, full-foot footbeds can improve golf performance and comfort.

• Because the way you carry your bag can impact your comfort and performance, look for a carrying system or strap that uses both shoulders symmetrically and that places the bag as close as possible to the center of gravity in the small of the back.

• Sport performance eyewear will reduce eye strain, reduce UV ray damage to the eyes, and will help the golfer gain visual acuity in changing light and weather conditions.

References

Frank, J.A. 1988. The country's clubs: American ingenuity was key to the advances in golf club design. *Golf Magazine* 30(3):110.

Frankel, V.H., and M. Nordin. 1980. *Basic Biomechanics of the Skeletal System.* Philadelphia, PA: Lea & Feabiger.

Golf shoes and turf wear — a story that won't go away. *1985 USGA Green Section Record* 23(4):12.

Gross, M.T. 1985. Lower quarter screening for skeletal malalignment — suggestions for orthotics and shoewear. JOSPT: *The Journal of Orthopaedic & Sports Physical Therapy* 21(6):389-405.

Hamilton, G.W., J.S. Gregos, D.R. Gean, and A.E. Gover. 1997. Golf shoe treads affect putting green quality. *Golf Course Management* 65(4):53-56.

Hunter, S., M.G. Dolan, and J.M. Davis. 1995. *Foot Orthotics in Therapy and Sport.* Champaign, IL: Human Kinetics.

Kaneko, Y., and F. Sato. 1993. The optimization of golf swing and its application to the golf club design. International Society of Biomechanics. Congress (14th: 1993: Paris, France). Societe internationale de biomecanique. Congress. (14: 199: Paris, France). In, *Abstracts of the International Society of Biomechanics, XIVth Congress, Paris, 4-8 July, 1993,* vol. I, Paris, s.n., 652-653.

Maltby, R.D. 1990. *Golf Club Design, Fitting, Alteration, and Repair: The Principles and Procedures.* Rev. 3rd ed. Newark, OH: R. Maltby Enterprises.

Milne, R.D. and J.P. Davis. 1992. Role of the shaft in the golf swing. *Journal of Biomechanics* 25(9):975-983.

Pagliano, J.W. 1994. Footnotes — orthotics. *Sports Medicine Digest* 16(7):5.

Pietrocarlo, T.A. 1996. Foot and ankle considerations in golf. *Clinics in Sports Medicine* 15(1):129-146.

Saggini, R., N. Tjoroudis, and L. Vecchiet. 1992. The role of orthotics in the football. International Symposium of Biomechanics in Sports (10th: 1992: Milan, Italy). In Rodano, R. (ed.) et al, ISBS '92 *Proceedings of the 10th Symposium of the International Society of Biomechanics in Sports.* Milan, Italy: Edi-Ermes, 301-303.

Seilbel, M.O. 1988. *Foot Function.* Baltimore, MD: Williams & Wilkins.

Tomaro, J.E., and S.L. Butterfield. 1995. Biomechanical treatment of traumatic foot and ankle injuries with the use of foot orthotics. JOSPT: *The Journal of Orthopaedic & Sports Physical Therapy* 21(6):373-380.

Torello, W.A., Yan Su, and C. Dixon. 1997. More options afoot for spikeless courses. *Golf Course Management* 65(4):57-61.

Injury Armor

For some reason, people who don't play golf think the sport is relatively easy on the body. In reality, few other sports demand the acceleration and control that is required to swing a golf club, nor do they require an athlete to precisely repeat the same motion more than 200 times during one sporting event. Golfers can get hurt in any number of ways, from muscle overuse to making improper golf swings — even while getting out of a golf cart.

Oh, Your Aching Back

Golf generates a surprisingly high number of injuries in the areas of the back, knees, feet, shoulders and elbows. Why? The golf swing is a powerful, stressful and repetitive motion. But between swings the golfer is not active, and the body's ability to keep the muscles warm during a round is thus curtailed. Other sports, such as tennis for example, require constant movement that keeps the muscles warm and prepared, which helps reduce injury. Golf, on the other hand, with relatively long times between shots, can generate injuries because the muscles don't stay warm between shots.

Additionally, poor body mechanics is often the cause of injuries since the body is placed in positions where muscle groups such as the back and shoulder are strained. Most golf injuries occur to the soft tissues of the muscles, skin, ligaments, tendons and cartilage. Injuries befall professional and amateur golfers alike. In the case of professional players, injuries occur from a powerful movement combined with a consistent swing. In fact, there is generally a correlation between lower handicaps and better swings, which place their own unique sets of stressors on the body. The more consistent the swing, the higher the tendency to sustain overuse injuries. Professional golfers cite back problems as the #1 injury problem they face.

Because injuries at the advanced levels of performance are caused by the overuse of certain muscles, preventing and treating injuries in top-level golf requires special strategies. If you are an advanced-level golfer, carefully plan your physical and golf training to include periods of rest with regular activity. This ensures that the muscle groups you use for golf are adequately rested and retain full capabilities in strength, flexibility and endurance.

The golf swing is a powerful, stressful and repetitive motion.

The more consistent the swing, the higher the tendency to sustain overuse injuries.

219

The likelihood of the common golf injuries occurring is significantly reduced with a consistent conditioning program.

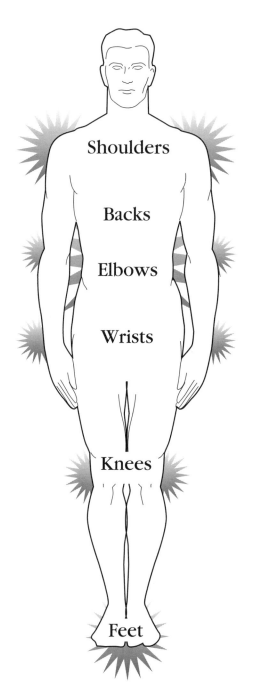

Shoulders

Backs

Elbows

Wrists

Knees

Feet

For less-accomplished golfers, injuries stem from a different set of factors, including the lack of consistent body mechanics and accidental "turfing" of the club head. Recreational golfers cite low-back problems as their #1 malady, with elbow and wrist injuries close behind. Women recreational golfers tend to suffer more elbow problems, with back injuries taking second place. Golfers with higher handicaps have a higher number of shots where they turf the club or mis-hit the ball. Recreational golfers have cited that their most common injuries are caused by "excessive practice." From a physiological perspective it's not the practice itself that is excessive but rather the low level of golf-specific conditioning with which many golfers enter into practice.

Factors in Preventing Injuries

Even with proper conditioning, failing to warm up before play or practice will increase the potential for injury. A good warm-up for golf is essential to decreasing your injuries because it prepares your body for activity. In one recent survey, it was found that fewer than 20% of golfers went through any kind of formal warm-up routine besides just hitting golf balls.

Fewer than 20% of golfers go through any kind of formal warm-up routine besides just hitting golf balls.

Fewer than 10% of the golfers surveyed had a routine that adequately prepared their bodies for golf. No wonder it takes four or more holes for most golfers to get into a rhythm!

A good warm-up for golf requires that you do more than hit 10 balls before you tee off. What most golfers do, when they warm up at all, is to run through a few stretches that aren't even specific to their injury potentials or style of play. What they should do is warm the muscles through movement, stretch lightly (if at all), then start hitting, starting with the shorter clubs.

Warm-up Phases for Golf

Phase 1: General Movement

The first phase of a warm-up should focus on general dynamic movement activity, such as calisthenics. This can include light jumping jacks, jogging in place, or even walking briskly to the practice tee. The body moves blood according to needs dictated by activity, and it takes a certain amount of activity to move the blood away from the body's core (trunk and vital organs) to the exercising muscles. Many golfers believe that stretching serves this purpose. But although stretching may be part of a warm-up, unless it is dynamic or movement-based, it won't improve circulation to the working muscles. Dynamic, active movements are the key in the first phase of a warm-up.

Phase 2: Extra Movement and Stretching for Problem Areas

The second phase of a warm-up is specific to injury prevention, and entails warming up and stretching the muscle groups that have been prone to injury in the past. In some cases this just requires basic movement, and in others it requires movement followed by specific stretching exercises. For example, golfers who need more shoulder flexibility and who don't focus on warming up this area before play have a tendency to injure it. Always start with general exercises, then add specific exercises for the joints and muscle groups that have been problems for you.

If shoulder injuries have plagued your game, follow general arm circles with front to back wing-like motions (see the chapter on Flexibility Training Exercises). This will warm up the shoulder area and stretch it at the same time. Muscles such as those in the back and hips require active movement and stretching with the aim of preventing injuries before you even hit the golf ball.

Phase 3: Hit Golf Balls

The next part of your warm-up should be to start hitting golf balls. Most recreational golfers focus on the long clubs when they first hit balls, but they should use the shorter clubs first, such as a sand wedge or pitching wedge. Short clubs require the use of more arm and shoulder muscles, which allows gradual and effective warming up of the back and hips as the transition is made to the longer clubs. You should hit at least five balls with a club before proceeding to the next (longer) club.

Phase 4: Continue Your Warm-up on the Tee Box

Continue your warm-up routine on the first tee box so that you don't cool down. It does more harm than good to go through a scientific warm-up on the driving range, only to lose the benefits of the warm-up in the ten minutes before your group tees off by standing around and getting cold. You can actually cool down enough in those 10 minutes to increase your risk of injury. Additionally, you won't score to your potential until four or more holes into your round. On the tee box and after the break at the 9th hole you should go through the dynamic warm-up routine described in the Training Programs chapter.

The first phase of a warm-up should focus on general dynamic movement activity, such as calisthenics. Dynamic, active movements are the key in the first phase of a warm-up.

The next part of your warm-up should be to start hitting golf balls.

Golf Injuries

Like other sports, golf produces its share of sprains, strains and muscle tears. A strain is a mild tear in a muscle, ligament or tendon, whereas a sprain is a more severe tear in a muscle, ligament or tendon. Most of the injuries caused by golf to the back, knees and shoulders are soft-tissue injuries, which means something other than bone is injured. Rarely are bones broken in golf.

The best way to deal with soft-tissue injuries is to prevent them in the first place. A proper conditioning program, along with the other tips in this book, can prevent many injuries. Overuse injuries, which are caused by repeated motions, are best prevented with strength training and developing assisting and opposing muscle groups. Many sprains and tears are the result of lack of strength in both key and opposing muscle groups.

Specific Areas of Injury Concern

Feet

If your feet can't maintain stable contact and balance, then your golf swing won't be powerful, efficient and consistent.

Golf is a game of balance, and the physical force you generate depends on your feet making consistent and solid contact with the ground. If your feet can't maintain a stable platform, then your golf swing won't be powerful, efficient and consistent. Any force you generate with the upper body, trunk or legs will be wasted if you're not secured to the ground.

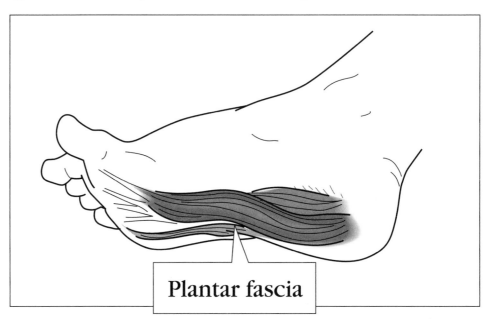

Plantar fascia

One of the most common injuries in golf is *plantar fasciitis*. A tendon-like structure, the *plantar fascia* extends along the bottom of your foot from the heel to just behind the toes. Think of your foot as a bow and the plantar fascia as the bow's string. The tension it generates helps the foot to push and also supports the foot so it doesn't roll to the inside (pronation) excessively during sports.

Almost 75% of all golfers pronate during golf and other activities. This means that, because of poor foot support, most people are targets for plantar fasciitis at some time in their athletic careers. Plantar fasciitis most often causes a tear close to the heel bone, hence the term "heel spur." The tear or subsequent spur is just slightly in front of the heel. The causes of this injury include having a rigid foot or a tight Achilles tendon and pronating excessively during activity. Improper arch and foot support in golf shoes is one of the causes of this irritation, and improperly fitted shoes (either too long, too short or too tight) contribute to the problem, as do worn-out shoes. Given the stress golf shoes take with each shot, they should be replaced yearly if not more often.

After-market insole replacements are both a performance and injury prevention tool because of their ability to increase foot support.

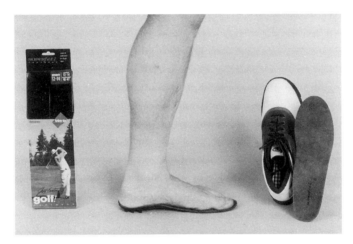

Plantar fasciitis doesn't show up during a round of golf but rather when you get up in the morning. It begins with a sharp pain on the bottom of the foot that goes away after about five or more minutes of movement. It generally starts as a minor ache and will intensify by the day until it is attended to.

If you get this type of injury, the first step is to rest and apply ice to the bottom of the foot. In addition, anti-inflammatory medication can aid the healing process. After the pain subsides, gently stretching the Achilles tendon will increase flexibility. You should be able to return to walking more of the course gradually as the pain subsides. You may also want to consider adding a custom insole to your golf shoe. Given the fact that most golf-shoe insoles do not give proper balance, comfort and support, investing in a custom insole or sport footbed is an excellent preventive measure.

Insoles come in two varieties: Those made by a podiatrist are called "orthotics," and "footbeds" are insoles not made by a podiatrist. Orthotics can be of a hard material, like plastic, or of softer material, like cork. A well-made insole will help support your foot and increase comfort and performance. In addition, custom insoles can help alleviate back problems because the stability they provide will make your swing more effective and efficient. A rigid orthotic requires a medical prescription and is both expensive and time-consuming to make. Most golfers would be well-served with a scientifically designed replacement footbed, which will be a substantial improvement over the insoles in most golf shoes.

A well-made insole will help support your foot and increase comfort and performance.

Backs

Low back pain affects over 80 million Americans every year and is the most common injury in golf. Even if you have a great swing you risk back injury because the swing uses the back for support and leverage. During the swing, the back is rotating along its own axis, which stretches ligaments and muscles. As you continue to the end point of your swing, your spine, shoulders and hips store a tremendous amount of muscular energy.

Training the erector spinae through exercises such as back raises will help strengthen the ligaments of the back.

In golf, your back is subject to major physical forces occurring in relatively short succession, including compression, rotation, and lateral bending along an axis (the length of the spine). Because of these forces, golfers are often subject to muscular strains and herniated disks. In one movement performed in a relatively short period of time you are asking your back to change position, resist torque and compress, as well as rotate along its own axis. In addition, the spine has limited range of motion at any given point because of the construction of the vertebrae, related ligaments and discs. Individually, each vertebra can move only slightly in any direction. The discs in the spine, which resemble small automobile tires, cushion each vertebra and allow for the limited movement.

Because the back takes the most stress as your hips rotate in the swing, most golfers' back injuries occur at the lower, or lumbar, region of the spine. It's important to note that a number of ailments, from stress reactions to kidney disease, can show up as back pain. It's important to have recurring back pain checked by a doctor.

Because the back takes the most stress as your hips rotate in the swing, most golfers' back injuries occur at the lower, or lumbar, region of the spine.

Prevention is the best remedy for back injuries. Your need for prevention is increased not only because of golf but also because of the stresses life places on your back. Most people have poor posture, don't get enough trunk exercise, and sit at a desk for a living. Even a minor back injury caused by golf can be very painful when combined with these other factors. In this sense, back problems can be cumulative: Although none of the aforementioned stresses, including golf, by itself may be enough to cause back pain or a back injury, add them together and you can develop or aggravate a back injury.

Improving golf swing mechanics is the first step in alleviating golf-related back pain. After that, the next best remedies are a regular strengthening and stretching program. Remember, few golf athletes have ever developed the strength or flexibility needed for golf just by playing golf. If they could, then the swings exhibited by senior amateur golfers would be mechanically similar to those of younger golfers.

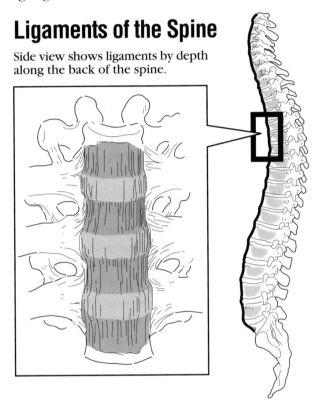

Ligaments of the Spine

Side view shows ligaments by depth along the back of the spine.

The back muscles themselves are only part of the answer to reducing your risk of back injury from golf. The hamstrings, a prime group targeted in the prevention of knee injuries, are important in reducing back pain and lessening the chance of injuries. Because the hamstrings connect to the pelvis, their lack of strength in most cases causes inflexibility, which in turn rotates the pelvis backward, changing the angle of the spine. When this happens, more stress is placed on the back. This is especially true in the rotational or twisting movements in golf. Performing hamstring strengthening exercises at least once a week is essential to low-back maintenance. Because the spine is a column that moves in a number of directions, you have to strengthen the major muscles, including the abdominals (front), erector spinae (back), and obliques (sides). Choose at least one exercise for each area to be performed with your other regular exercise sessions, and once a week during the golf season.

Strengthening the trunk muscles is as important as stretching them. Use the body-weight-resistance exercises for the trunk region demonstrated in the Resistance Training Exercises chapter to begin.

Because the hamstrings connect to the pelvis, their lack of strength in most cases causes inflexibility, which in turn rotates the pelvis backward, changing the angle of the spine.

The golf swing is dependent on proper functioning of the spine, which requires both strength and flexibility.

Your hips and their major muscles connect to the pelvic girdle, which is connected to the spine. Thus, hip strength and range of motion in a number of directions is also essential for proper golf mechanics. Without hip strength, you have one more weak link that can add to back stress during golf. Slide board training is an excellent way to develop hip strength and endurance.

Flexibility for the spine and trunk is sensitive, because too much flexibility training can potentially loosen the ligaments of the spine. Yet with too little flexibility you can't turn the spine properly and will increase stress on the shoulders and hips. In isolating stretches needed for the trunk area, strive to use static, or reach-and-hold, methods to reduce the risk of further injury. Use the stretches demonstrated in the flexibility exercises chapter on a daily basis, at least for back extension and rotation.

Proper mechanics during lifting and bending movements also will reduce your chances of back injury. When removing your bag from the car, place one leg on the bumper or step and use that as a brace to lift the bag to your waist, or your center of gravity. Avoid bending over the trunk and lifting the bag out in an extended position. Instead of bending over on the course to pick up your ball, use one leg as an axis point. Rotate around your hip, and use a golf club as a balance point if necessary with the other arm. By letting your upper body go forward as the other leg moves backward for balance, you will shift the axis point to the hip, and not the back.

Finally, losing weight if you are overweight may be one of the best ways to lower your risk of back problems. Excessive weight, especially for men, tends to be deposited in the stomach area. A "pot belly" causes the back to arch backward significantly, forcing movement that causes further muscular imbalances. The result: You place extra stress on discs and support structures.

Shoulders

Golf is a unique sport because of the range of motion the shoulders need during the swing. The rotator cuff muscles and their surrounding tendons are subject to a number of injuries. These muscles are not only active in the golf swing, but they are stabilizers in just about every movement involving the shoulders. They help lock the shoulder joint to allow other muscle groups to work, and they move the shoulder joint and arms as well.

Golfers over the age of 60 tend to lose significant strength and support in this area, so it is no wonder that shoulder injuries are a prime concern for older golfers. Common injuries to this area involve bursitis (the irritation of the bursa sac, a cushioning mechanism) and tendinitis (inflammation and irritation of the tendons). You also can irritate or tear the muscles of the rotator cuff as well as irritate and tear the attachment to the bones.

Shoulder Injury Prevention Strategies

- General rotator cuff strengthening
- Specific external rotator strengthening (rear of shoulder)
- Stretching internal rotators (chest, front of shoulders)

Strategies for the reduction of shoulder injuries in golf involve both resistance training and stretching.

Strong rotator cuff muscles are the key to preventing and rehabilitating injuries in this area. This requires specific exercises. Any time you perform a chest or back exercise, especially those that use the pectorals, anterior deltoid and teres major (or those rotator cuff muscles that rotate the shoulder internally), you must counterbalance with the rotator cuff muscles that rotate the shoulder externally (teres minor and infraspinatus).

In many cases, the external rotator cuff muscles, the infraspinatus and the teres minor, are much weaker than the internal rotator cuff muscles. Most golf athletes tend to perform more pushing or pressing exercises, such as the bench press, rather than pulling exercises, such as bent rows. This means they become even more out of balance. With all this in mind, the best ways to prevent golf injuries to the shoulders are to:
- Develop a pre-season exercise routine that stresses the rotator cuff group.
- Perform stretches for the chest/anterior deltoid area on a regular basis because the internal rotators get overly strong and therefore overly tight.
- Spend extra time strengthening the external rotators through exercises such as bent rows with external rotation, side-lying flyes, side-lying L-flyes and rear deltoid raises.
- Perform 2 sets of external rotation exercises that involve a pulling movement for every pressing movement.

Strong rotator cuff muscles are the key to preventing and rehabilitating injuries in this area.

Knees
The rotational movements of golf, which the knee joints are not designed to withstand, are a contributing cause of knee injuries. Although the leg muscles of the front and back of the thigh don't generate most of the power for hip turn in the swing, they *are* essential and are used during the golf stance. Knee injuries occur in the non-target or back leg because it takes the weight shift, then helps transfer the body forward during the swing.

The knee joint is not like the ball-and-socket joint of the hip and is dependent on the support of ligaments and tendons. When bent, the knee joint is less stable. The ligaments and tendons around the knee can suffer strains and

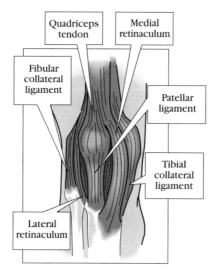

Anterior view

Knee stability is dependent on gaining strength in the ligaments and tendons, which is improved through resistance training.

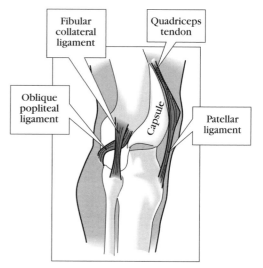

Lateral view

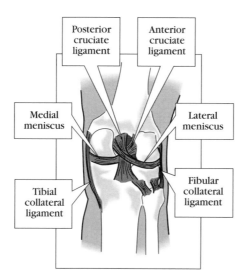

Posterior view

sprains, as well as tear completely during a mis-hit, an off-balance shot or by slipping on wet grass. Lack of ligament strength and support can contribute to cartilage tears.

Strengthening your legs is probably your prime defense against knee injuries in golf. Resistance training over time will improve the strength of the ligaments and tendons. However, these tissues grow much slower than muscle because they have a greatly reduced blood supply compared to muscle. This is an important reason for beginning and continuing resistance training, especially when you get older, when there is a natural tendency for these tissues to lose strength and elasticity.

The backs of the knees are a major area of concern, because if you tear or injure this area, it could keep you from golf for up to a year. The back of the knee is supported by the cruciate ligaments and the tendons from the biceps femoris, or hamstring group. In contrast, the front and sides of the knee are stronger in ligament and tendon strength. This is why in forward movements, where there can be a stop-and-start component as in basketball, the cruciate ligaments are strained or torn. The back of the knee simply doesn't have the natural stability to keep the joint together in these movements.

Resistance training over time will improve the strength of the ligaments and tendons.

Leg curls are a cornerstone of an injury prevention program using resistance training.

Early research demonstrated that if the hamstring group is at least 70% as strong as the quadriceps group, there is a decreased chance of hamstring injuries. This means that if you can lift 100 pounds in a leg extension with the quadriceps, then a leg curl motion using the hamstrings should lift at least 70 pounds. Although this is not a guarantee against a torn cruciate or knee instability, it is still good prevention strategy.

Unfortunately, few exercises strengthen the hamstring group, whereas many daily activities such as walking strengthen the quadriceps group. The result is that, without supplemental training, the quadriceps group gains strength over the hamstring group with normal activity. One of the few activities that would build the hamstring group, if you can perform it enough, is walking uphill, which places more emphasis on the hamstrings. Some major exercises such as lunges and dead lifts can improve hamstring strength, but attendant orthopedic problems such as low back pain can make these impractical. Strive to include at least 3 sets of hamstring exercises, such as leg curls, per leg training session, and at least once per week in the golf season.

Research demonstrated that if the hamstring group is at least 70% as strong as the quadriceps group, there is a decreased chance of hamstring injuries.

Golfers do get "tennis
elbow," which is
essentially a strain to
the tendon on the
outside of the elbow.

Wrist and Elbow Injuries

If you hit the ball improperly or have poor body mechanics, the body parts taking most of the shock will be the wrists and the elbows. Any time there is acceleration and deceleration of the arm as in golf, there is a greater potential for injury. Wrist and elbow injuries are a top concern for golfers, and elbow injuries are the #1 problem for women golfers.

Even though the average golf ball weighs 45.5 grams, when your club strikes the ball at almost maximum velocity, that's still a great amount of force bearing on your arm and wrist joints. These joints have to move from one position at the top of your backswing to another at impact. Generally this is with both arms fully extended, with the wrists "snapping" or following through over the target shoulder. The majority of elbow and wrist problems are impact injuries, and even though they occur more on the target side, they easily can occur on the other side as well.

Golfers do get "tennis elbow," which is essentially a strain to the tendon on the outside of the elbow. "Thrower's elbow," a strain to the tendon on the inside of the elbow, is more rare. Tennis elbow occurs in golfers for two reasons: weak forearm muscles and less than full extension at impact. Over time, these will over-stress the elbow area. In women, a general lack of sports experience and experience with resistance training leaves their elbow areas vulnerable to injury. Women golfers often don't have enough arm strength to fully extend the club properly during the takeaway, which contributes to poor swing mechanics.

Wrist injuries in golf are similar to elbow injuries in that impact and poor body mechanics can contribute to strains and sprains. Like elbow injuries, lack of strength in the forearm muscles is a factor in wrist injuries. Poor wrist flexibility is also a secondary cause and results from both a lack of strength and flexibility.

Exercises such as
reverse triceps extensions
or press-downs and
reverse wrist curls are
useful in preventing
wrist and elbow injuries.

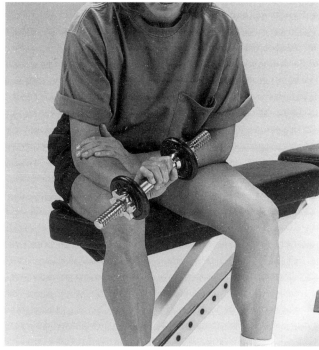

The first steps in handling elbow or wrist injuries is to take a break from golf and to apply ice and use anti-inflammatory medication. After the pain and swelling subside, a common step with cases of tennis elbow is to strengthen the forearm muscles with the arm fully extended. This takes some of the strain off the affected tendon as well as makes you conscious of straightening the arm as much as possible in the swing. Gripping exercises (squeezing a ball, dumbbell wrist flexion and extension) are recommended because they strengthen the affected muscles and tendon. Make sure your triceps are strong with some type of weekly triceps exercise such as extensions or press-downs.

The prevention of wrist injuries should follow the same type of strengthening activities yet also add flexibility. Start with exercises such as wrist curls and reverse wrist curls (see the chapter detailing resistance training exercises). Remember, the wrists and forearms respond better to more frequent training, so you should try to exercise them 2 or 3 days a week if they are problem areas. For stretching, use the wrist flexion and extension stretches in the chapter detailing flexibility exercises.

Wrist and hand injuries are aggravated by gripping the club too tightly, then impacting an object or piece of hard ground. Gripping the club lighter is one answer, as well as increasing hand and forearm strength. However, if your hands are wet, or the conditions are humid, then you will have a tendency to grip the club with more force. This significantly raises injury potential, decreases swing consistency and causes a loss in distance and accuracy. If you are one of the many golfers who suffers from sweaty palms, then use one of the antiperspirant lotion products designed especially for hands. These lotions will allow you to grip the club lighter, which significantly increases performance and lessens the chance of injury.

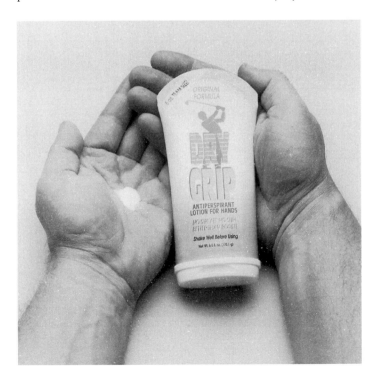

Anti-perspirant hand lotions can decrease the amount of grip pressure needed to overcome sweaty or humid conditions.

When You Are Hurt

The first step is to seek medical attention even if you think an injury is a recurrence of one you had last golf season. This is generally the time to quit playing golf, possibly take a break from all activity, and rest the affected joint. Right after an injury, use the RICEEE method:

- **Rest.** Take a break from activity using the affected joint.

- **Ice.** Place ice on the injury for 20 or more minutes, 2+ different times per day.

- **Compression.** Apply light compression to the area with an elastic bandage.

- **Elevation.** Raise the affected joint to help reduce swelling.

- **Evaluation.** Seek evaluation from a sports medicine physician or other qualified professional.

- **Exercise.** Continue to exercise the other muscles in the body, especially in the case of arm or leg injuries. Exercising the unaffected limb actually imparts a training effect to the injured limb.

The greatest amount of swelling in injuries occurs in the first 3 days. The chances are that you have broken some blood vessels, which prevents your body from draining fluid effectively. Once swelling and pain have subsided and you have medical clearance, a commonly prescribed regimen is to lightly exercise the affected area, gradually building strength and flexibility. This is also the time where anti-inflammatory medication and ice will provide tremendous benefit.

It's generally best to return to golf only when the muscle group or joint in question has full capability. In most sport injury situations, full capacity involves range of motion, strength, and endurance in the affected area. If you try to come back too soon and the muscle group or joint isn't ready, you will change your body mechanics by compensating with other muscle groups. The result could be a worse injury than the one you started with.

Injury Armor KEY POINTS

- Golf injuries are common to feet, back, shoulders, knees, wrists and elbows.

- A good warm-up before play can significantly reduce your chances of injury and should include calisthenics, movement-based stretching, and static stretching if you have time.

- You should begin hitting golf balls only after you've sufficiently warmed up with other movements.

- Most injuries in golf include sprains, strains, and tears of ligaments, tendons and muscles, which in many cases are preventable.

- Proper golf swing mechanics will decrease the chances of some types of injury.

- Foot injuries hurt golf performance because of the relationship between foot stability and effective swing mechanics.

- Relieving plantar fasciitis is a matter of stretching, rest and, in many cases, adding a footbed or orthotic to golf shoes for support.

- The best prevention for back injuries is a daily strengthening and stretching program for all muscle groups in the trunk.

- Preventing shoulder injuries involves stretching the internal rotators (pectorals and anterior deltoids) while strengthening the external rotators (teres minor and infraspinatus).

- The stability of the knee joint can be enhanced with exercises such as leg curls and leg extensions, which will strengthen the ligaments that support the knee.

- For both back and knee injury prevention, hamstring strengthening is essential.

- Wrist and elbow injuries stem from impact, with contributing factors of lack of strength and flexibility as well as poor swing mechanics.

- Strengthening the wrist and forearm muscles on a regular basis is important because they are critical in golf yet remain untrained through normal activity.

References

Arendt, E. and R. Dick. 1995. Knee injury patterns among men and women in collegiate basketball and soccer. NCAA data and review of literature. *American Journal of Sports Medicine* 23(6):694-701.

Arnold, J.A. et al. 1979. Natural history of anterior cruciate tears. *American Journal of Sports Medicine* 7:305-313.

Batt, M.E. 1992. A survey of golf injuries in amateur golfers. *British Journal of Sports Medicine* 26(1):63-65.

Brendecke, P. 1990. Golf injuries. *Sports Medicine Digest* 12(4):1-2.

Buchan, J.F. 1990. Golf injuries: Treatment and prevention. In S.D.W. Payne, ed., *Medicine, Sport and the Law*. Oxford: Blackwell Scientific Publications.

Callahan, M.P., C.R. Denegar, and C.A. Segree. 1993. The effects of vacuum-molded orthotics on lower extremity overuse injuries. *Journal of Sport Rehabilitation* 2(4):251-260.

Craton, N., and D.C. McKenzie. 1993. Orthotics in injury prevention. In P.A.F.H. Renstroem, ed., *Sports Injuries: Basic Principles of Prevention and Care*. Boston: Blackwell Scientific Publications.

Cunningham, C. 1993. Golf injuries: Common sites of involvement and possible mechanisms. *Sport Health* 11(4):18-20.

Duda, M. 1987. Golf injuries: They really do happen. *The Physician and Sportsmedicine* 15(7):190-192, 194-196.

Gerbino, P.G., and L.J. Micheli. 1995. Back injuries in the young athlete. *Clinics in Sports Medicine* 14(3):571-590.

Glazebrook, M.A., S. Curwin, M.N. Islam, J. Kozey, and W.D. Stanish. 1994. Medial epicondylitis: An electromyographic analysis and an investigation of intervention strategies. *Journal of Sports Medicine* 22(5):674-675.

Halle, J.S., R.J. Franklin, and B.L. Karafala. 1986. Comparison of four treatment approaches for lateral epicondylitis of the elbow. *Journal of Orthopedic Sports Physical Therapy* 8(2):62-68.

Harris, N. 1992. Preventing golf injuries through exercise. *Sideline View* 13(10):1-4.

Hosea, T.M., and C.J. Gatt. 1996. Back pain in golf. *Clinics in Sports Medicine* 15(1):37-53.

Hubley-Kozey, C.L., and W.D. Standish. 1984. Can stretching prevent athletic injuries? *Journal of Musculoskeletal Medicine* 1(9):25-32.

Kohn, H.S. 1996. Prevention and treatment of elbow injuries in golf. *Clinics in Sports Medicine* 15(1):65-83.

Liemohn, W. 1978. Factors related to hamstring strains. *The Journal of Sports Medicine and Physical Fitness* 18(1):71-75.

Mallon, B. 1996. *The Golf Doctor.* New York: MacMillan.

McCarroll, J.R. 1996. The frequency of golf injuries. *Clinics in Sports Medicine* 15(1):1-7.

McCarroll, J.R., A.C. Rettig, and K.D. Shelbourne. 1990. Injuries in the amateur golfer. *The Physician and Sportsmedicine* 18(3):122-126.

McFarlane, B. 1987. Warm-up Design Patterns. *National Strength and Conditioning Association Journal* 9(4):22-29.

McGregor, R.R., and S.E. Devereux. 1982. *EEVeTec.* Boston: Houghton Mifflin Company.

Murray, P.M., and W.P. Cooney. 1996. Golf-induced injuries of the wrist. *Clinics in Sports Medicine* 15(1):85-109.

Nicholas, J.A., and E.B. Hershman. 1990. *The Upper Extremity in Sportsmedicine.* St. Louis, MO: Mosby.

Schenk, R. 1995. Prevent low back injury with the prone pressup. *Strength and Conditioning* 17(4):32-33.

Tanner, S., and J. Harvey. 1988. How we manage plantar fasciitis. *Physician and Sportsmedicine* 16:39-48.

Voss, M.W. 1983. Golf injuries. *Sportsmedicine Digest* 5(7):1-2.

Wallace, L. 1988. Foot pronation and knee pain. In R. Mangine, ed., *Physical Therapy of the Knee.* New York: Churchill Livingstone.

Williams, K.R., and P.R. Cavanagh. 1983. Mechanics of foot action during the golf swing and implications for shoe design. *Medicine and Science in Sports and Exercise* 15(3):247-255.

Williams, P. 1974. *Low Back and Neck Pain.* Springfield, IL: Charles C. Thomas.

Wysocki, R.J. 1989. Bowling and golf injuries. In S.I. Subotnick, ed., *Sports Medicine of the Lower Extremity.* New York: Churchill Livingstone.

It's All in the Mind

Life tends to get in the way of a regular exercise program. Some golfers find that the desire to play an extra round can be just one more excuse to avoid working out. When it's nice outside and golf season is in full swing, you'll want to hit balls rather than lift weights or stretch. For many golf athletes, sticking to an exercise program is tougher than scoring an eagle. Yet resistance training and cardiovascular conditioning are important to both golf performance and health, and you can't expect to benefit from a program if you don't stick with it.

The body simply doesn't remember what you did 2 months ago, let alone 2 weeks ago. High-level fitness must be maintained or it is lost. For example, elite marathon runners start going downhill in their aerobic fitness levels within a few days of halting training. Likewise, the average golfer must maintain aerobic fitness, strength, and flexibility away from the course. And by now it should be clear that playing golf will not in itself maintain your hard-earned fitness. The reality is that you need constant motivation to start and maintain your golf fitness regimen.

The reality is that you need constant motivation to start and maintain your golf fitness regimen.

A Motivating Foundation

Motivation is the psychological spark behind everything you do. Have you ever noticed that it's easy to motivate yourself for certain tasks yet quite difficult to get others accomplished? This is why making lifestyle changes is tough. And sticking with exercise to improve your golf game is just as difficult and challenging as it is to make any other changes in personal habits. In the same way that a planning book is a useful tool to help you organize your schedule, exercise is a facilitator — a tool to help you reach a goal. In this case the goal is becoming a better golfer. You've got to wholeheartedly accept your exercise routines as useful tools, or you'll quit. If you are serious about your golf game, you'll find ways to stick with it and make exercise a habit. The more exercise becomes a habit, the better your golf game will be!

Commitment to Change, *Not* More Information

Once you have decided to exercise, sticking with it over the long term is the next challenge. "Exercise adherence" is the technical term for complying with, or sticking with, an exercise program. Some of the research on this process indicates that adherence is not a matter of information or intelligence. In other words, understanding the relationship of fitness to improved golf performance does not significantly increase the likelihood you'll still be exercising for golf a year from now. The reams of information now available that link unhealthy lifestyle choices (especially lack of exercise and poor nutritional habits) to heart disease hasn't spurred many people to work out. If information was the answer, we'd all be exercising up a storm—and we're not. The key is to choose to change personal habits.

Chances are that if you're reading this book you've made the decision to start an exercise program. Deciding to exercise and choosing specific forms of exercise are important steps in the change process. The next step is overcoming all the barriers (real or perceived) to transforming your intentions into habit. Some of the barriers to golf exercise include time constraints, the availability of a nearby fitness facility, the availability of exercise experts and trainers, conflicts with golf practice time, and lack of encouragement. It's sometimes difficult to separate excuses from reasons, isn't it?

Goal Setting as the First Step

If you want to turn that interest in exercise into action, start with goal setting. You don't have to run a Fortune 500 company to set goals; you just need to know what you want. Goal setting translates what you want to do into easy, clearly defined steps. For example, your goal could be to add distance to drives. That could entail adding more hip strength, more shoulder flexibility, and developing a good warm-up routine.

The best thing about setting goals is that it makes you think about what you really want to accomplish. Thinking about your goals helps clarify your life priorities. And that's useful no matter what your level of commitment or past experience, because people are motivated where their priorities are concerned. As you think things over, you'll be able to pinpoint your real golf priorities, and your natural motivation will help you overcome any obstacles to realizing them.

Goal setting should start with long-term objectives, which then form the basis for intermediate goals. The long-term objective simply provides the focus for short-term and intermediate goals. These are your goals for the next six months. For example, to "play to a 9 handicap in two years" might be a reasonable goal, but what do you do to reach that goal? This is where secondary goals enter the picture. Playing to a 9 handicap probably will require building additional strength and flexibility and then maintaining those improvements with in-season conditioning. The secondary goals break down long-term goals into clear steps that can be acted upon.

The goal-setting process also will help you refine your goals so that they are attainable, rather than so far out of reach that you'll be disappointed. You

---

Some of the research on this process indicates that adherence is not a matter of information or intelligence. The key is to choose to change personal habits.

Goal setting should start with long-term objectives, which then form the basis for intermediate goals.

might decide that the time it will take to train for the 9 handicap is not realistic, so you readjust your goal for a 12 or 14 handicap. There's nothing wrong with readjusting long-term goals. In fact, this is a natural part of the goal-setting process. Even the best goal-setting plans should be updated every 3 months or so. High-level achievers say that life circumstances such as schedule, job or family situations often force them to change their goals. That's okay, and it's part of the process. Priorities do change.

Goals: Realistic, Specific and Measurable

Goals should be realistic and reflect what you are able to accomplish. They should also be specific and measurable. For instance, you might decide to perform 3 sets of key weight-training exercises for maintenance of shoulders, back, trunk and legs for 30 minutes on Mondays. You may set a long-term golf goal of gaining consistency. You may then decide that additional flexibility is necessary to improve your consistency, so you plan to stretch every other day in the off-season using three stretching exercises each for your shoulders and legs. You have just upped your chances for success because you converted a long-term goal into specific and measurable short-term action.

When starting or adding to an exercise program, mentally allow yourself less than full compliance with your target exercise routine. This will give you some latitude when everyday life affects your training and golf plans. To be flexible, your goals need to reflect what you hope to accomplish over 3 or 4 weeks. Focus on the process, not on short-term success or failure. Sticking to

> **Focus on the process, not on short-term success or failure.**

Goal Setting

Long-term   *Lower handicap to 9*

Intermediate

1. *Improve strength by 20% in one year.*

2. *Improve flexibility in hamstrings.*

3. *Maintain aerobic endurance.*

Short-term

1a. Perform resistance training 3 times per week, 24+ exercises per session off-season.

1b. Perform resistance training 2 times per week, 24+ exercises per session, in season.

1c. Increase hamstring strength via leg curls, 3 times per week off season.

2a. Stretch hamstrings daily after golf and exercise.

3a. Treadmill walk at grade in-season 1 time per week, 30 minutes with target heart rate at normal aerobic levels.

3b. Recumbent cycling 1 time per week, 40 minutes with target heart rate at normal aerobic levels.

Example of a goal-setting chart that can be used to plan physical and mental training for improving golf performance.

the process is what leads to accomplishing your goals for golf fitness. Averaging the number of golf training sessions over three or four weeks gives you the latitude to add or subtract exercise in any given week without feeling guilty or less inspired.

Lower Your Own Expectations

Combining golf and physical training for golf is a balancing act yet can be done.

If training for golf is your first experience with exercise, or if you are beginning an exercise program again after an inactive period, lower your goals a notch. One of your goals should be to establish exercise as a habit, even if it's a small habit — you might not be able to exercise every single day. You can always increase the amount of time you spend exercising once it's become a regular part of your schedule. By tailoring your goals to fit your circumstances, you'll increase motivation and sustain drive. As a result, it will be easier to start and maintain your ideal golf training program.

Sticking with the Program

Learn to make exercise a part of your daily life if you really want to improve your golf game. This is what exercise psychologists call the "adoption phase." It's probably the most difficult part of establishing an exercise program. Most people have so much going on in their lives that thinking about adding exercise can be overwhelming. To circumvent this, learn to see exercise as a stress-reducer as well as a golf-performance tool.

It's best to set a regular time for exercise in order to take advantage of its stress-reducing qualities. And because establishing new habits is not always easy, allow for a certain amount of difficulty. Most golf exercisers make three attempts at establishing an exercise program before discovering the pattern that works best for them. It's all part of the process of discovering how exercise can fit best in your life.

Once you've adopted an exercise routine that's best for your golf game and your lifestyle, focus on maintaining the regimen. The same things that helped you begin and refine your program also can be used to provide ongoing motivation. Goal setting definitely helps because you focus on specific factors contributing to your success. And because exercising regularly is a new experience for many golfers, it's necessary to consider the connection between training, golf performance, and quality of life. Link the outcomes you desire with the specific actions or exercises you have planned and you will enhance your own motivation. Think specifically about the toughest hole on your home golf course: How will more endurance, strength and flexibility lower your average score on that hole? Would you have won the club championship if you had had more aerobic endurance and energy over the last 6 holes?

Record Keeping: Tangible Reinforcement

One of the most effective ways to stay motivated is to keep records of your progress. The process of simply logging what you did each day and noting progress will form a basis for new, desirable habits. If you start with 5 pounds in dumbbell bicep curls and progress to 25 pounds, your self-confidence and motivation will increase.

Remember, exercise is physical: You can see your progress in pounds lifted or calories burned. This is a powerful motivator and reinforcer. That's why resistance training is so popular among athletes in a wide variety of sports. The tangible gains in the weight room lead to increased self-confidence in all aspects of life, both inside and outside the gym. And resistance training results in self-confidence gains more often than does aerobic activity or flexibility training. Record keeping is "proof," a daily reminder of what you've accomplished. Most athletic clubs have forms for recording weight-training progress. If you train at home, use a spiral notebook to record your workouts, or use the form at the end of this book.

Timing Is Everything

If you want to be successful, set a fixed time for your exercise regime. Although there is no best time to exercise, there is a best time for you. Finding it will decrease your stress and improve your overall performance. Why? It's simple: You'll be more focused. Your best time to exercise depends on your work schedule, psychological makeup, and the availability of facilities. Pick a time when you're the least distracted. For many people this is first thing in the morning, before business and social obligations intrude. Some people prefer to work out at noon or after work. The most important thing is to stick with a specific time, during golf season and after.

Set up Your Environment for Success

The exercise environment is important, especially for new exercisers. This applies to people who work out at fitness facilities as well as those who exercise at home. If you will be using a facility, pick one where you feel comfortable, where the employees' attitudes toward exercise seem in sync with your own. Golf is not bodybuilding, so the gym where Mr. Universe works out may

One of the most effective ways to stay motivated is to keep records of your progress.

The tangible gains in the weight room lead to increased self-confidence in all aspects of life, both inside and outside the gym.

Because of the time requirements of golf, in addition to time spent traveling to and from the gym, exercising at home — if it's possible — makes the most sense for most golf athletes.

not be the best place for you to work on improving golf fitness. To be successful, you've got to feel comfortable with the facility, its staff and its programming. Look for the following when choosing a fitness facility:

- Fitness staffers who have formal training (a four-year degree) in exercise science, cardiopulmonary resuscitation training (CPR), and appropriate certifications from nonprofit educational certifying organizations, including the National Strength and Conditioning Association (NSCA), the American College of Sports Medicine (ACSM), and the American Council on Exercise (ACE).
- Staffers who are sympathetic to your golf fitness goals and who don't seek to convert you to their personal fitness agenda or routine.
- State-of-the-art equipment and machines that are scrupulously maintained and cleaned.
- Month-to-month memberships so you can go elsewhere if you change your mind.

If you exercise at home, spend time to lay out your exercise area or room conveniently. Place some golf posters or pictures in strategic locations. Don't set your equipment permanently right away. Instead, during the first few weeks experiment and adjust the layout. A pleasing and functional home environment will make exercise easier. Pictures and posters not only motivate you but will serve as a constant reminder of the link between physical conditioning and performance. Because of the time requirements of golf, in addition to time spent traveling to and from the gym, exercising at home — if it's possible — makes the most sense for most golf athletes. When setting up your home exercise area, remember:

- Integrate equipment like stereos, radios, televisions or headsets to help make the time pass pleasantly.
- Include a stretching area with mat so you will get in the habit of stretching after exercise.
- Don't skimp on equipment: Make sure you have as many quality tools as you can afford.
- Consider a separate exercise room if you have more than one piece of exercise equipment.

Why People Fail in Exercise Programs

The biggest reason for failure is underestimating the commitment needed to change behavior.

There are a number of reasons why people abandon their exercise routines. Understanding those reasons ahead of time will help you design a better program for golf, a system that helps you work out consistently. The biggest reason for failure is underestimating the commitment needed to change behavior. The process generally takes more time than most people anticipate, and when that becomes obvious, many people stop.

For most golf athletes, the toughest thing is to maintain in-season programs. Golf is physically and mentally taxing, and it's tough to make the time for physical maintenance while you're practicing and playing. Most golf athletes find off-season training is easier because they can't play much golf. Even if you work out only one or two days per week, establishing an in-season routine is important. You can always add time later in the golf season once the exercise habit is set.

Try and Try Again

It usually takes some trial and error before most golfers are able to make exercise a lifelong habit. But remember, this is a natural part of the change process. Relapsing does not mean you won't ultimately be successful. It simply means you'll have the information to help you discover why you weren't successful the first time. A lapse is simply a temporary interruption, and if viewed as such it won't prevent you from establishing exercise as a habit.

The golf culture abounds in stories of people who, in their first quest for a major victory, erred in preparation, physical training or mental execution. They viewed these failures as learning experiences. They made changes and came back to win the next time. Take this long-term perspective with your golf exercise and not only will you relax, you'll reach your goals.

Positive results are the best motivators in the world. Two areas you should focus on as you work to achieve positive results are score improvement and enhanced well-being. Sticking with your program long enough to see these results in your golf game and your life will produce the motivation that will keep you going.

A lapse is simply a temporary interruption, and if viewed as such it won't prevent you from establishing exercise as a habit.

It's All in the Mind KEY POINTS

• As you improve physically, especially in areas such as resistance training, expect a corresponding boost in self-confidence.

• Discover your best time of day to exercise and plan your program around it.

• Set goals. They will help you determine a plan of action, which will make it easier for you to exercise.

• In setting goals for exercise, plan a realistic number of exercise sessions averaged over three or more weeks. This technique provides the psychological latitude that will be necessary if you need to rebound from a day or week when events interfere with your workouts.

• Determine whether you prefer working out at home or in a gym.

• Keep in mind that it usually takes more discipline to exercise at home, whereas it takes more time to work out in a facility.

• Keep an exercise log. It will motivate you and elevate your self-confidence from tee to green.

• Analyze successful experiences in your life to help you understand what motivates you and to give you ideas on how to integrate golf exercise into your daily life.

• Some exercise is better than no exercise, so find things to do that you enjoy and will perform with regularity.

• Remember that a partial workout on a hectic day reinforces your psychological resolve and has some fitness benefits.

References

Ajzen, I., and M. Fishbein. 1980. *Understanding Attitudes and Predicting Social Behavior.* Englewood Cliffs, NJ: Prentice-Hall.

Dishman, R., ed. 1988. *Exercise Adherence.* Champaign, IL: Human Kinetics.

Emery, C.F., E.R. Hauck, and J.A. Blumenthal. 1992. Exercise adherence or maintenance among older adults: one-year follow-up study. *Psychology of Aging* 7:466,470.

Glasser, W. 1976. *Positive Addiction.* New York: Harper & Row.

Martin, J.E., and P.M. Dubbert. 1984. Behavioral management strategies for improving health and fitness. *Cardiac Rehab* 4:200-208.

Maslow, A.H. 1954. *Motivation and Personality.* New York: Harper.

McAuley, E. 1993. Self-efficacy and the maintenance of exercise participation in older adults. *Journal of Behavioral Medicine* 16:103-116.

Morgan, W.P., and S. Goldston. 1987. *Exercise and Mental Health.* New York: Hemisphere.

Morgan, W.P., J.A. Roberts, F.R. Brand, and A.D. Feinerman. 1970. Psychological effects of chronic physical activity. *Medicine and Science in Sports and Exercise* 2:213-218.

O'Block, F.R., and F.H. Evans. 1984. Goal setting as a motivation technique. In J.M. Silva III and R.S. Weinberg, eds., *Psychological Foundations of Sport.* Champaign, IL: Human Kinetics.

Rajeski, W.J., and E.A. Kenney. 1988. *Fitness Motivation: Preventing Participant Dropout.* Champaign, IL: Life Enhancement Publications.

Selicki, F.A., and E. Segall. 1996. The mind/body connection of the golf swing. *Clinics in Sports Medicine* 15(1):191-201.

Shimer, Porter. 1996. *Too Busy to Exercise.* Pownal, VT: Storey Publishing.

Tucker, L.A. 1993. Comparison of the effects of walking and weight training programs on body image in middle-aged women: an experimental study. *American Journal of Health Promotion* 8:34.

Wankel, L.M. 1985. Personal and situation factors affecting exercise involvement: The importance of enjoyment. *Research Quarterly for Exercise and Sport* 56(3):275-282.

Whitehouse, F.A. 1977. Motivation for fitness. In R. Harris and L.J. Frankel, eds., *Guide to Fitness After Fifty.* New York: Plenum. 171-189.

Wolkodoff, N. 1995. Psychological tweaking: motivation and adherence for the inactive market. *Certified News* 5(1):5-7.

Special Golfers, Special Training

Some golfers have special needs in their physical training. If you're a senior, for example, or a woman whose first physical activity is golf, or an adult with arthritis, you should alter your approach to physical training. Although you may look at exercise as key to improving your golf game, if you are in one of these groups, exercise also is key to improving your health and quality of life.

Seniors

If you're over 55, your approach to golf and golf fitness should be different from someone who's 25. This is because aging changes your responses to exercise: You don't maintain what you don't use and you have to work harder to build and maintain your fitness. Research points out that as you get older you can train just as hard as you did when you were younger. The difference now, however, is that it takes longer to get a training effect or fitness benefit, and you don't recover as quickly.

In our society, you become a "senior" at age 65. However, the physical effects of aging, especially those that relate to golf performance, begin to take effect after age 28. Whether you are 35, 45 or 55, you can't ignore these changes. If you start training now, you can maintain and even improve your physical abilities. The key to fighting the aging process with exercise is to never stop exercising. Exercise, to be effective, has to be a daily dose — not a one-time vaccination. If you develop and maintain the key components of fitness, there is no reason your golf swing when you're 67 should look different than it did when you were 33. It all depends upon maintaining your abilities in strength, aerobic capacity, flexibility and coordination. Regular exercising might even make you look better!

Golf and the Aging Process

Most golfers reach their peaks in strength when they are in their late 20s. After this point, strength and power begin to decline with each passing year. By age 65, *with no physical training,* you will lose at least 20% of the strength capacity you had at your peak. Most of this strength loss comes from loss of actual

> Exercise, to be effective, has to be a daily dose — not a one-time vaccination.

> Research points out that as you get older you can train just as hard as you did when you were younger.

muscle, mostly the fast-twitch (FT), or explosive, type of muscle fiber. The reduction in FT muscle fiber is part of the reason that, with age, most people see a lessening of their resting metabolism. Less muscle means less active tissue to burn calories all day long.

Aerobic capacity or endurance also declines with age. Theoretically, you could lose 50% of your aerobic capacity from age 25 to 65. With the loss in aerobic fitness comes less peripheral blood flow in the muscles and reduced stroke volume, or the amount of blood the heart pumps.

Aging takes a toll on your flexibility, a key golf component. Your body loses flexibility because of increased rigidity in the tendons. Collagen is the structural basis for tendons, and there's a degeneration or loss of collagen with age. In addition, there is a connecting or "cross bridging" between individual tendon fibers as you get older, which also decreases flexibility. Although training may not significantly affect the loss of collagen, it will retard and slow the loss of flexibility from this linkage between tendon fibers.

By age 65, *with no physical training,* you will lose at least 20% of the strength capacity you had at your peak.

Physical training retards the effects of the aging process in the key areas of muscular strength, aerobic capacity and flexibility.

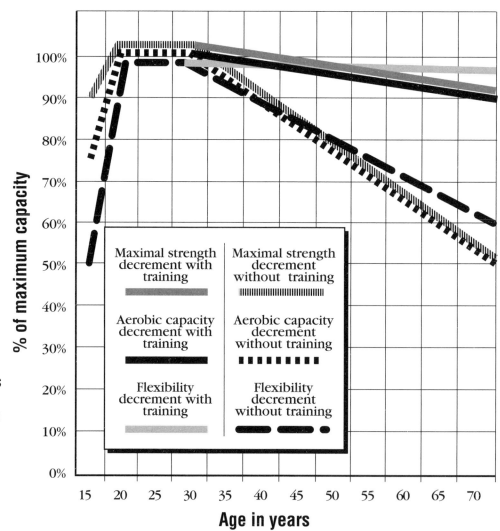

Exercise, Aging and Fitness Factors

% of maximum capacity

Maximal strength decrement with training

Maximal strength decrement without training

Aerobic capacity decrement with training

Aerobic capacity decrement without training

Flexibility decrement with training

Flexibility decrement without training

Age in years

Coordination and timing decline with age as well. Reaction time is shown to decrease with advancing age, as does the ability to activate your muscles quickly. You can't react as fast, and when you do, it takes you longer to get there or to perform the sport movement. Needless to say, it's easier to be a 60-year-old golfer than a 60-year-old boxer. But the good news is that if you remain active, research shows you can maintain the reaction time of adults in their 20s.

Aging and Exercise: A Fountain of Youth

The foregoing physiological changes alter your response to exercise. Your ability to make gains from any training program decreases with age: It takes 10% longer to get the same training effect for every decade over age 30. For example, if you can gain 20% in strength in two weeks when you're 25, when you're 65 it will take almost four weeks. And it takes longer to recover from exercise because of the decrease in blood flow to the muscles. You may be able to train as hard, but it will take longer to get to a certain level and to recover from each training session.

The good news for your golf game — and your life — is that these and other physiological factors can be altered through a consistent fitness regimen. If you exercise and exercise regularly, you'll come close to maintaining your physical abilities as you age.

Your True Age

To explain this concept, exercise scientists have differentiated between chronological and functional age. Chronological age is your actual age in years. Functional age is the sum of your abilities in fitness as well as your health status. The research is clear: Your chronological age can increase, but your functional age can *decrease*. This is why your golf swing should look no different when you're 65 than it did when you were 35: You can maintain and even build your strength, flexibility and endurance as you age.

The key to maintaining fitness is to use training methods and levels that fight the effects of aging. Most golf athletes gravitate toward easier activities as they get older. For example, the toughest area for most senior golfers to maintain is strength and power because of the natural loss of FT muscle fibers. So it's no wonder that most older golfers prefer aerobic exercise and shy away from resistance training. They don't have the strength, so it's harder to perform resistance training. If you want to fight the aging process, not only do you have to exercise but you have to spend more time resistance training than you might have anticipated.

> **Your chronological age can increase, but your functional age can *decrease*.**

Training Recommendations for Senior Golfers

- To effectively fight the aging process and its relationship to declining performance in your golf game, exercise regularly, focusing on all the fitness components, including strength, flexibility, aerobic capacity and even coordination training.
- Increase your warm-up and cool-down time as you get older to make up for reduced circulation.

- To fight the effects of aging on your muscles, perform resistance training at least two times per week.
- To maintain strength, resistance training should progress to the level where you perform 6 to 12 repetitions maximum (RM) per exercise.
- Flexibility training should be practiced on a daily basis, especially after a round of golf.
- Regular aerobic or cardiovascular training will help to maintain your aerobic abilities, which aren't significantly improved by merely walking a golf course.
- To maintain your coordination, engage in sports like racquetball, squash, and basketball in the off-season, if possible. These force you to move in a number of directions while planning and reacting to information.

Women and Golf

Without adequate physical preparation, many women golfers will not progress in their games and will risk a higher level of injury.

According to the National Golf Foundation, women comprise approximately 1/3 of the 2 million new golfers each year. However, without adequate physical preparation, many women golfers will not progress in their games and will risk a higher level of injury. Although exercise is the key to improvement, in some areas the basic golf programs outlined in this book need to be modified for women's needs.

On average, most women golfers have not had the athletic or training opportunities that male golfers have had. Until recently, most women have not had the opportunities to engage in sports in school, nor have they had the same access to physical training methods that most men in our society have had. The result is that most women are not adequately prepared to get the most from their golf games.

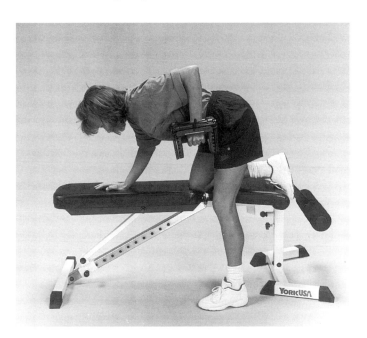

Women should perform more resistance training, especially upper-body exercises, to improve golf performance.

The Strength of the Swing

The general lack of training experience hinders a woman golfer's physical abilities because without physical training a woman's muscles will not have had the chance to develop to their full potential. As a consequence, most women golfers find it difficult to keep the target arm straight during the initial takeaway, which requires upper body and triceps strength, and to have the shoulders work as a unit during both the backswing and initiation forward. The most common injuries in women golfers occur to the elbow, and both elbow and shoulder injuries occur more frequently in female golfers than in male golfers — the direct result of a lack of upper-body strength.

Grip and hand strength are definitely important to both the short game and the regular swing. Female golfers should spend extra time each week on developing grip strength. A general lack of leg strength also can be a problem for the woman golfer. Without specific resistance training, the inside of the knee, known as the medial side, does not develop the ligament support needed for golf. The non-target, or back, leg must take the weight shift during the backswing, then help move the body in the other direction. Poor inside-knee ligament support presents a higher potential for injury during the swing.

Grip and hand strength are definitely important to both the short game and the regular swing.

Too Flexible for Power?

Women generally have higher flexibility levels than men. In golf this can be a hindrance to developing club head speed because extending the swing arc too far means you can't use elastic energy to develop a powerful swing. If you can swing too far back without building elastic tension and the stretch reflex in the muscles, your swing will probably not have the power it would otherwise be capable of generating. So if you're a woman who is serious about golf, you may want to discontinue flexibility training for a while in the hips and shoulders in order to build the ability to develop elastic muscle energy. Athletes often use resistance training through a more limited range of motion (ROM) to reduce flexibility in areas where it is too high.

Training Recommendations for Women Golfers

Women golfers should pay attention to the following suggestions in order to maximize training for golf:
- Spend more time on resistance training for the upper body, especially for the arms, shoulders, upper back and forearms.
- Perform specific resistance exercises such as squats, leg extensions and leg curls to strengthen the important ligaments in the knee.
- If you're too flexible and your swing isn't powerful, reduce flexibility training temporarily and use resistance training with limited ROM to take your flexibility to an appropriate level for golf.

Arthritis

You don't have to play on the senior tour to be affected by arthritis. In fact, one of every seven Americans has arthritis. As the population ages, this will continue to be a major problem for a growing number of golfers. If you have arthritis, exercise is one way to manage the condition. If you don't, prudent exercise can help you from getting arthritis.

Types of Arthritis

By definition, arthritis is inflammation of a joint. This is not exclusively a disease of old age. Many golfers in their 20s and 30s develop arthritis and simply ignore the warning signals. There are over 100 different types of arthritis, ranging from very rare to very common.

Osteoarthritis, one of the most common forms, is the progressive loss of cartilage, the substance on the surface of the joints. Without that lubricating and shock-absorbing surface, the joint is constantly irritated. Any joint that bears weight or functions as a shock absorber is a target for osteoarthritis. For golfers, the susceptible joints are in the feet, knees, hips, spine, fingers and hands.

Rheumatoid arthritis is the most severe form of arthritis. Not only does it cause inflammation of the joints, but it can spread to other areas — including organs, such as the heart and lungs, and the skin.

Arthritis and Golf

It's beyond the scope of this text to provide more than a basic look at how to train for golf if you have arthritis. Your physician or arthritis specialist can provide comprehensive advice. Nonetheless, if you have arthritis, there are some things you can do in order to continue playing golf, to train for golf and even to improve your score. These ideas are meant for golfers with mild cases of arthritis only.

Safe Exercise

Playing golf and training for golf if you have arthritis is possible, and that possibility depends upon a couple of key concepts. First, exercise is important in fighting arthritis, but it must be "safe" exercise. The exercise should improve the condition in the long run, not make it worse. You must choose the mode and intensity of both aerobic and resistance training exercise very carefully in order to effectively work around arthritis.

Exercise is important in fighting arthritis, but it must be "safe" exercise.

Part of the problem with arthritis and exercise is that people with arthritis tend to become inactive because of the pain and discomfort. With that inactivity comes inflexibility and loss of both aerobic and strength capacities. Although it might provide relief in the short term, not exercising tends to make arthritis worse over the long term. The second key concept is that, when exercising with arthritis, never work out to the point where joint pain or discomfort is worse than when you started.

Range of Motion Priorities: Warm Up and Cool Down

Spend more time stretching and going through range of motion exercises. The dynamic stretching routine profiled in the chapter "Flexibility Exercises" provides general exercises that are suitable, with modification, for maintaining and developing ROM in golfers with arthritis. The session should be extended if you have arthritis because you want to gradually warm up the joints and muscles without achieving too much ROM too soon in the exercise session.

Your cool-down should also be tailored to your condition. It should look very much like your active warm-up, but at a slower pace. This is because ROM is crucial to fighting arthritis, and a slow cool-down is one more opportunity to build and maintain ROM.

Adjusting Aerobic Exercise

Aerobic training also has to be adjusted to meet the special needs of golfers with arthritis. Golfers without arthritis are free to choose almost any mode of aerobic exercise they enjoy, but the effect of arthritis on weight-bearing joints necessitates modification. Choose aerobic exercise that is either low-impact or completely non-weight-bearing. Swimming and cycling (especially using the stationary bicycle models with movable arms) are two excellent exercises that meet these criteria.

Some electronic bicycles have "random" settings where the resistance changes up or down periodically, and this can torque or twist joints. If you use a stationary bicycle for your aerobic workout, choose a resistance setting or program where the speed or difficulty is constant. In general, the constant-pace programs will be safer and just as effective aerobically.

ROM is crucial to fighting arthritis, and a slow cool-down is one more opportunity to build and maintain ROM.

Using a recumbent bicycle with a constant workload setting is a safer form of aerobic training for arthritis.

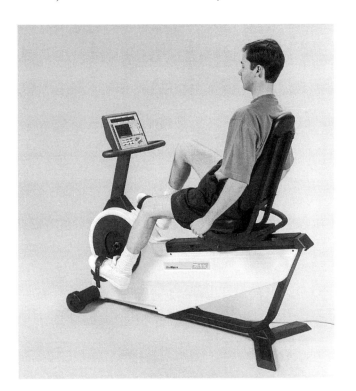

Strength and Arthritis

Resistance training is important in combating arthritis from a number of perspectives. Because golfers with arthritis may not be as active as other golfers, for them, resistance training is key to strengthening the ligaments and tendons supporting the joints. This enhanced stabilization can help minimize the effects of other physical activity that may twist or torque the joints. And resistance training maintains muscle mass, which is crucial to keeping metabolism levels up. Without this you will gain weight, and that extra weight will negatively affect your joints. Additionally, multi-joint exercises such as lat pull-downs are useful in many cases because they spread the exercise stress to more than one joint. When performing conventional resistance training, make sure you lift the weight in a controlled, systematic manner. And you probably will need to use the first few sets as a warm-up.

Multi-joint exercises are a safer form of resistance training for arthritis.

Recommendations for Golfers with Arthritis

The keys for golf training if you have very mild arthritis are:

- Check with your physician or arthritis health-care professional about how to modify the exercise programs presented in this text.
- Continue to exercise and exercise regularly, using a modified program.
- Perform a more extensive warm-up and cool-down, using active movements to develop and maintain range of motion.
- Adjust your resistance training program and use more multi-joint exercises, which spread the stress over more than one joint.
- Pay special attention to any of the devices or techniques you can use from the ergonomics chapter, including custom clubs, footbeds, alternative spikes and carrying systems.

References

Altman, R.D. 1991. Classification of disease: Osteoarthritis. *Seminars in Arthritis and Rheumatism* 20:40-47.

Anniansson, A. et al. 1981. Muscle morphology, enzymatic activity, and muscle strength in elderly men and women. *Clinical Physiology* 1:73.

Avlund, K., M. Schroll, M. Davidsen, B. Lovborg, and T. Rantanen. 1994. Maximal isometric muscle strength and functional ability in daily activities among 75-year-old men and women. *Scandinavian Journal of Medicine & Science in Sports* 4(1):32-40.

Bick, E.M. 1961. Aging in the connective tissues of the human musculoskeletal system. *Geriatrics* 16(9):448-453.

Bruce, R.A. 1984. Exercise, functional aerobic capacity and aging — Another viewpoint. *Medicine and Science in Sports and Exercise* 16:8.

Crews, D.J., J.H. Shirreffs, G. Thomas, G.S. Krahenbuhl, and H.M. Helfrich. 1986. Psychological and physiological attributes associated with performance of selected players of the Ladies Professional Golf Association Tour. *Perceptual and Motor Skills* 63(1):235-238.

Dummer, G.M., P. Viccardo, and D.H. Clarke. 1985. Muscular strength and flexibility of two female master swimmers in the eighth decade of life. *The Journal of Orthopaedic and Sports Physical Therapy* 6(4):235-237.

Evans, W.J. 1996. Aging and exercise: preventing muscle loss in older adults. *American Fitness* 14(1):20-21.

Fiebert, I.M., K.E. Roach, T. Armstrong, D.W. Mandel, and M. Donohue. 1995. Dynamometric grip strength assessment of subjects sixty years and older. *Physical & Occupational Therapy in Geriatrics* 13(4):27-40.

Fleg, J.L. 1986. Alteration in cardiovascular structure and function with advancing age. *American Journal of Cardiology* 57:33c-44c.

Fries, J.F., and L.M. Crapo. 1986. *Vitality and Aging: Implications of The Rectangular Curve.* San Francisco: W.H. Freeman and Company.

Frontera, W.R., C.N. Meredith, K.P. O'Reilly, H.G. Knuttgen, and W.J. Evans. 1988. Strength conditioning in older men: Skeletal muscle hypertrophy and improved function. *Journal of Applied Physiology* 64:1038-1044.

Gordon, Neil F. 1993. *Arthritis: Your Complete Exercise Guide.* Champaign, IL: Human Kinetics.

Grelsamer, R.P. and S. Loebl, eds. 1996. *The Columbia Presbyterian Osteoarthritis Handbook.* New York: Columbia Presbyterian Hospital.

Heinonen, A., P. Oja, H. Sievanen, and I. Vuori. 1993. Effects of equivolume strength training programmes of low, medium and high resistance on maximal isometric strength in sedentary women. *Scandinavian Journal of Medicine and Science in Sports* 3(2):102-109.

Ilke, R.W., R.M. Lampman, and C.W. Castor. 1989. Arthritis and aerobic exercise: A review. *The Physician and Sportsmedicine* 17:128-138.

Kasch, F.W. et al. 1990. The effect of physical activity and inactivity on aerobic power in older men (a longitudinal study). *The Physician and Sportsmedicine* 18:73.

Larson, L. et al. 1979. Muscle strength and speed of movement in relation to age and muscle morphology. *Journal of Applied Physiology* 46:451.

Leaf, A. 1973. Getting old. *Scientific American* 229:45-55.

Montoye, J.J., and D.E. Lamphiera. 1977. Grip and arm strength in males and females, age 10 to 69. *Research Quarterly* 48:109.

Porter, M.M., A. Myint, J.F. Kramer, and A.A. Vandervoort. 1995. Concentric and eccentric knee extension strength in older and younger men and women. *Revue Canadienne de Physiologie Appliquee/Canadian Journal of Applied Physiology* 20(4):429-439.

Samples, P. 1990. Exercise encouraged for people with arthritis. *The Physician and Sportsmedicine* 18:123-126.

Smith, E.L. 1984. Special consideration in developing exercise programs for the older adult. In J.D. Matarazzo, S.M. Weiss, and J.A. Herd, eds., *Behavioral Health: A Handbook of Health Enhancement and Disease Prevention.* New York: John Wiley & Sons.

Spirduso, W.W., and P. Clifford. 1978. Replication of age and physical activity effects on reaction and movement time. *Journal of Gerontology* 33:26.

Stockton, D., and P. McCleery. 1992. Why women need a different setup: The two-time PGA champion and 1991 U.S. Ryder Cup captain's tip: take into account the flexibility factor. *Australian Golf Digest* (March):36-38, 41.

Thomas, S.G. et al. 1985. Determinants of the training response in elderly men. *Medicine and Science in Sports and Exercise* 17:667.

Toski, B., J. Flick, E. Merrins, P. Runyan, and G. Wiren. 1977. Do women play a different game than men? *Golf Digest* 28(10):102-105.

Welch, G.L. 1995. The other arthritis. *American Fitness* 13(5):23-27.

Wells, C. C. 1985. *Women, Sport and Performance. A Physiologic Perspective.* Champaign, IL: Human Kinetics.

West, W., A. Hicks, L. Clements, and J. Dowling. 1995. The relationship between voluntary electromyogram, endurance time and intensity of effort in isometric handgrip exercise. *European Journal of Applied Physiology and Occupational Physiology* 71(4):301-305.

Training Equipment Comparison

When using or purchasing equipment for a golf training regime, keep in mind a few general and specific guidelines. Since the exercise industry is relatively new, it is often difficult for consumers to select the best equipment for their needs. This task is even more complicated because golf has specific requirements for training.

Generally, there is a correlation between equipment costs and the quality of the exercise experience. Most exercisers make club or commercial equipment a reference point for home purchase.

It is important to consider a ratio of costs, training benefits and safety. By matching the general features of the targeted equipment with the key decision points listed, you will be a more informed consumer and will have a better chance of meeting your golf fitness goals.

Consider a ratio of costs, training benefits and safety.

Resistance Training Equipment

Resistance training equipment options are dominantly free-weight systems, which include both barbells and dumbbells and multi-station weight machines.

Free Weights

The best way to use free weights, and especially dumbbells, is with an adjustable workbench, which provides support for a number of exercises. While barbells are appealing because of their connection with traditional exercise, dumbbells offer more versatility for golf, as well as for regular exercise and health purposes. To perform chest exercises effectively and safely with a bar versus dumbbells, you need a bench with arm supports for the bar, which greatly increases space requirements.

Decision points:

- Bench should have wide platform/legs for stability.
- Bench should have a separate leg-brace attachment for use in decline exercises.
- Bench adjustments should go from decline to full military press with pop-pin adjustment for time efficiency and ease of use.
- Leg extension/leg curl attachment is a must with height adjustment being optimum for proper alignment with the knee joint.
- Dumbbells to save space should be push-pin adjustments or spin-on collars and plates.
- Barbells should have collars to keep the weights from falling off during unbalanced movements.

Weight Machines

Home multi-station gyms have become popular in the last five years because of their increasing technical ability to simulate commercial, single station weight machines. In general, the more expensive the machine, the better the exercise quality.

Decision points:

- Exercises that work out the intended muscle group.
- Support when appropriate in exercise positions, such as full support for a seated row or military press.
- Easily adjusts to change exercises.
- Adjusts to fit different sizes of persons in adjusting axis points/seats on such exercises as leg extensions.
- Range of motion adjustments.

Aerobic/Energy System Equipment

The adage "you get what you pay for" is definitely true in aerobic equipment. If you want the equipment to accommodate a wide variety of exercise levels, and have the sophisticated programming options to create custom workouts for golf, expect to pay close to commercial prices. Remember, electronic displays are not the same as electronic control, which adjusts exercise level or intensity — a real plus in developing golf-specific training programs.

Treadmills may be
the most sport-specific
piece of aerobic
equipment for golf.

Treadmills

Because golf is a walking game, treadmills may be the most sport-specific piece of aerobic equipment for golf. The quality of workout and its applicability to golf are tied to both the cost of the materials and the features.

Decision points:

- Electronic speed control of 0-10.0 miles per hour in .1-mile-per-hour increments.
- Electronic grade control of 0-15% grade in .5 degree increments.
- The motor should be at least 2.0 horsepower, continuous duty rating.
- The treadmill should allow you to program workouts for your specific golf needs.
- Emergency shut-off/stop switch.
- Heart-rate monitoring.
- Heart-rate control based on both speed and grade.

Basic Power/Electrical Guidelines

- Make sure the power outlet is the same as required, such as 110 for 110 and 220 for 220.
- A 3-prong outlet is not a guarantee the circuit box is grounded, always check.
- Try not to use an extension cord with electronic equipment because of the potential for drawing excessive current.
- Don't use power surge strips: they add length to the electrical system and often are not grounded.
- Unplug the machine when not in use to further protect the circuitry.
- When cleaning or adjusting electronic equipment, make sure it is off and unplugged.
- Never use electronic equipment with standing water or when wet.
- Consult your owner's manual for procedures specific to the function of your equipment.

Stair Climbers

Stair climbers are excellent aerobic training machines because they are space efficient. While an excellent workout for the legs, they don't involve the upper body much during the workout.

Models with club-like features generally cost close to club-like prices.

Decision points:

- Electronic readouts and electronic controls are different, so look for a stair climber that is electronically controlled.
- Independent stair climbing action where one pedal is not connected in motion to the other pedal — allows for individual leg range of motion.
- Programming should allow development of golf-specific programs through changes in speed at specified intervals.
- Upright handlebars, which allow for climbing in a more back-friendly position.

Basic Cleaning/Maintenance Guidelines

- Remember, no exercise equipment is maintenance free.
- Dust and dirt is the number-one electronic enemy, so vacuum around equipment once a week, vacuum under the machine bimonthly and in the case of treadmills, carefully vacuum around the motor area once a month.
- Use a light cleaning solution, such as window cleaner, or a damp cloth weekly on cleanable parts.
- When cleaning or adjusting electronic equipment, make sure it is off and unplugged.
- In a damp area, use a flooring surface such as a rubber/plastic mat under equipment.
- Yearly service check by authorized dealer on complex electronic pieces such as treadmills.
- On treadmills, make sure the belt is properly aligned in the center of the running surface.
- Use only manufacturer-approved and -recommended lubricants according to owner's manual.
- On resistance machines and equipment, check bolts, nuts and screws for tightness once a month and perform a visual inspection of all moving parts such as cables and pulleys.
- Consult your owner's manual for procedures specific to the function of your equipment.

Stationary Bicycles

Stationary bicycles are still a mainstay of athletic training, offering golfers a non-impact form of cardiovascular training. Recumbent and dual-action bicycles (using both arms and legs) are the best choices for golf athletes.

Decision points:

- Air or electronic resistance provides both a better workout and the ability to easily and precisely change workloads versus tension strap or belt resistance.
- Both the seat height and pedal straps should adjust for individual size.
- The ability to program a workout electronically boosts your results for golf and fitness.

Aerobic Riders

While aerobic riders have become popular over the last few years, not all are created equal. There are definite differences in the ride mechanics as well as resistance variations. Mechanics and resistance determine how effective the machine will be for your golf program as well as potential back discomfort.

Decision points:

- Electronic resistance is generally superior to body weight or pneumatic resistance.
- Ergonomic design to lower stress on the back/knees by allowing more leg use versus arm dominance.

Total Body Exercise Machines

When selecting one of these pieces of equipment for your golf program, the more muscle groups used in the exercise, the better the applicability to golf. In addition, the lack of impact during the motion is a plus for the ability to increase exercise intensity.

Decision points:

- Electronic resistance and programming is generally superior to other forms of resistance in that it allows for custom programs that can enhance golf performance.
- Arm and leg motion is generally superior for burning calories than just leg motion.

Slide Boards

Slide boards offer the benefits of building both strength and aerobic endurance. They also are excellent developers of the lateral and pivot muscles in the hips.

Decision points:

* Non-skid surface on the bottom of the board.
* Angled bumpers or end ramps to lessen impact shock.

Heart Rate Monitors

If you don't use equipment that either monitors or controls the energy-system workout, then the use of a chest strap/watch monitoring system will help ensure you are training at the proper intensity. Monitor systems run the gamut from a watch/strap system that simply monitors your heart rate to systems that will store and download information to a personal computer.

Decision points:

* For most exercisers, simple monitoring features are the most used.
* The watch and heart-rate strap should be water resistant to account for sweat or humid conditions.
* Batteries should be easily available for both the heart-rate strap and the watch.

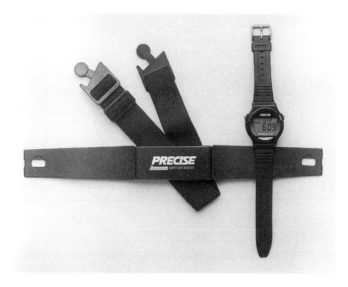

Flexibility Development Equipment

Your two best options for development of golf-specific flexibility are standard floor exercise mats and vertical or posture-specific stretching devices. Mats can easily be stored and are applicable to a wide variety of exercises. Because of the posture-specific benefits of stretching in a posture like the golf swing, posture-specific devices have great potential.

Posture-Specific Flexibility Devices

Because of the posture-specific benefits of stretching in a posture like the golf swing, posture-specific devices have great potential.

Posture-specific devices allow you to stretch more than one muscle group at a time — in a golf-posture, for the best benefit. These devices can be used both in a home exercise center as well as golf clubs and athletic clubs.

Decision points:
- The vertical column of the stretching device should be attached securely to the floor or platform allowing for use of body weight as a stretching mechanism.
- Cables or cords at a variety of heights and angles to accommodate various stretches and flexibility levels.
- Ample width or wing span of the device so combination stretches can be performed.

References

Cardinal, B.J. 1994. Six steps to selecting exercise equipment. *Athletic Business* 18(9):39-40,42,45,47.

Draper, C. 1992. Exercise equipment review: multistation gymnasiums. *Ultrafit* 7:67-69

Exercise equipment: hip and thigh machines — review. 1992. *Ultrafit* 10:68-69,72.

Kato, D. 1992. A buyer's guide to exercise equipment. Guide pour l'achat d'appareils d'exercices. *CAHPER journal/Journal de l'ACSEPL* 58(2)38-39.

McKeon, M. 1994. Become a console conqueror: your guide to mastering the controls of hi-tech aerobic exercise equipment. *Ultrafit* 19:22-25.

Pinachio, P., S.F. Loy., W.C. Whiting, and K. Wyatt. 1996. Aerobic Riders: Can you ride your way to a healthier body? *Fitness Matters* 2(3).

Ramotar, J. 1993. Injuries from exercise equipment. *The Physician and Sportsmedicine* 21(2):59.

Robergs, R.A., and L. Kravitz. 1994. Making sense of calorie-burning claims: help your clients understand the truth about caloric expenditure and exercise equipment. *IDEA Today* 12(8):27,29-32,34.

Shafran, J. 1995. Stay in, work out: home-exercise equipment that you'll want to spend some quality time with. *Women's sports & fitness* 17(8):57-60.

Schwarzkopf, R. and E.F. Kreighbaum. 1996. Aerobic exercise equipment. In, Kreighbaum, E. and M.A. Smith (eds.), *Sports and fitness equipment design*. Champaign, IL: Human Kinetics. 157-177.

Stamford, B. 1997. Choosing and using exercise equipment. *The Physician and Sportsmedicine* 25(1):107-108.

Webb, D.A., and M.J. Stevenson. 1994. Life-expectancy costing of exercise equipment. NIRSA journal: *Journal of the National Intramural-Recreational Sports Association* 18(2):28-30.

Wolkodoff, N. 1993. Exercising equipment options for the home. *Rocky Mountain News: Special Health & Fitness Issue* 3-5.

Wolkodoff, N. and M. Macro. 1994. Recommending home equipment: part 1—energy system training. *Certified News* 4(3):7-8.

Wolkodoff, N. and A.M. Miller. 1995. Recommending home equipment: part 2—strength training. *Certified News* 5(1):9-10.

Wolkodoff, N. 1995. *ExerTrends 1995 Consumer Treadmill Study*. Denver, CO: ExerTrends.

Glossary

Active Flexibility. The use of opposing muscle groups by the individual to move the joint or set of joints through a motion.

Aerobic Capacity. The actual amount of oxygen that can combine with fat and carbohydrates in the muscle cell to produce steady or constant muscular work, which is influenced by training variables.

Anaerobic Metabolism. Where the body cannot provide the necessary fuel for muscular work from the combination of oxygen, fat and carbohydrates and shifts to a form of metabolism or energy production where carbohydrates without oxygen can be used for a short period of time, generally less than two minutes.

ATP-PC. Adenosine triphosphate/Phosphate creatine, or the actual fuel the muscle uses for short-term work of less than 20 seconds.

Ballistic Stretch. Any stretch or movement with enough force or speed to activate the stretch reflex resulting in a rapid movement the other direction.

Cardiovascular Fitness. The general ability of the body to perform long-term exercise or activities lasting 20 minutes or more without fatigue.

Concentric contraction. Muscular work where the muscle shortens, generally raising a weight or lifting body weight away from gravity.

Cross Training. The rotation of different fitness activities within an exercise session or within a training cycle or phase to promote general fitness or physical recovery, or to relieve psychological or physiological boredom.

Delayed Onset of Muscular Soreness (DOSM). The aftereffect of heavy muscular work, either severe energy system or resistance training, that causes the muscle to have physical trauma, including internal swelling, generally becoming greatest 24 to 48 hours after the exercise session.

Dynamic Flexibility. The use of any method that involves movement to increase range of motion around a joint or set of joints.

Eccentric Contraction. A muscular contraction in which the muscle actually lengthens, generally against an external resistance such as a weight or gravity.

Energy System Training. Any major body movement training, such as cycling, stair climbing or jogging, where intensity or difficulty can vary from aerobic to anaerobic levels.

Exercise Duration. The actual length of any exercise bout or session measured in minutes.

Exercise Frequency. The number of specific exercise sessions of any type or total during the period of one week.

Exercise Intensity. The effort of the exercise, which in energy system training is generally a percentage of aerobic capacity or maximum heart rate, and in the case of resistance training is the number of repetitions performed within a given time frame with a specific resistance.

Exercise Mode. The actual specific exercise type within a category, such as using a treadmill for energy system training or free weights for resistance training.

Fast Oxidative Glycolytic Muscle Fibers. Referred to as FOG fibers, those muscle fibers or units of movement that have almost equal aerobic and power characteristics and are trainable in either direction.

Fast Twitch Muscle Fibers. Those muscle fibers or units of movement commonly labeled FT, that are strength and power oriented with relatively low muscular endurance.

Flexibility. The demonstrated ability to move specifically through a range of motion either statically or dynamically.

Hypertrophy. The changes in muscle fiber resulting in physical gains in size, mainly from resistance training of eight to 12 repetitions maximum.

Isokinetic Contraction. Muscular movement that is the same speed or almost the same speed, generally controlled by a sophisticated exercise machine, or occurring in a sport like swimming, with the main application of rehabilitation from injury.

Isometric Contraction. Muscular movement that is almost stationary against a resistance.

Kcal. The kilocalorie, or the amount of energy required to raise one kilogram of water one degree Celsius; the measure of food energy and human work, expressed as kcals.

Maximum Oxygen Uptake. The maximum amount of oxygen that can be used during energy system activities measured in the amount of oxygen in milliliters per minute per kilogram of body weight or ___ml/kg/min-1.

Muscular Endurance. The general or specific ability to repeat a movement without fatigue or a decrease in coordination or performance.

Muscular Failure. A level of work where the muscle cannot continue because of lack of fuel, lack of recovery or neurological failure, known as MF.

Passive Flexibility. The level of flexibility where an external force, such as an exercise partner or trainer, pushes a joint or set of joints through their range of motion.

Perceived Exertion. The perception of effort in aerobic/energy system activities on a numbered scale that correlates with actual energy expended or target heart rate, where work is given a corresponding RPE number.

Plyometric Training. Training in which a rapid eccentric movement is followed immediately by a quick and powerful concentric movement, such as catching and then throwing a medicine ball.

Power. The ability to move as rapidly as possible against a resistance or through a movement.

Proprioceptive Neuromuscular Facilitation. Known as PNF, a set of varied stretching techniques that use combinations of contractions, relaxation and movement of muscles and joints in question.

Range of Motion. Termed ROM, the collective movement through a joint or set of joints, which is influenced by muscle, ligament, tendon and skin resistance.

Repetition Maximum. Known as RM, the maximum amount of resistance or weight that can be performed for the goal number of repetitions. For example, a 15 RM is the weight or resistance that can only be performed for 15 repetitions, no more or less.

Resistance Training. The use of any resistance — primarily weight machines or free weights — to improve a specific muscle group or groups in some aspect of muscular endurance, strength or power.

Resting Heart Rate. Taken first thing in the morning upon arising, RHR is a measure of overall aerobic fitness, training levels and reaction to stress.

Set. A group of repetitions performed consecutively or nearly consecutively.

Slow Twitch Muscle Fibers. Those muscle fibers or units of movement that are endurance oriented with relatively low muscular power levels, known as ST units.

Static Flexibility. The ability to move through ROM and hold a position.

Strength. Defined as force against or through a resistance regardless of how much time the effort takes.

Stretch Reflex. The reaction of the muscle spindles, or protective mechanisms inside the muscle, when stretched too far, sending a signal to the brain and back to the muscle to contract, protecting the body from injury and aiding movement.

Training Heart Rate. Known as THR, a relatively easy means to measure energy system training intensity to ensure the desired benefits and training effects.

Training Load. The quantifiable amount of training stress put on the system or muscle in any given exercise that can be measured in kcal per hour, speed, grade, resistance or VO_2 for energy system training, and actual resistance used in resistance training.

Training Variety. The use of different modalities in training to produce a cross-training effect.

V0$_2$. The maximum volume of oxygen that can be used in aerobic work, a measure of fitness, which is express is milliliters of oxygen per kilogram of body weight per minute, or ___ml/kg/min-1.

Workload. The actual amount of work imposed on the system in an energy system activity that can be measured in speed, grade, resistance, watts, kcal per hour or mets.

Index

A

Abdominal, 10, 12-13, 16, 23, 25-26, 70, 75, 91, 107, 129-132, 140, 177, 182, 215, 225

Abduction, 16, 20, 23, 26, 144, 177, 180, 184-185

Abductors, 24, 144, 152

Active external rotation, 150, 175-176, 179, 183

Active flexibility, 79, 81, 83-84, 86, 88-89, 93, 96-97, 152, 159, 163-164, 172, 265

Active stretches, 26, 29, 79, 81, 83-84, 86, 88-89, 93-94, 96-97, 147, 150-152, 158, 162-164, 181-182, 185, 221, 226

Active wrist extension, 164, 181, 185

Active wrist flexion, 163, 181, 185

Adaptations, 49, 58, 60, 77

Adduction, 20, 143, 177, 180, 184-185

Adductor, 17, 23, 143, 145

Adductor brevis, 17, 23

Adductor longus, 143

Adductor magnus, 17, 23, 143

Adenosine Tri Phosphate (ATP), 61, 100, 265

Aerobic

    capacity, 1-5, 7-13, 28-30, 33-41, 43-49, 51-57, 59-71, 75-77, 79, 81, 83-84, 86, 88, 92, 95-96, 98, 100, 145, 148, 170-175, 178, 181-182, 184, 186-189, 192-193, 204, 209-210, 212, 219, 223, 226, 232, 235, 237-239, 241-247, 249, 253-255, 257, 260-262, 264-268

    fitness, 2, 35-38, 40-41, 44, 48, 175, 181-182, 186, 237, 246, 267

    riders, 46, 180-181, 185, 261, 264

    training, 2, 35-36, 38, 40, 51, 175-178, 180, 185, 196, 251, 259

Aging, 1-5, 81, 192, 245-248, 254

Air-resistance, 44

American College of Sports Medicine (ACSM), 49, 242

American Council on Exercise (ACE), 242

American Heart Association (AHA), 195

Americans, 1, 195, 224, 249

Amino acids, 196

Anaerobic metabolism, 35, 39, 57, 60, 265

Anti-perspirant lotions, 231

Arm circles, 89, 149, 175-176, 179, 183, 221

Arthritis, 85, 245, 249-254

Physical Golf Exercise Log

Training phase:

Name: _____ Date: _____ Off-season ___ Pre-season ___ In-season ___

Warm-up Exercises

Exercise	Sets/Repetitions	Date	Notes

Resistance Training

Exercise	Sets/Repetitions	Resistance	Date	Notes

Energy System Training

Exercise	Target Heart Rate	Duration	Date	Notes

Flexibility Training

Exercise	Repetitions	Date	Notes

Reproduce as needed.

Physical Golf Exercise Log

Training phase:

Name: _____ Date: _____ Off-season ___ Pre-season ___ In-season ___

Warm-up Exercises

Exercise	Sets/Repetitions	Date	Notes

Resistance Training

Exercise	Sets/Repetitions	Resistance	Date	Notes

Energy System Training

Exercise	Target Heart Rate	Duration	Date	Notes

Flexibility Training

Exercise	Repetitions	Date	Notes

Reproduce as needed.

Physical Golf Exercise Log

Training phase:

Name: ———————————————— Date: ——————— Off-season ——— Pre-season ——— In-season ———

Warm-up Exercises

Exercise	Sets/Repetitions	Date	Notes

Resistance Training

Exercise	Sets/Repetitions	Resistance	Date	Notes

Energy System Training

Exercise	Target Heart Rate	Duration	Date	Notes

Flexibility Training

Exercise	Repetitions	Date	Notes

Reproduce as needed.

Physical Golf Goal Setting Form

Name ——————————————————— Date ——————————

Long term

_____

_____

Intermediate		Short term

1. _____

2. _____

3. _____

4. _____

1a _____

1b _____

1c _____

2a _____

2b _____

2c _____

3a _____

3b _____

3c _____

4a _____

4b _____

4c _____

Reproduce as needed.

Physical Golf Goal Setting Form

Name ——————————————————— Date ———————————

Long term

————————————————————

————————————————————

Intermediate

Short term

1. ————————————————

2. ————————————————

3. ————————————————

4. ————————————————

1a ————————————————

1b ————————————————

1c ————————————————

2a ————————————————

2b ————————————————

2c ————————————————

3a ————————————————

3b ————————————————

3c ————————————————

4a ————————————————

4b ————————————————

4c ————————————————

Reproduce as needed.

Resource List

The following products or services are listed on this page as a service for readers who seek further information. This information is provided as a service only and does not constitute an endorsement by KickPoint Press.

American College of Sports Medicine
Certification Resource Center   (800) 486-5643

American Council on Exercise   (800) 825-3636

Bite Golf Shoes   (800) 248-3465
                                                 www.biteshoes.com

Reebok/CCS Fitness   (800) 344-0444
                                                 www.ccsfitness.com

Dimension Z Golf Clubs   (888) 271-1889
                                                 www.dimensionz.com

Flatspikes/Highlander Golf   (800) 577-4630
                                                 www.flatspikes.com

National Strength and Conditioning Association   (719) 632-6722

Performance Zone Nutritional Products   (800) 960-0025

PowerBlock Dumbbells by IntellBell   (800) 446-5215

SUPERFeet Sport Footbeds   (800) 634-6618
                                                 www.superfeet.com

Tri-Bar Gripping System   (888) 874-2271
                                                 www.tribar.com

True Treadmills   (800) 426-6570
                                                 www.truefitness.com

Vectra Fitness, Inc.   (800) 283-2872, press "5"
                                                 www.vectrafitness.com

Neil Wolkodoff/MaxPerformance Training Services www.maxperform.com

To order additional copies of *Physical Golf*...

If you borrowed this book from a friend or library, and wish to purchase your own copy, and do not have distribution through your local bookstore, *Physical Golf* can be ordered direct by calling (800) 966-4767 toll-free.

Inquiries on special market orders, premiums, trade markets, and gift sales should be directed to KickPoint Press at (303) 571-9335.